"[A]n essential read for everyon[...]
TORONTO.COM

"Fred Sasakamoose played in the NHL before First Nations
people had the right to vote in Canada. This page turner will
have you cheering for 'Fast Freddy'as he faces off against
huge challenges both on and off the ice—a great gift to every
proud hockey fan, Canadian, and Indigenous person."
WAB KINEW, LEADER OF THE MANITOBA NDP AND AUTHOR OF *THE REASON YOU WALK*

"The most moving and plain-spoken account to date . . . of
the Indigenous experience in the racist white world that
constituted much of both the NHL and the Canada of Fred
Sasakamoose's day."
WINNIPEG FREE PRESS

"Freddy Sasakamoose is the epitome of hard work and
perseverance. His story reveals the hardships he faced while
overcoming the impossible. He will be an inspiration for
generations to come."
BRIGETTE LACQUETTE, OLYMPIC MEDALIST AND FIRST FIRST NATIONS HOCKEY PLAYER
TO BE NAMED TO CANADA'S NATIONAL WOMEN'S TEAM

"A heart-wrenching story of survival in the face of
injustice and tragedy."
DAN ROBSON, BESTSELLING AUTHOR OF *QUINN: THE LIFE OF A HOCKEY LEGEND*

NATIONAL BESTSELLER

Praise for *Call Me Indian*

"Fred Sasakamoose is an icon. Any Indigenous hockey player skates in his footsteps. His trailblazing hockey career has been well documented in recent decades, and now, his riveting life story has been published in his own words. *Call Me Indian* is a powerfully essential account of Sasakamoose's journey, from his Cree upbringing on the land to the bright lights of NHL arenas. His voice throughout is candid, heartfelt, and astute, as he reveals the triumphs and tragedies of his life. Sasakamoose's resilience and dedication to his family, his people, and the game of hockey is nothing short of awesome, despite the brutality he endured at residential school and the racism that followed him on the ice and beyond. *Call Me Indian* is an inspiring and enlightening saga that's a must-read for Indigenous communities, hockey fans, and all Canadians."

—Waubgeshig Rice, author of *Moon of the Crusted Snow*

"More lasting and impactful than the usual sports memoir."

—*Publishers Weekly*

"A heart-wrenching story of survival in the face of injustice and tragedy. In his unflinching memoir, Fred Sasakamoose shares his journey from being a residential school Survivor to becoming the NHL's first Indigenous player—on the arduous road to finding the peace and pride he was long refused. Canada's pastime and the nation's darkest sins collide in a beautifully told tale of resilience, passion, and ultimate triumph."

—Dan Robson, bestselling author of *Quinn: The Life of a Hockey Legend*

"Fred Sasakamoose's story is gripping and powerfully told—a story of triumph and tragedy, of great success and the perils of excess. There is laughter and tears here aplenty, but also inspiration. Characters as large as Gordie Howe and Bobby Hull are easily matched by the likes of Moosum, Freddy's grandfather; Father Roussel, the only good to be found in residential school; George Vogan, who always believed in Fred—and Loretta, who loved him, gave him family, and ultimately saved him."

—Roy MacGregor, bestselling author of *Chief: The Fearless Vision of Billy Diamond* and *Canadians: Portrait of a Country and Its People*

"Fred Sasakamoose played in the NHL before First Nations people had the right to vote in Canada. This page turner will have you cheering for 'Fast Freddy' as he faces off against huge challenges both on and off the ice—a great gift to every proud hockey fan, Canadian, and Indigenous person."

—Wab Kinew, Leader of the Manitoba NDP and author of *The Reason You Walk*

"*Call Me Indian* is not only an excellent memoir about the first Indian hockey player with treaty status in the National Hockey League. Just as importantly, it is also the most moving and plain-spoken account to date, from the inside, of the Indigenous experience in the racist white world that constituted much of both the NHL and the Canada of Fred Sasakamoose's day—which was not so very long ago. . . . The hot heart of this story begins and ends within the wider Indian experience. . . . Sasakamoose's graphic recollection of every imaginable form of abuse at St. Michael's will stand for decades to come as one of the most damning indictments of the residential school system."

—*Winnipeg Free Press*

"Freddy Sasakamoose is the epitome of hard work and perseverance. His story reveals the hardships he faced while overcoming the impossible. He will be an inspiration for generations to come."

—Brigette Lacquette, Olympic medalist and first First Nations hockey player to be named to Canada's National Women's Team

CALL ME INDIAN

From the Trauma of Residential School to
Becoming the NHL's First Treaty Indigenous Player

FRED SASAKAMOOSE

with MEG MASTERS

PENGUIN
an imprint of Penguin Canada,
a division of Penguin Random House Canada Limited

First published in Viking Canada hardcover, 2021

Published in this edition, 2022

4th Printing

Copyright © 2021 by Fred Sasakamoose
Foreword © 2021 by Bryan Trottier

Distributed by Penguin Random House Canada Limited, Toronto.

LIBRARY AND ARCHIVES CANADA CATALOGUING IN PUBLICATION
Title: Call me Indian : from the trauma of residential school to becoming the NHL's first treaty
Indigenous player / Fred Sasakamoose.
Names: Sasakamoose, Fred, 1933- author.
Identifiers: Canadiana 20200238493 | ISBN 9780735240032 (softcover)
Subjects: LCSH: Sasakamoose, Fred, 1933- | LCSH: Cree Indians—Saskatchewan—
Biography. | CSH: Native hockey players—Canada—Biography | LCSH: Hockey players—
Canada—Biography. | CSH: Indians of North America—Saskatchewan—Residential
schools | LCGFT: Autobiographies.
Classification: LCC E99.C88 S28 2022 | DDC 971.24/004973230092—dc23

All photographs in the book are courtesy of the author unless otherwise specified.

Cover and interior design: Matthew Flute
Cover image © Jason Franson

Printed in the United States of America

www.penguinrandomhouse.ca

Penguin
Random House
PENGUIN CANADA

To my parents and grandparents, especially Alexan, whose love gave me strength. And to Loretta and my children, whose love always brought me home.

CONTENTS

FOREWORD

by Bryan Trottier

I admired Fred Sasakamoose for decades before I had the chance to meet him. When I was young, my father would tell me stories about him. When my dad first saw Fred play, it was the early 50s in Moose Jaw, when Fred was playing junior with the Canucks. In those prairie towns in the 40s, 50s, and 60s, hockey was the main entertainment. It was the lifeblood of the town, everyone went and watched hockey games on Friday and Saturday nights. There is nothing better than live hockey—these days, you can watch any game from almost anywhere, but it isn't the same as seeing it unfold at breakneck speeds right before your eyes. Watching the game is so much more exciting when you can feel the impact of every hit, hear the echo of every shot. After my dad saw Fred play for the first time, he came home and told me that he had just watched the fastest skater he had ever laid eyes on. That Freddy Sasakamoose was faster than a jack rabbit. That's what a lot of people still remember about Fred—that he was so incredibly quick. If you ask NHLers—those lucky enough to play with Fred—about him, to this day they all say, "Oh my god could he skate, oh my god could he fly." That is quite something, to have people still talking about your skating seventy years later. My dad spoke about Fred with such reverence, such pride, the stories he told stuck with me. He was so proud that this fast, star player was First Nations. I kept that pride and inspiration with me as I embarked on my own hockey career, and when I was a kid I used to practice saying his name because it was hard to pronounce. I knew one day that I would meet him, and I wanted to be able to say it.

Fred will always be a hero in my life, and I kept his inspiration top of mind as I went on my own NHL journey as both a player and later as a coach. He is a pioneer and hero for all First Nations, Métis, Inuit players; he was fast and strong and his shot was intimidating. He had a massive impact on my life, and the prospect of finally meeting the man who was a legend in my mind was a bit daunting. Fred is a huge part of hockey history, Indigenous history, and an inspiration to so many people, but more than that—he is nice. It's quite something to meet your boyhood hero, but it just blows your mind when your boyhood hero turns out to be nicer than you had even imagined they would be. I think that's a big part of what made Freddy and guys like him—like Gordie Howe, Jean Béliveau, Stan Mikita—such great hockey players: they are just really good people.

When I finally met Fred, we were at an event in Frog Lake, speaking to First Nations kids; I think it was in the early- to mid-2000s. This man I had heard about for so long, the man who everyone spoke of in legendary terms, was now right in front of me. The first thought I had was, *Where is all the grey hair?* Fred was in his 70s at that point and looked so young and handsome. He had boundless energy and wasn't shy at all. After we both gave our talks, I told Fred about my dad coming home and saying that he skated like a jack rabbit, and Freddy looked at me and said, "Bryan, you won't believe this, but when I was at school, the priests would say, 'Skate like you are chasing rabbits.'"

Now, that's how we greet each other—we say, "Chasing rabbits?"

I was quite small when my dad first started telling me about Fred. I had a hard time pronouncing his name—Sasakamoose is a tricky name for a kid! I grew up knowing that he was the first full Treaty Indigenous player to break into the NHL. That meant a lot to me and to all of us. It made us all really proud of our heritage. When my siblings and I were in school and playing sports, kids would call us names. Kids can be awful when you are different. But Fred's accomplishments made us proud, seeing Fred succeed made my dad beam. When he watched me play, my dad would tell me "Fred would be so proud to see you play," and that would make me beam.

The name-calling and discrimination that we experienced as kids was different from what Fred went through. Fred will tell you about it in this memoir. My dad, who is Cree Métis Chippewa, went through similar experiences when he was young—he and Fred are of the same era. The things that happened to them when they were young are truly horrible. They were too young to really understand what was going on, but that doesn't change the pain that was inflicted. Seldom do we ever talk about discrimination from that time, and everything that happened. I didn't face the same things in the NHL that Fred faced, because he did it before me.

I love talking to First Nations communities and sharing stories from my career and my journey to the NHL, but one of the highlights is bumping into Fred, which happens often at these events. Fred is the kind of guy who, when he is speaking to you, makes you feel like you are the centre of the universe. You can ask him one question and he will go on for ten minutes talking to you like you are the dearest friend to him in the world. Every time I bump into Fred my cheeks get sore from smiling. He always has so many stories. One that I really love, which you'll get to read in this memoir, is from when Fred was playing junior hockey with two teammates who were particularly special to him, and how he made sure that he honoured them when he made it to the NHL. That's the kind of guy Fred is—if you are dear to him, if you had an impact on his life, he never forgets you. Those linemates who meant so much to Fred, they all experienced discrimination and jealousy, and supported each other through it.

One of the greatest gifts Fred has given the world is not *just* being the first Treaty Indigenous player in the NHL, but also his talent for speaking about his life. He has dedicated so much of these past decades to sharing his story and encouraging kids—and the way he carries himself, it's unbelievable. Fred isn't a tall man—he isn't 6 foot 6 but he has a 6 foot 6 personality. He has a real energy around him and he is just so proud of who he is, of what he was accomplished, of his heritage. The power in his voice and the way he expresses himself, he exudes sheer joy when he is speaking. His gift for sharing his stories continues to amaze me, even after I've listened to him speak for years now. After a while, I had to tell him how great he was at speaking, how wonderfully he came across, and he told me, "We come from story-tellers, we love to tell stories, it is in our blood." His words amazed me all over again.

So here is Fred's story, in the way only he could tell it.

We are all so lucky that Fred has decided to write some of his stories down in this memoir, so we can return to them again and again. The legacy that Fred has left on the ice is really important and lasting, but everything he has done after retiring is monumental. He inspires so many people and takes the time to make everyone feel important. He takes such pride in being Cree, it's infectious. It makes us all proud to be First Nations. It's an honour to introduce his story to you. Fred's words will take you through all the ups and down of his life—the good stories and the devastating ones, as well. This is the story of how Fred became who he is, a proud Cree man, one who inspires so many. A boy-hood hero who is even stronger, kinder, and more generous than I'd ever dreamed he could be. A lot of people ask why Fred didn't have a longer career in the league, why didn't he achieve more in the game but to us, he made it. That's the biggest deal, he made it to the greatest hockey league in the world and broke the barrier for the First Nations players who would come after him. He made it possible for all the kids who didn't think it would be possible. He stands taller than all of us, and is revered by all of us. My life has been changed by the man who is always chasing rabbits, and I know yours will be as well.

Bryan Trottier
November 2020

AUTHOR'S NOTE

Readers will notice that I use the word "Indian" throughout this book. I know many of my people do not like it. Because of that, non-Indigenous people should avoid the word. But "Indian" is the term I grew up with and use for myself and others. I will explain my feelings about the word in more detail later.

Also, the reserve that has always been my home was called Sandy Lake until 1986, when its name was changed to Ahtahkakoop to honour one of our greatest Chiefs. I use "Sandy Lake" throughout most of the book. (The lake on the reserve is labelled "Hines Lake" on most maps. But it was always known to my people as Sandy Lake.)

And finally, it's pretty challenging to describe things that happened six, seven, eight decades ago. I know I have told my story in different ways, sometimes with different details, over the years. Take my friend Ray Leacock, from the Moose Jaw Canucks. In the past, whenever I've told stories about him, I've called him "Al." Was Al a nickname he used? One I gave him? Or did I just misremember at some point? I have no idea. All I can say is, in putting my life story on paper, I have done my best to draw from the deep well of memory. My family, friends, and editors have helped me piece together timelines or details that have faded with the passing years. In the end, I have told my story as accurately and, most importantly, as honestly as I can. In some places, that honesty meant I had to change the names and identifying features of some people to protect their privacy.

As a man, long grown, I was told this: On the night I was born, an old woman said that I was special. People say she blessed me. And she gave me a song. She said she saw my future in the stars.

No one told me about the old woman when I was a child. I never heard a word of this. But still, I knew that the world had something wonderful in store for me.

It was my grandfather, my moosum Alexan, who told me this.

Alexan was deaf and mute. But for the first seven years of my life, he was the one who spoke to me the loudest.

He was the one who spoke to me of my future. A future that I hope I have lived up to.

I

ahtahkakoop otaskiy

AHTAHKAKOOP'S WORLD

I was born at Whitefish Lake, on what is now called the Big River First Nation. My mother's home. Among her people. When I was very young, we moved to my father's reserve—Sandy Lake. This was the land that the great Chief Ahtahkakoop chose when he and other Indian Chiefs were forced to move our people onto reserves.

Ahtahkakoop was my great-great-uncle. His brother, Sasakamoose, was my great-grandfather.

Some of my earliest memories are of hearing the stories about Ahtahkakoop and the choices he made for our people. About his understanding of the challenges the white world brought us. About his wisdom in picking a safe course when the waters moved against us. I heard tales of Ahtahkakoop's foresight—and his innocent miscalculations. The way the white men would break his trust, the way they would force their ideas of land ownership and property on him and his people. About how, despite Ahtahkakoop's remarkable leadership, our people would suffer. Those early stories about Ahtahkakoop would convince me that the white world was not made for the Cree people, and despite every effort our great Chief made to embrace it, that world would not embrace him—or us, his family, his kin, his people.

Ahtahkakoop was born in 1816, in the Saskatchewan River country, to a Métis or French-Canadian father, Antoine Chatelain (also known as Charles or Louis) and a Swampy Cree half-breed mother thought to have been named Okimawinotook. He had four brothers: Mususka-poe, Ahenakew, Nāpēskis, and my great-grandfather—Sasakamoose. "Ahtahkakoop" can be translated into English as "Starblanket." "Sasakamoose" is thought to come from the Cree words meaning "one who adheres."

Ahtahkakoop's roots, my roots, in this country are deep. We nēhiyawak (the Plains Cree people) have lived in the woods and meadows of what is now known as the province of Saskatchewan for hundreds of years. Hunting buffalo, moose, deer, and elk. Fishing in the lakes and rivers of this fertile land. We roamed the hills and grass-lands freely, settling in winter hunting grounds and moving to follow the buffalo when the snows melted. Travelling in all directions to meet and trade. Sometimes riding south into Montana and North Dakota to raid horses from the Blackfoot there.

When the fur traders arrived, we trapped and traded with the môniyâwak, the white men, from the Hudson's Bay Company. When the permanent trading post Fort Carlton was built, Ahtahkakoop and his men were among its chief suppliers of fur and pemmican. But with the arrival of the môniyâw settlers, and then the Métis from the Red River Valley, things began to change for my people.

The white man hunted the buffalo for sport and trophies, wiping out huge numbers of the beasts that were our medicine. Food became scarce for those who depended heavily on the buffalo. Many of us starved. Traders brought in enormous quantities of alcohol to blur our judgment during trade. Smallpox and other diseases arrived with the traders and settlers, killing us by the thousands. First the Hudson's Bay Company, then the Canadian government and the settlers claimed the land, sometimes protecting with force what they had seized. In just a few generations, our world had changed.

And so Ahtahkakoop faced the uncertain future head-on. The môniyâw government had signed treaties with bands in the south and east (Treaties 4 and 5). The treaties promised specific areas where our people could live without fear of môniyâw settlers or Métis encroaching. It was a strange idea. Nēhiyawak recognized that some land was traditionally inhabited by other Indigenous nations, but no one could "own" the land the Creator had provided for men and beasts. That was against wâhkôhtowin, or kinship, the connection between people, the land, the natural world.

The môniyâwak did not live in the world this way. Ahtahkakoop saw this, understood that the freedom his people had always known was disappearing. The only freedom they might now have was on this land that the white men were offering to "give" them. The only freedom left would be on the reserves.

A number of other Plains Cree Chiefs and leaders, including the famous Big Bear (Mistahimaskwa) and Poundmaker (Pitikwahanapiwiyin), were distrustful of the môniyâwak and did not want to enter into treaties with them. Ahtahkakoop, however, sadly accepted that there was no way to stop the great shifts that were happening. He wanted to negotiate an agreement with Canada's Queen, to touch a treaty paper with his hand in order to protect the rights of his people. And he believed nēhiyawak needed to gain a greater understanding of the white ways in order to survive. He wanted his people to raise crops so they could feed themselves when hunting was poor. He wanted his children to learn to read and write English. He wanted to learn more about the way white men worshipped God, who he assumed was the same as the Creator his own people prayed to.

I heard all about this as a child. I also heard many stories of the Reverend John Hines and his influence on my family.

In 1874, Ahtahkakoop met Hines, an Anglican minister newly arrived from England. Hines had been sent by his mission to teach both Christianity and farming to the Cree of northern Saskatchewan. Ahtahkakoop invited Hines to live among his people. At the time, the band was settled semi-permanently at Fur Lake, not far south of Sandy Lake. John Hines advised Ahtahkakoop that the land was not ideal for farming. So Ahtahkakoop began to look for a better location to be his people's permanent home. Travelling past Sandy Lake, he climbed to the top of the crest we now call Lonesome Pine Hill. Sitting there, he looked out across the sloughs, the woods, and the open spaces. This, he thought, was the place his people would find their best future. The land had abundant fresh water and fishing spots—Sandy Lake, the Asissipi River, the many sloughs. There were fine stands of big trees to provide lumber for cabins. Deep woods for trapping and hunting. Good soil, hay fields, and meadows where they might start farms. And it was close to where his good friend and cousin Chief Mista-wasis and his band had settled. He wanted their two reserves to adjoin—or at least be close enough that white settlements couldn't be made between them.

In 1876, the Cree Chiefs, headmen, and leaders gathered at Fort Carlton to negotiate land guarantees with the Queen. Ahtahkakoop would claim for his people all the land he had seen from Lonesome Pine Hill.

Not everyone at the meeting came prepared to trade freedom for territory. At one point during the talks, the Cree leader Poundmaker shouted out, "This is our land! It isn't a piece of pemmican to be cut off and given in little pieces back to us. It is ours and we will take what we want."

The truth of Poundmaker's words would not safeguard his people. He and Big Bear both refused to sign the treaty for many years. In that time, their bands would starve as the shortage of buffalo worsened, and both Poundmaker and Big Bear would be charged with treason and imprisoned.

Ahtahkakoop was hoping that touching the treaty paper made with the Queen would protect his people from that kind of suffering. He and Mistawasis bargained with Alexander Morris, the Lieutenant-Governor of Manitoba and the North-West Territories, for more than just land. They also negotiated for government help in cases of famine and sickness and the provision of farming supplies. They decided to trust the claim that Morris made about the treaties: the agreements would last as long as the sun shines, the grass grows, and the rivers flow. Mistawasis was the first Chief to sign Treaty 6. Ahtahkakoop was the second.

Ahtahkakoop was satisfied with the compromises he had made and the guarantees he'd got from the Queen. But when the official survey of Sandy Lake was done, the government agent redrew the boundaries, reducing the reserve in size, from seven miles by eleven to seven miles by ten, and reshaping it so the length ran north to south instead of east to west. The new configuration meant land that had already been worked by Ahtahkakoop's people lay outside the reserve. And worse, the reserve no longer adjoined Mistawasis's land. A full seven miles now separated the two nations.

As long as the sun shines, the grass grows, and the rivers flow. It had taken almost no time for that promise to be broken.

It was a sad sign of things to come. The reserve would provide Ahtahkakoop's people with a permanent home, but it could not stop the injustices they would suffer from the Canadian government.

In 1876, there were 276 people newly settled on the Sandy Lake reserve, including Sasakamoose, who was the first of the four headmen. Reverend Hines was given land to build a home and school. Barley and wheat were sown in the newly plowed fields. Vegetable gardens were planted. And cabins were built. Living in these permanent buildings, Ahtahkakoop's band came to be known as wāskahikaniwiyiniwak, or "House Cree," to the surrounding Indigenous population.

Ahtahkakoop believed that as the world was changing, the nēhiyaw spiritual practices must change as well. But it was not always easy for him and his people to take on the new religion Hines was offering. Hines insisted that none of the Cree spiritual beliefs were compatible with Christianity—worshipping the Creator was not the same as worshipping the Christian God. The old ways were pagan and "evil" and had to be abandoned. No more traditional ceremonies, like the Sundances or feasts to honour the dead inhabiting the spirit world, no more Sweat Lodges to commune with the Creator and heal mind and body. In fact, according to the Elders of my youth, when Hines began his conversion of Ahtahkakoop and his headmen, he told them to bring their medicine bundles to him. These bundles were used in our ceremonies, and each contained sacred items given to us by the Creator. Pipes, rattles, hand drums, eagle whistles, even the essence of our ceremonial songs. Hines then insisted that Ahtahkakoop and his men bury the bundles in the ground, saying they were heathen relics and, as Christians, the people of Sandy Lake would no longer have use for them. The Elders also told stories of how Hines, accompanied by an Indian agent and a North-West Mounted Police officer, went from home to home confiscating these holy bundles, which he threw into a huge bonfire outside the little Anglican church. When my Elders talked about this destruction of their holy treasures, it was if they were describing the death of a beloved child. Confusion and heartbreak coloured their words.

My great-grandfather Sasakamoose struggled greatly with the move to Hines's Christianity. He was a member of the mitēwiwin, a secret and powerful spiritual society, and was considered a great shaman. He also had two wives (a third wife had left Sasakamoose with their two daughters and a son, Seeseequasis, to return to her people, who lived in the Duck Lake area). Hines insisted that Sasakamoose and his two remaining wives could not be baptized until Sasakamoose lived with only one of them. Sasakamoose loved his wives, and he had children by both. He would not abandon either of them. The older of the two, Okeke Okima, later called Mary, wanted to be baptized. In the end, because Mary was old and sick, Hines agreed to baptize her. Later that day, she passed away. She would be the first woman buried in the new Anglican graveyard.

Eventually, Sasakamoose converted, taking the name Jacob. (Although he never truly gave up his traditional spiritual beliefs and refused to surrender his medicine bundle.) His second wife, Apistiskwesis, took the name Margaret, or Maggie. They had their children baptized and educated at Hines's little school as well. Sasakamoose even allowed Reverend Hines to informally adopt his son Joseph and daughter Margaret. Joseph taught school before he died at twenty. And Hines married Margaret off to a forty-two-year-old Scottish man when she was fifteen. But other family members, including Sasakamoose's son Alexander, hung on to the traditional ways even as they worshipped as Christians.

I heard all of this from my Elders, including my father, Roderick, who was born to Alexander. Alexan, as my moosum was called by his family, could not hear. Could not speak. Yet he was a smart, handsome man and seemed to have no trouble finding a wife. When his first wife, Rosella, passed away not long after they were married, he wed my kokum Julienne "Julia" Favel, and together they had eight children. (She was a member of a Métis family from the Poundmaker reserve, where that Chief's people had eventually settled. Her father had even been a scout in the 1885 North-West Rebellion.)

The story of how my own parents met has been lost. My mother, Judille or Judith, but known by everyone as Sugil, grew up about one hundred miles north of Sandy Lake, on Green Lake. At some point, she and her family moved to the Whitefish Lake area, only about thirty miles from Sandy. My father was a logger, so maybe he crossed paths with my mother and her family while he was north of home, working in the camps.

My mother's mother, Veronica Bear, had been born a member of the Whitefish First Nation (which is now part of the Big River First Nation) but lost her treaty status and her right to live on the reserve when she married a Métis man, Joe Morin. Sadly, my mother didn't know her father well. He died when she was about eight, shortly after his return from World War I. For most of my mother's childhood, her mother raised the kids alone. Eventually, Veronica wed another Métis man, Gaspar Morin.

As soon as my parents fell in love, no obstacle could keep them apart. My father had a daughter from a previous relationship with another woman, Georgina Sahpwassum. My mother wasn't bothered by this. She would come to consider little Sapphire, or Sophia, a daughter, although she didn't tell us, her own children, about our half-sister until we were in our teens.

What might have been a bigger problem was their religious differences. My father was Anglican, but my mother had been raised Catholic. At the time, that difference often kept people apart. But my parents didn't care one bit about it.

My father agreed to marry my mother in a Catholic church and to live for a time at Whitefish Lake. He also followed the Plains Cree custom of letting his children be raised in their mother's traditions and faith, although that would have consequences neither of them could have imagined.

My parents' first child together was my brother Frank, born in 1931. Then on Christmas Day, 1933, I came into the world.

My mother gave birth to me at the home she and Dad shared with her parents. An older woman named Myrtle Duquette, or Meegwais, helped deliver me. I've been told that on that night, Myrtle and others blessed me, gave me a song, and predicted that the future had special things in store for me. Myrtle also followed a traditional Cree practice— placing a baby's umbilical cord in a spot that symbolized the family's hopes for the child's future. Myrtle apparently took my cord to a frozen pond, a place where many buffalo skulls had been found. She left the cord lying on the ice.

Myrtle also gave me my Cree name, Ayahkokopawiwiyin, which describes the steadfast spirit of a young buffalo. In English, it means "to stand firm." I was a hefty little guy, with strong legs, so maybe that's why she chose it. The name I was baptized with, however, was Frederick Patrick George Joseph Sasakamoose. But no one called me Frederick until I was taken far from home. At home, I was nick- named Toosaw, after a famously strong man who'd lived in the area years before.

As I have said, I never heard any of those birth stories when I was a child. What I did hear from Myrtle was that I had interrupted her Christmas.

She was at a party, in the Catholic church on the Big River reserve, the night my mother went into labour. The music was playing. She was just about to start dancing with my grandfather. That's when my dad burst into the room. Without a word, he hustled her out the door and into his sled. He pulled her two or three miles through the night so she could help deliver me.

"Ah, Toosaw," she used to say, laughing, "eki-wiyakitayin ninīmi-towin, eki-wiyakitayin manito kisikaw." You ruined my dance. You ruined my Christmas.

I don't know what brought my parents back to Sandy Lake.

Perhaps my father wanted to return there because he longed to rejoin his own family. Alexan and Julia. His brother Joe. Joe's wife and children. His cousins, aunts, and uncles.

Perhaps it was the draw of the place itself. The beautiful mix of grassland and trees, hills and water. The promise of the land that Ahtahkakoop had chosen. The land where Sasakamoose, my great-grandfather, had lived out his life.

If so, I understand that draw.

This land, the country that Ahtahkakoop gazed at from the top of Lonesome Pine Hill, the land he claimed—wherever I have travelled, wherever I have lived, this land has always called me home.

2

nīkihk

HOME

When my parents returned to Sandy Lake in the mid-1930s, we moved in with my father's parents for a while. Julia and Alexan had a little farm just west of the northern tip of Sandy Lake. My parents then chose a spot some distance east of the lake, where the land sloped down to a bright blue slough ringed with poplars and spruce. There they felled trees to build a simple cabin. The log walls were chinked with a mixture of clay-rich mud and grass. Lime whitewash brightened the inside of our little home.

It was a small place, this house—just twenty by twenty-four feet. There was no electricity or running water anywhere on the reserve at the time. We collected water from the slough in the warmer months. In the winter, when the slough froze, we melted snow for drinking and bathing. Smoky coal oil lamps were our only light. A small wood-burning stove stood in one corner of the cabin. On mild days the stove managed to keep us cozy, but in the frigid winter months the cabin could get very cold. We didn't have a lot of furniture—just a tall cupboard along the wall, where my mother kept food and cooking equipment. And a small bed in one corner, where she and my father slept. We children slept together on the floor, wrapped in soft, warm covers that my mother made by layering silky rabbit fur and heavy Hudson's Bay wool blankets. It was a simple home, but one where we were safe, happy, surrounded by love.

By the time I was four or five, our small cabin was home to seven of us. First there was my brother Frank and me. After us, two sets of twins were born—two girls and then a boy and a girl. I have little memory of the first pair, as the girls died while I was still a toddler. Then my brother Peter arrived.

My father was a big man, tall and strong. He walked straight as an arrow. His skin was dark with the sun. He hunted, trapped, and fished, but he spent most of his time working as a logger in the camps north of Big River. Those camps would employ 100 or 150 men, and my father told us that he and his friend Frank Cox could cut more timber in a day than anyone else. In the winter, they'd stack those logs on top of the frozen river. When spring came and the ice melted, the loggers would run in spiked boots along the top of the floating boom with picaroons, guiding the logs down to the sawmill at Big River. When I was older and working in the camps, I would see my dad perform this feat. But even when I was a small boy, I could picture it. Dad was agile and athletic, a terrific soccer player. He could make even the most difficult move look easy. Dad loved his work, sharpening his crosscut saw until its edge was fine as a razor before heading off north, but logging meant he was gone all winter long, from October to March. He would even miss Christmas. It was too difficult to make the long journey from the lumber camps to Sandy Lake in the deep snows. During the spring and summer, he would be home, although fishing, hunting, and trapping trips would take him away from the reserve for days at a time. He would also trek about fifty miles to the edge of Prince Albert National Park to collect Seneca root, which was used as traditional medicine to treat asthma and colds. He could sell it for ten cents a pound to the local people. And he spent weeks working for the white farmers whose fields threaded around Sandy Lake and between the reserves. In the fall, he might stook for them, but much of the time he spent hauling rocks out of stone-filled fields.

My mother never complained—she was one of the hardest workers I have ever known. She was tough, disciplined, resourceful. Not only did she make our bedcovers, she also pieced and stitched soft hides into moccasins, shirts, and pants, which she decorated with delicate bead-work. Other clothes she made out of Hudson's Bay blankets. She grew potatoes, turnips, and carrots in a small garden beside the house. She baked bannock, made pemmican, and cooked up big pots of stew. We ate mostly rabbit and prairie chicken, but also deer, moose, beaver, muskrat, and fish. And berries—chokecherries, blueberries, saskatoons.

My father and my grandfather weren't the only ones who hunted and trapped. In the winter months, my mother would often bundle up us kids in the sled, covering us with our rabbit-fur blankets. Then she would set off, a .22 strapped to her back, hauling the loaded sled behind her.

My first memory of these trips is still crystal clear. I am lying in the sled on my back, under the warm fur, staring up at the trees. And suddenly they are a blur.

"nimāmā, mītosak oki e-waskawipayicik," I shout. Mom, Mom, the trees are moving!

And my mother begins to laugh. "moya, toosaw. ēkamā aniki mītosak. kiyanaw anima." No, Toosaw. The trees aren't moving. We are.

Every so often, after my mother had pulled the sled for a while, it would come to a halt. And then we'd see her take the rifle off her back and lower it, focusing on something in the distance. There'd be a bang, and then she'd be holding up our next supper: a prairie chicken. Sometimes the sled stopped so she could lay snares for rabbits and weasels. Many of the pelts would become clothing, but she also traded ermine and rabbit fur at the Hudson's Bay post just outside the reserve for grocery items and other supplies.

When Mom wanted to visit her mother and stepfather, Veronica and Gaspar Morin, and the rest of her family at Whitefish Lake, we travelled the same way. But for this long journey, she'd get us in the sled even before the sun had come up in the sky. Once we were seated, she'd take the clothes irons she'd heated on the wood stove, wrap them in extra blankets, and bury them at our feet. Then we would be off. Since Frank was older, he'd sometimes run along with her. At some point in the journey, Mom was sure to shoot a rabbit. Then she'd stop, build a fire, and roast the rabbit on a little vertical rack she'd made. While we were eating and warming ourselves by the flames, she'd put the irons into the embers to reheat them. We'd spend the whole day like that, as she pulled the sled the twenty miles to her former home. Later, we would have a horse to pull the sled, but when I was very young, we walked or snowshoed everywhere.

We had only one close neighbour, a fellow named Albert Snake. The rest of the three or four hundred residents of Sandy Lake were spread out over the seventy square miles of the reserve. Only about four families were Catholic—the rest were Anglican. Reverend Hines's church and the little school he'd set up in the parish hall were at the south end of Sandy Lake, but of course, since the church was Anglican, only my father attended, and then only once in a while. I went to the school a couple of times, but I wasn't keen on it. Besides, it was at least five or six miles from our house—a long way, especially in winter, when the snow was deep. And yet, spread out as we were, as isolated as some of us might seem to have been, we were a strong community. We visited our friends and relatives on the reserve as often as we could, and people dropped by to see us. When anyone was sick, healers would arrive with traditional medicines. Midwives helped when women were having babies. (My mother was one of these midwives.) When someone killed a moose or came into a great bounty, they would always share with others. At Christmas, our retired Chief, Ahtahkakoop's son kāmiyoastonin, or Basil Star-blanket, would kill one of his cows and hold a huge feast for everyone in Sandy Lake.

Sharing was the way my people had always survived, and even with all the changes that had been inflicted on us, that didn't stop. I can still see my mother getting us all ready to set off for a visit or to pick berries. She would place some pieces of bannock and a pot of tea on the stove. As she got us all out the door, she would turn to me and Frank and say, "kipahmok iskwatem, kaya maka ka-apihkohamik." Close the door, boys, but don't lock it.

"maka nikāwiy," I said, the first time she did this, "tansi maka kīspin awiyak otinaki ōhi?" But Mom, what if someone comes and takes our things?

"kikwaya maka kotinakihk?" What are they going to take? she asked. "ekosi oma mana pahkwesikan ekwa maskihkīwāpoy, kīspin awiyak katakosi, ekwa ka-nohtehkatet, kahki-asāmsōwak." Besides, that's what the bannock and tea are for. If someone stops by and is hungry, there's some food for them. And then she added, "kaya waneyihta, toosaw, misawac aniki kapetawak kīkway." Don't worry, Toosaw, they will bring a little something in return.

And she was right. Whenever we got home to find the bannock eaten and the tea finished, a short time later someone would drop by with a little gift—maybe tea or other groceries from the store in town.

My mother loved to laugh. And she loved to dance. Our traditional round dances did not take place on the reserve. Reverend Hines, of course, had not allowed them, and then, in 1895, the Indian Act officially prohibited them, as well as Sundances. But some reserves still managed to hold them. We would travel to nearby communities or as far as Mom's parents' home on Whitefish Lake to join the dances. The round dance—that was our waltz. The dancers would perform in a circle, stepping lightly to the rhythm of the drums, for two or three nights in row, resting only in the day. Many would not eat or sleep during the whole time.

Oh, my, I loved to watch my mother dance. She was a beautiful woman, made even more stunning by the bright colours and beaded headbands and belts she wore to the dances. As she moved, her salmon-hued skin would begin to glow, and her glossy black braids would bounce against her back.

One of my favourite memories is seeing her when I was very small at a Christmas dance in Sandy Lake. The music was lively. A fiddler and drummer were playing jigs. Feet were tapping, people were turning on the dance floor. Then the door of the hall opened. And there stood an extraordinary man. He was shining and sparkling, the lamp light shimmering off the thousands of tiny beads that decorated his buckskin jacket and his tall leather mukluks. He had on a fur cap and wore huge beaver-pelt mitts. He stood tall and regal. I was struck by wonder. Taking his mitts off, the stranger moved towards my mother.

"astam nitānis." Come here, my daughter, he said. "wichi-nimihtomin." Come dance with me.

And then my mother was spinning on the floor with him, the two of them a blur of colour and light, her orange and purple silk dress flashing along with his beaded jacket. It was magical.

I would later learn his name was Jerry Rabbitskin. He was a trapper from up north, one of my mother's relatives. A traditional Cree man greatly respected for his knowledge and skill. In fact, he was so admired, after he was widowed twice and was quite old, he was offered the hand of a beautiful young woman as his third wife.

But I didn't know any of that then. All I knew was that this mysterious, striking figure had singled out my mother, drawing everyone's attention to her beauty and grace.

Even when my mother wasn't at dances, she would celebrate them. One of her favourite songs was one she had learned from her mother-in-law, Julia. It was about Alexan's half-sister Margaret, who had married a much older man. In the song, Margaret's husband is begging his young wife to come back from a round dance, where she has been for days. "astam nicimos pekiwe, ki-pēpīm māhto. wipac ka-wāpa. pekiwe . . ." my mother would sing. Come home, my sweetheart, come home. Your baby's crying. It will be daylight soon. Come home . . .

Round dances weren't our only trips. Sometimes we would pack up a few things and journey to the Big Stone, about twenty-five miles south of our home, in rolling grasslands. The rock was smooth-edged and huge—about eleven feet high. A buffalo stone, worn smooth over the centuries by the great beasts who rubbed and scratched against it. There, along with Alexan and Julia and my mother's parents, Veronica Bear and Gaspar Morin, and other families and Elders, we would set up our tents. This, we were told, was the very place where Chief Ahtahkakoop and Chief Mistawasis and their people camped, trapped, and feasted during the winter months. We would spend a couple of weeks in the area, hunting as well, the Elders singing feast songs each evening. Before we left, my moosum Alexan would always tuck small twists of tobacco into the crevices in the rock—an offering to the earth.

Despite being Catholic and the child of a Métis father, my mother embraced Cree ways, just as Alexan did. She relied on the Medicine Man and knew a lot about traditional healing herself. When any of us were sick, she made remedies from bark, rat root, balsam needles, bear fat, frog leaves, and other local plants. She collected sweetgrass for smudging ceremonies. And she believed in the power of Sweat Lodges. Once, when she had her hurt foot badly, she called upon a local healer, who built her a Sweat Lodge near our home. A few days after her time in the lodge, her foot was better and she was walking again.

My father was much more leery of traditional ways. He had been born just twenty years after Reverend Hines left Sandy Lake, and had attended the Reverend's little school for a year or so. Even though several members of his family, including his own father, never let go of Cree spirituality and practices, he seemed to be more strongly affected by Hines's influence. But he never interfered with my mother's way of doing things. He always let her lead the way.

As lively and direct as my mother could be, that was how quiet and mild my father was. Though he could speak English well, he only talked with the family in Cree. (My mother could speak a little French, and English was a foreign language to her.) But perhaps because his own father was deaf and mute, my dad was a man who spoke little in any language. He never raised his voice. He didn't waste words, not even on instructions. I remember an early spring day when he took me with him to cut some wood. When he got to the tree he wanted to fell, he started in on it with the swede saw. I stood a little distance off. Soon I became cold and started to complain. He stopped sawing. Built me a little fire. From the warmth of the fire, I watched him as he worked, stopping now and then to wipe his brow. A few more minutes passed before I figured it out. I went to the other end of the saw and began to pull. In no time, I was warmer than the fire could make me.

When I was about five or six, my grandmother Julia passed away. Alexan moved from his little house to live with my uncle Joe, who also had a house on the reserve. But after a short while, Dad brought Alexan back to stay with us.

My brother, sisters, and I were happy to have him so close again. We had always loved our time with our moosum. A small man, with a fair complexion and red beard, he walked with a bit of a slouch, yet he was tough and surprisingly strong. He used to lift the front end of horses off the ground to amaze us. Indeed, he seemed to have a special relationship with children. He always paid us plenty of attention, and when his good friend our neighbour Albert Snake visited, the two of them would team up to entertain us. Albert, who apparently had coined my nickname, Toosaw, was originally from the Young Chippewayan band (and was its hereditary Chief). He would often tell us stories of his younger days. How he would travel to hunt in Maple Creek and the Cypress Hills—the only places you could still find buffalo in the late 1800s. How he and members of his band would go to Medicine Hat, four hundred miles away, to meet with other Indians and trade medicine. And how the government thought his band had supported the Métis uprising of 1885, so had cut off support, forcing the starving band members to leave their reserve and join other bands. (Ahtahkakoop and Mistawasis had turned down Riel and Dumont's invitation to join the uprising. They remained neutral throughout the conflict.) That's how Albert had come to us. Sometimes Grandpa would pull out a sacred pipe from the medicine bundle that his father, Jacob, had kept hidden from Hines for so many years. The pipe was packed in a small case, surrounded by healing herbs. It was coloured red and blue—red from cranberries, blue from saskatoons. We understood that it may have been the pipe stem used at Fort Carlton during the signing of Treaty 6. At other times, the mood was sillier. Moosum would dance jigs while Albert played tricks, like pretending to pull peppermints out of his bum and giving them to us to eat.

We weren't always easy on our moosum. Frank and I would run into the fields that he tended and jump on the haystacks he'd made. He would come after us, waving his hands, yelling, in his way, but we would only laugh.

"We're faster than Grandpa. He can't keep up with us." (We learned this cockiness was a mistake when the snow was really deep.) But we knew our moosum would never stay angry at us.

Perhaps it was because I was a small child and had also been without language not so long ago, or perhaps it was something else, but I'd always felt a deep connection to Alexan. Since he couldn't hear and he couldn't speak, he mostly used hand gestures to communicate. Sometimes he would murmur to draw attention. He could feel the vibrations when people walked or tapped their feet. He always knew when someone was behind him. But Moosum and I didn't need to talk to understand each other. He would look over at me and smile, and I immediately understood what he was thinking. We'd often go for long walks together. He'd hold my hand or rest his palm on my back, and with each footstep I felt as if what was on his mind was floating through the air to me.

Even though he couldn't say a word, my grandpa was a great teacher. He taught me and Frank how to fish. He showed us how to hunt. His ability to track animals was extraordinary. When he found animal prints in the earth, he'd squat down and run his fingers over the impressions. From that, he could tell if the animal was long gone or close by. If he felt it was near, he'd point to his eyes and then to the direction he wanted me and Frank to go so that the three of us could circle around the animal. We knew the animals could smell us if we got close, but Alexan seemed to have an ability to sense them too. I think he learned that from his father and all of those other great hunters of the past.

Like my mother, Alexan was a believer in the Sweat Lodge—as a place to heal and to worship. He always built his some distance from the house, in the clear grasslands, where the ground was clean and open. First he would dig a pit in the earth, about a foot deep and two and a half feet wide. Then cut and bend willow branches over it to form a wide dome, many feet across. He'd cover this with a large piece of canvas he kept for this purpose. Then he'd build a fire outside the lodge. In that fire would go the rocks that would eventually heat the interior.

He worked with care and intensity. My moosum was a deeply religious man, and even constructing the lodge was a way to honour the Creator.

When the rocks were very hot, he'd bring five into the lodge. The first four represented the directions—east, then south, then west, then north. In the middle was the rock that signified God's creation. He'd put tobacco on each of these stones. It was a mixture he made for himself to smoke—a combination of tobacco, scraped willow bark, cranberry leaves, and dried cranberries.

We'd have to take all our clothes off to go into the lodge. My moosum would toss water on the rocks until great clouds of steam filled the canvas. If other men were in the lodge with us, they'd sometimes talk about our relations who'd passed before us, about wâhkôhtowin (kinship and connection) and about God, the Creator. And then they would begin to sing. Since my moosum had no voice, he'd use a rattle or drum to create music. He would gesture for me and Frank to join in, but I didn't know the songs. Often he'd put the drum on his knees, tapping it with one hand while the other rested on my head or Frank's. We knew it was an act of love and protection—he was praying, praying for our long lives and good futures.

After about fifteen minutes, we'd need to take a break, go outside. Then more rocks would be brought in for a second round, then a third and fourth, until the pile of rocks at the centre of the lodge numbered forty-eight.

As the cleansing and worship continued, different herbs and barks would be placed on the stones, perfuming the air. My favourite was diamond willow fungus, which produced the deep rich scent of anise. It was a beautiful smell.

Near the end of our sessions, Grandpa would bring out food for us: kinosêw (fish), corn, berries, whatever he'd been able to gather. We would eat some of it, but we always saved a portion to put on the fire, an offering for people who had passed on.

Grandpa also once took me to see a Shaking Tent that had been built by some Indians visiting from South Dakota. Shaking Tents are used at night to call forth spirits who might give guidance about things like where to find game and how to restore health. But I didn't understand what was happening in the dark tent and became frightened. Years later, as an adult, I would attend another Shaking Tent ceremony. A number of people suffering from various illnesses had gathered that night, hoping to receive help. The shaman had his wrists and arms tied with rawhide ropes and was then covered in a blanket. He crawled inside a tiny tent just big enough to hold him. As he called forth the spirits, we could hear the sound of rattles and the tent began to shake. Suddenly the rawhide ties, somehow still knotted, came flying out of the tent. They landed on me. It's hard to describe what happened around that tent—the sounds and the sights, suggesting spirits were present—but it unnerved me, just as it had when I was a child. And

I remembered the relief I'd felt when Grandpa took hold of my hand and led me away, his warm touch making me feel safe again.

My moosum made me feel special. It was as if he saw something in me, and without words he let me know that he believed in this vision. So I was not surprised when, one cold winter's day, he put me in a sled, took me down to the frozen slough, and produced a pair of bobskates. Before we left the cabin, he had dressed me with five pairs of socks under my moccasins. Now, at the lake, he strapped the double blades onto my feet, picked me up, and set me down on the ice. When I fell, he gently raised me and set me on my feet once more. He did that again and again and again.

I would later discover there was a little French community in Debden, not far from the reserve, that had an outdoor rink where some of the men played hockey. From time to time, Grandpa would make the trip into town to watch the games. And I guess, for some reason, as he looked at the players, he thought of me.

Day after winter day, Moosum and I would head down to the lake in the early afternoon. Sometimes Frank would come with us, but there was only one pair of skates, and they were too small for Frank's feet. Frank would slide around the ice as I shuffled forwards on my blades, but he soon became bored of this and left Grandpa and me to our new afternoon routine.

As soon as we got to the slough, Grandpa would shovel off the snow and tie my blades on. Once I had started to skate, he'd cut a hole in the ice. He'd settle himself on an overturned bucket and drop a fishing line into the water, while I skated around and around and around. Sometimes, if it was really cold, he'd go to the shore after an hour or so and build a little fire so I could warm myself before heading back onto the ice.

One afternoon, just before we headed home for the day, Grandpa disappeared into a stand of willows on the shore of the slough. He came out with a long willow branch. That evening, sitting in the dim light of the oil lamp, he began to whittle, stripping the bark and smoothing the surface. Then he bent one end and placed the branch on the stove to dry. The next afternoon, when we got to the slough, he handed me my new hockey stick and showed me how to push a frozen cow patty across the ice with it. I didn't know it at the time, but Grandpa had just turned me into a hockey player. I played with the stick and "puck" for hours, until it was time for Grandpa and me to return to the cabin and our chores before the sun dropped from the sky.

This was my world. A nēhiyaw world. A nēhiyaw life.

It was not easy. Underlying everything we did were the rules and regulations laid out by the Indian Act, enforced by our local Indian agent. He was the one who issued our treaty cards and the passes so my father could leave the reserve to work and to trade. He was the one who doled out the coupons we had to use to get our ration of sugar or tea from the reservation store. He was the one who determined who would receive farm equipment or building supplies. This white man was the one who made all the rules on our reserve. As Indians, we didn't have the rights of Canadian citizens. We couldn't even own property or vote. And we were poor, that's the truth. But I didn't know that.

What I knew was that home was full of song, dance, and tradition. It was full of wonder and mystery. It was full of family, love, and community.

And then one day, in 1941, when I was just seven, all of that was taken away.

To be honest, I don't remember a lot about the beginning of that last day of my childhood. I don't know what Frank and I were doing, only that we were outside. My father was home, chopping wood out back.

I remember that, at least. And it was fall. Perhaps we were helping dig potatoes out of the ground before the first hard frosts touched them. I don't know. The twins must have been in the cabin. Maybe three-year-old Peter was with them. It felt like a normal day, the kind you have over and over until they all blend together, stretching to the edges of memory.

Everything is a bit cloudy until the moment a huge canvas-covered grain truck appears in front of our little cabin. Three men get out of the cab. One I recognize—the reserve's Indian agent. Another is wearing a uniform. An RCMP officer. And the third is a pale white man with a hard face. He is wearing a long black robe that billows slightly behind him as he walks. He's talking to my mother, and my father is coming around to the front of the cabin, but I can't make out what anyone is saying. All I can hear is the sharp, jagged sound of crying. Crying children. It's coming from under the canvas of the truck.

And then someone is lifting the canvas flaps at the back of the vehicle. And one of the men is grabbing Frank and lifting him into the truck. My moosum is pulling me in behind his back, is standing in front of me with his arms spread. I'm peeking around him, and I see one of the men coming towards us. My grandpa tries to push him away, but he's swept aside and falls to the ground. My strong, protective moosum, the man who is mighty enough to lift the front end of a workhorse clear off the ground, is shoved aside as if he is nothing. And then I'm being hoisted into the crush of crying, trembling children. I can see my moosum struggling to get up. He is making desperate sounds, sounds I have never heard before. My mother is hanging on to my father, her shoulders heaving. My big, strong father looks helpless.

The last thing I see before the engine starts and the flaps are dropped in front of me is my moosum, lying on the ground, shaking and crying.

And then we are gone.

3

kiskinwahamākēwikamik

THE SCHOOL

I don't know how long we were travelling. There were about thirty of us crushed into the eight-by-five-foot back of the truck. Frank and I had no idea where we were heading. We were given nothing to eat or drink. We sat on the wooden floor, terrified, crying, as hour after hour passed. Kids were forced to relieve themselves where they sat. The truck reeked. I leaned against Frank, numb with fear.

Eventually the truck stopped, and the robed man gestured for us to get out. We were at a wide, fast-moving river, and there was a long, flat boat waiting at the shore. To our amazement, the truck drove onto the boat, and then we were forced to follow it. The ferry moved slowly across the water and we gulped in the fresh air. Once we arrived at the other bank, we had to climb back inside the dark, stinking bed of the truck. We began to bump along the dirt road once more.

A few hours after that, the robed man appeared at the back of the truck again. When we got off this time, oh, man. In front of us was a huge grey-brick building. It rose into the air, windows on top of windows on top of windows. Four storeys high. I had never seen anything like it. It was terrifying.

And then we were being hustled into the building. Frank and I were separated. We were marched into a room where nuns set about cutting off our beautiful braids with huge pairs of scissors and shaving off the rest of our hair with clippers. Then we were forced to take our clothes off and shuffle into a windowless brick-walled room. There, coal oil, the stuff we used in our lamps at home, was poured over our bare heads. The foul-smelling liquid dripped into my ears, stung my eyes, burned down my back.

Hot steam began to billow out from a pipe near the ceiling of the small room. Water, soap, scrub brushes. After all those hours in the filthy truck, I guess some of the kids needed a good bath. But this wasn't a bath. It felt like those nuns and priests were trying to scrub the colour right off our skin. As if they didn't care that my mother made sure we were washed every day, our hair clean and brushed, carefully braided, neatly tied at the ends.

I have no idea how long we were kept in that steamy shower room, but it felt like hours. We came out half-blind, our eyes red and running, our skin raw. Finally, we were taken into another room and given stiff brown-striped canvas pants, coarse shirts, running shoes. Those beautiful wraparound moccasins my mother had made for me were gone. All my other clothes too. I have no idea what happened to them.

I don't remember if we were ever given anything to eat that night. All I remember is the huge room filled with tiny cots and crowded with boys. I had never seen so many children in my life.

Each cot was stamped with a number. Mine was 437. I noticed this number on all my clothes, my shoes, my bedding too. I would come to realize that it even replaced my name. As the priests and nuns got to know us, they'd use our "Christian" names. But mostly we were numbers.

A strange new routine started the very next day. Up at 6 A.M. to dress, wash our faces, and brush our teeth so we could be in the chapel for morning prayers. Then we filed back into the school to the long, narrow tables in the dining hall. Here the older girls would serve us lukewarm, lumpy porridge and a small glass of skim milk for breakfast. The nuns and priests sat at a raised table at the end of the room, chewing on bacon and eggs, sipping tea and cream-laced coffee.

After breakfast, we'd do our morning chores and spend a few hours at desks in the classroom. A small lunch, then we all had jobs to do around the school for the afternoon. Dinner might be a skimpy portion of baloney, head cheese, or watery stew. And bread. That was the best part of most meals. Boy, the girls baked good bread. Evenings would be spent playing sports or games in the fields outside or in the "playroom." The playroom had a ping-pong table we could use, or the priests might run some sort of organized game. Then it was time to wash up, say our prayers, and go to bed.

St. Michael's might have been called a "school," but it was really a work colony. The main building where the two hundred or so students lived sat on several acres of land, surrounded by a high fence of page wire. A large vegetable garden was planted with potatoes, turnips, carrots. The barn held about sixty dairy cows. There was a pigpen, a slaughterhouse, a woodshop. And we kids did the work. Girls would be in the kitchens, or bent over sewing machines and knitting needles, making all the clothes we wore. They did all the laundry and cleaned the school as well. The older boys milked the cows twice a day and fed the livestock. We were taken to the railway station in Duck Lake to shovel coal off the trains into a horse-drawn cart. Back at the school, we'd stoke the school's two huge boilers. The younger boys scrubbed floors, collected garbage, made beds, and cleaned the barns. Everyone laboured in the garden. We worked every day, in every type of weather. Our only time off was Sunday afternoon, after church.

Frank and I didn't know anyone else at the school. The priests and the Indian agents had forced only Catholic children to attend St. Michael's. The Anglican kids in Sandy Lake were allowed to stay at home. But all of the new kids at the school struggled, even if they were joining siblings and neighbours. Everyone was homesick and confused. We quickly learned that we weren't supposed to speak Cree. But many of us couldn't understand much English, and we'd whisper questions to each other in our language. Speaking Cree got us punished. And that punishment was harsh.

If you got caught taking food you weren't supposed to have, you went without lunch or supper. Instead, you knelt in front of the table where the priests and nuns sat and watched them eat. But punishments were often worse than that. If you did something else "wrong," like explaining something to another child in the language they could understand, the priests would march you into the middle of the dining hall. You'd have to take your shirt and pants off. Then a big leather strap would be brought down across your back, your arms, your legs, your backside.

What a shock to see that happen for the first time. My parents didn't hit us. I had never seen *any* adult beat a child. But at St. Michael's, grown men and women were always beating kids. Most of the time, it wasn't a formal punishment, like in the dining hall. If a priest or nun or one of the brothers who was training to be a priest saw you someplace they didn't think you should be, or maybe thought you were walking too slowly, or doing a sloppy job at something, they would take a swipe at you or kick you or bang your head into the wall or on the floor. (One friend got a perforated eardrum from one such blow. And my younger brother Peter would have permanent damage to one of his eyes from being struck by a priest when he arrived at St. Michael's.) You got hit for crying. Some of the adults were worse than others. You quickly got to know which ones you should avoid if you could, and when to brace yourself if you couldn't. But even the men and women who weren't as likely to slap or kick you wouldn't do a thing in the presence of one their own who was beating a student. They simply stood by, letting it happen.

It was only we children who were sometimes stopped when things got violent. If boys were caught fighting, the priests would say to the larger boy, "If you want to fight with someone, you're going to fight someone bigger than yourself." Then they'd take the boy into the playroom, make a little boxing ring out of the benches, and force the kid into the ring with one of the priests or young men who were training to be priests. The children were never any match for the grown men. More than once, a poor boy got knocked right out.

The voices of the nuns, priests, and brothers were never soft or conversational. They barked at us or blew whistles to get our attention or signal an order. Some of the French-speaking staff referred to us as "*les sauvages*."

The few hours we spent in the classroom each day were focused on English, a bit of math, and music. The nuns and priests seemed to believe that learning to sing and play a musical instrument was good for us, and I did enjoy that. But subjects like history or science, those they must have thought were completely unnecessary. Mostly, what we were taught was that our traditional ways of life, our traditional beliefs, were pagan, sinful. They were the ways of the devil. And that our Cree language was backward. I'm amazed, when I think about it, that we came away with any education at all, as we learned in fear, and you can't really learn anything in fear. I don't mind saying it—I hated it in that classroom. Sure, sometimes, as I shovelled out the horse barns or mopped a floor, I felt like a slave, but I would always rather work than sit at those desks.

Our days were long and tiring, but nighttime—nighttime was the most difficult.

Once we were all in our narrow beds in the huge, crowded dorm room, the lights would go out. When the priests and nuns had disappeared, the muffled sobs would begin. The new arrivals, sure. But others too. Worse than the crying, the pad of footsteps or the thumps of a struggle. Sometimes you could see black robes who had returned in the middle of the night, drifting through the darkness. Other times the shape of older boys would hover over the beds of smaller kids. One night I woke to the sound of Frank's cries. I quickly shut my eyes, put my hands over my ears. I didn't have any words for what was happening to him. What happened on other nights to other boys. And there was nothing I could do.

There was no safety in that huge, dark room. Yet the thought of leaving it at night was even more frightening. I never got out of my hard little cot, even if my bladder was bursting. I guess I wasn't alone in this. Under the rough, scratchy sheet on each bed was a stiff rubber pad. In no time, the damp and the heat created by the rubber had covered my body with a stinging red rash. I noticed angry raw patches on the backs and legs of many others as well.

We boys understood we were not alone in this suffering. The terrible things that happened in our dorm room were also happening on the other side of the wall to the girls. One day, I was sent to the principal, Father Latour, to deliver something. Two girls were sitting outside his office, trembling and crying. As I left, Father Latour called them in, told them to shut the door. I felt sick.

Some of the lucky kids—if you could say any of us were lucky—lived close to St. Michael's and were allowed to escape the odd time for a short visit home. Sandy Lake was too far away for that. But one Sunday afternoon, an old man showed up at the school asking for me and Frank. His name was Joe Seeseequasis. He was the father of one of the other boys at the school, Herb Seeseequasis, and was, apparently, a relative of ours, a descendent of one of Jacob Sasakamoose's sons, the one who had moved to Duck Lake with his mother. It seems my father had got word to him we had been taken to St. Michael's and asked him to try to look out for us. Joe took us to his home for dinner. After that, during the week, Joe's fatherly face would sometimes appear by the high wire fence. When we noticed him, Frank and I would sneak over. Joe would drop a few candies into our hands, then move away quickly before he was spotted. When Joe's daughter Grace, who was training to be a nun, worked at the school for a few months, she would sometimes sneak in a little fruit or bannock for us.

To be introduced to cousins and other family members, to be surrounded by people speaking Cree, to be eating familiar food, oh, boy, that was such a comfort. So often at the school, I felt I was losing my family, I felt I was losing my home. Those Sunday afternoons with Joe, his brother James, Herb, and the rest of the family, those brief visits at the fence—they were never enough for me, but they kept homesickness and hopelessness away for a sliver of time.

In warmer weather, we were allowed to go swimming in the lagoon. As I got older, I realized that this water was where the sewage from the school drained, but the priests and nuns didn't stop the kids from playing in it.

Singing and music also provided us with some cheerful breaks. I played the trombone in the school band. I don't suppose I was very good at it, but I enjoyed it. It was kind of nice to be allowed to make noise, to not be invisible, yet receive no punishment for that. But for me, the biggest distraction from all the homesickness and misery was sports. And fortunately, athletics was something the priests really seemed to believe in. We played ping-pong and basketball in the playroom all year long. The priests taught us how to box. In the spring and fall, there was soccer and baseball outside in the field. And in the winter—my favourite—hockey on the outdoor rink.

Even so, the first year at the school was very hard. But harder still was finding out Frank and I and the rest of the new arrivals wouldn't be going home for the summer. While all the other kids would spend about eight weeks with their families, it was too soon for us. I guess they thought that in ten months we hadn't lost enough of our Indian ways, our Cree language, our attachment to our homes and families. They didn't understand that while we might get used to eating their food and speaking their language, we would never stop missing those things.

When we'd finished our second year, we were finally allowed to crawl into the back of the three-ton grain truck with the older students for the long, bumpy journey home.

What a feeling. To catch a glimpse of that Lonesome Pine Hill on the horizon. After almost two years away. To know that we were only six or seven miles south of the reserve, six or seven miles from Mom, Dad, Moosum, the rest of the family.

Yet the first time we arrived home, it didn't go exactly as I'd imagined for those two long years.

When the truck stopped, Frank and I leapt from the back and ran to where our mother stood. She hugged us and brought us inside. But the familiar log cabin seemed strangely empty.

"tânte nīsotewak?" we asked my mother. Where are the twins?

She told us they had gotten sick and passed away when we were gone. We looked around, stunned. How could that be? Why had no one at the school told us?

But someone else was also missing. "mosōm ci kwaskwepichiket?" Is Moosum fishing? I asked. "tanehki moya ōta kāyāht?" Why isn't he here?

"nikosisak," my mother said with great sadness. Oh, my sons. "nakataskew, moya-ana kinwes kakīsepwehtayin kanakatasket. mistahi kaskeyitam. nikan ki-wanihew wiwa. aschi kiya ekwa. kinwes mana wayawītimihk nīpawiw. asko mina mana kinwes nitopapāmohtew ekwa tepiyahk koskwawatapew. asko mina mana sakā nitopapāmohtew ekwa kinwes mana moya-niwāpamanan." He is gone too. He didn't last long after you left. He got lonely. First he lost his wife. Then he lost you. He'd stand around outside for hours. Sometimes he would go for a long walk, but then he'd come home and just sit and sit. Sometimes he'd disappear into the bush, and we wouldn't see him for days.

It felt as if the earth had been pulled from under my feet. My moosum. Gone. The man who had spent so many hours with me, teaching me, who seemed so connected with the past and the future. The man who had always made me feel there was a special place for me in the world. Our quiet times together, walking in silence . . .

All those months in school I had missed him but never felt his absence, even though he was gone from the world. I wondered why. And I thought, He is still with me.

He will always be with me.

Even after the shock of Moosum's death eased a bit, I didn't tell my parents about the awful things that happened at the school. Neither did Frank. For one thing, by that time we'd figured out that if our parents tried to remove us from the school, or refused to send us back, they would have been arrested. They weren't even permitted to come visit us, as trips off the reserve required a pass from the Indian agent. And he was unlikely to give one for such a purpose.

But it was more than that. It was just too difficult to talk about. And we knew it would only make my mother suffer more than she already was. We could see that she had missed us, that it was devastating not to have her kids at home when just about everyone else on the reservation did. But she thought we were at least getting a good education and being kept safe by the priests and the nuns. We didn't want her to know that none of those things were true.

Yet thinking back to the day we were taken, I was sure that my moosum Alexan had seen the truth. He had known, as soon as he saw the truck, that something dark was waiting for Frank and me.

Despite all of our losses, Frank and I were happy to be home. We spent the summer helping Mom and Dad—working in the garden, chopping wood, fishing, picking berries. It wasn't like working at the school. There were no whistles or shouted orders. We were free to run through the trees and fields. To camp with our relatives. To speak Cree with them. To hug our parents and siblings. To sprawl on the floor under our rabbit-skin blankets at night, knowing we were safe.

As the years passed, each summer at home would be both a comfort and a reminder of the life we were missing. Sometimes we'd come back to find out that new siblings had arrived. Leo was born in 1943, Clara in 1947. Another boy came into the world but passed out of it again while still a baby. A little girl too. Those births and deaths made you realize how much time had slipped away while you were gone. More proof of that was the way it became harder and harder to talk to my mom and the other Elders who spoke only Cree. It got to the point where I couldn't find even the simplest words, and I'd have to point to a spoon or a fork to let my mother know that I wanted one. My language, the language of my people, was draining from me. When I realized that, I decided I would risk the beatings and have more whispered conversations in Cree at the school.

And every fall, that damn grain truck would show up on the reserve. Frank and I, and eventually Peter too, would have to climb in and say goodbye once again to everyone we loved and the place that was our only home. What would we find when we got home the next time? Would more people be missing? Would this world, our world, be changed again?

I think it was sometime in my third year that I tried to escape, to go home for good.

The priests and nuns were so hard on all the children—it was impossible to understand. Or to recover, in that place. The children, carved up by pain, confusion, anger, some turned to cruelty themselves. Usually, if an older kid tried to bully me, Frank would be there to protect me, would take the roughing-up himself. But of course, we weren't always together.

It was a Saturday afternoon, when I was about ten years old. My friend Pete and I were out in the fields, snaring gophers. The gophers made a mess of our garden, and the priests would pay Pete and me a penny for each one we killed. We'd just started out when a group of older boys came up to us, surrounded us. While a couple of boys held me, the others dragged Pete into the nearby bush. I could hear him crying and yelling, but I couldn't get to him. A priest was standing a few hundred yards away. His back turned. He must have heard our cries, but he didn't look around. Then I was being dragged into the trees too. The boys pulled off my clothes, wrestled me to the ground. Then they raped me.

I don't know how long I lay in that bush, sobbing. When I finally got up, I was all alone. I struggled back into my clothes and took a few steps. I felt something trickling down my legs. Blood. I hurt all over.

There was nobody around when I got out of the trees. I was relieved. I didn't want to face anyone, didn't want to go back to the school. I wanted to die.

I stood there for a while, trying to decide what I should do. I could hear the sounds of kids laughing and shouting. The voices were coming from the lagoon. They must be swimming, I thought.

I wanted to find Pete. I headed towards the voices.

He was standing a short distance from the lagoon, watching the other kids.

"Pete," I said. "What are you doing?"

"I'm not going back into the school," he said.

I felt the same. There was no life for us here. "Let's go home, Pete," I said.

We couldn't travel along the road, because we knew we'd be spotted by the priests. Instead, we ducked into the bush beside the gravel and started to walk. It was too early in the season for berries, so there was nothing to eat. We walked and walked, and when the skies darkened and the bush filled with shadows, we lay down on the underbrush and tried to sleep. The sun woke us the next morning and we started off again. By mid-morning, we had reached the Saskatchewan River.

The river was wider in those days than it is now, or at least in memory it seems so—about three or four hundred yards across. And it was deep and running quickly.

Pete said, "I'm going to swim across. I don't care if I drown."

He took his clothes off and waded into the water. He didn't get far before the current began to drag him downstream. I grabbed a large stick from the ground and ran along the bank, reaching it towards him. He managed to get hold of it, and I pulled him to shore.

When he came out of the water, he pulled his clothes back on and looked down the river.

"Where is the ferry crossing?" he asked.

We knew that somewhere along the river was the Wingard Ferry. Each time we were brought back and forth to school on the truck, we took it to cross the river.

"I don't know," I said. "I don't even know where we are."

We decided we'd walk downstream, hoping we'd find either the ferry or a narrower, shallower spot to cross.

We had only been going for about twenty minutes when we saw the ferry off in the distance. It was crossing the river to our side with a few cars on it. We headed towards it.

When we got to the ferry dock, the boat had arrived and the cars were gone. The ferryman appeared from out of his hut. He looked at us.

"You boys hungry? Want something to eat before you cross?"

Oh, boy, were we hungry. We nodded just about as hard as we could. He took us into his shack and put out some bread and jam.

I don't know how long we sat there, eating and resting, before we heard the sound of tires on the gravel road. A truck pulled up and out came Father Latour and another priest who had just arrived at the school—Father Roussel.

Apparently, the ferryman was used to the appearance of children who'd run away from St. Michael's. He would phone the school, then keep them occupied until the priests came to collect them.

We knew our escape was over. We walked over to the truck. But Father Latour shook his head.

"You are going to walk back," he said. "You made it this far, you can make it back."

And so we walked, hour after hour after hour, as the two priests followed us in the truck. By the time we got to the town of Duck Lake, it was evening. We still had a mile to go to get to the school. Father Latour stopped the truck beside us.

"Give me your shoes. And your socks. You will walk the rest of the way in bare feet."

My feet were already covered in blisters. After a few minutes on the sharp gravel road, they were bleeding. By the time we got to the school, I could barely put one foot in front of the other.

Somehow, Pete and I staggered into the school and into the dining hall. We were told to kneel in the middle of room, where the other kids could see us. A piece of bread and some water were placed on the floor in front of us. After we'd eaten, we were told to take our shirts off. One of the priests took a strap to our backs. After our whipping, our hair was shaved off and coal oil poured over our bare heads.

The punishment continued for a week. Bread and water for every meal. The strap each day. The priests were setting an example for the other kids—running away would only make your life more miserable.

I know, during my years at St. Michael's, other kids tried to escape. I'm not sure any made it. But there were disappearances.

If kids got sick, I mean really sick, with things like tuberculosis, they were moved out of the dormitories to another floor of the school. We often didn't see them again. We were never told what happened to them, but there were rumours. I understand that in the surviving school attendance records, there are notes beside some students' names. "Ran away." "Sick." "Hospital." "Discharged." Nothing more than that.

Yet, there was a little graveyard next to the chapel. From time to time, a few boys would be brought out there, given shovels, and told to dig. We weren't there when the long, deep holes were filled. And no signs or plaques marked the freshly mounded earth. I've been told, all these years later, that in 1898 Chief Poundmaker's son passed away at the school, and that in 1910 it was estimated that 50 percent of the children at the school had died in the previous few years. By the time I was there, I suppose things were better, but I know first-hand how dangerous it still was to get sick at that school.

One day, during our fifth winter at St. Michael's, I noticed Frank was missing from our evening meal. I asked the other kids about him. Someone told me he'd been feeling ill. The priests had ordered him to rest on a bench in the playroom. When supper was over, I snuck in to see him. He was lying on the wooden bench, his eyes closed. He was moaning.

"Don't worry," said the priest who'd come into the room after me. "He's just got a bellyache."

That night, Frank did not come up to the dorm room. He was kept downstairs on the bench.

He was still there the following day. And the day after that. I tried to slip into the playroom whenever I could to check on him. The priests kept shooing me away. Insisting he would get over his tummy ache. But I could see my brother was in agony. On the third or fourth day, I saw blood trickling out of his mouth. I ran to find Father Latour.

I guess Father Latour must have reached my parents somehow. They showed up a while later. They took Frank away.

I didn't know if my brother was alive or dead. For three months, all I knew was he was gone. I felt as if a piece of me had been ripped away.

I later found out they had brought him straight to the hospital in Prince Albert, where they were told his appendix had burst. If another day had passed without treatment, the doctor said, Frank would have died. He stayed in hospital for over two months before he was well enough to go home.

When I finally got back home in the summer, Frank was there to greet me. He raced over to the back of the truck and was hugging me almost before my feet hit the ground. As the truck rumbled away, he was jumping and jumping, so excited to have me back, so excited to tell me what had happened. And so excited to announce that he was never going back to St. Michael's. He was close to aging out anyway, and no one figured St. Michael's would make a fuss about his absence, since they'd almost let him die. So while I was happy that Frank was finally free, I was also sad that I'd no longer have his companionship at school. Now, I thought, I'd have no connection at all to my family in that place. I would be even further away from home in a way. (Peter would start at St. Michael's in the coming fall, but I wasn't thinking about that then.)

There was only one thing that made the thought of returning to St. Michael's bearable. And that was hockey.

4

The St. Michael's sīsīpak

THE ST. MICHAEL'S DUCKS

With all the misery at that school, the best relief for me was always sports. Soccer, softball, basketball. And more than anything else— hockey. When the priests and the older boys began to build a rink beside the school the first winter I was there, oh, was I happy. A lot of the boys who were new to the school weren't sure what it was for, but I knew.

And when we got on the ice, I was one of the few new arrivals who could manage to stay up on skates, could propel myself forwards, could move with a stick in my hands.

Not that we were given skates or real sticks. The little bit of equipment we had was old donated stuff. The few pairs of beat-up hockey skates were strictly reserved for the older boys. Same thing for a couple of sets of old shin pads and worn hockey gloves. We younger kids slid around on the ice in our boots. We'd sometimes make shin pads for ourselves with cardboard we salvaged from the garbage or pieces of wood we shoved down our socks. And we'd cut branches from the caragana bushes that surrounded the school to make sticks, just as my moosum had done with willow. None of the students, young or old, had hockey sweaters or pants.

Skates were, of course, the most prized possession. Once you'd worked at the school for about five years, you could "earn" skates, which meant you were assigned one of the pairs of decent skates the school had. So a number of the older boys had their own.

Boy, did I envy them.

Every Sunday, we would be given our one treat of the week. Usually an apple. Very rarely, a bowl of ice cream. But I didn't care about the food. I cared about skating. So in the winter months, when the rink was up, I'd trade with an older boy—my apple for his pair of hockey skates for a few hours. Then, in our free hours of Sunday afternoon, I'd get on the rink. The skates were big on me. It didn't matter—they sliced into the ice, so I could glide and race. I felt powerful and free and alive. The school and everything that happened there melted away for a few hours.

Many of the priests were French Canadian and were huge hockey fans. On Saturday nights during the winter, they'd set up a radio in the playroom, and we would all gather on the concrete floor to listen to *Hockey Night in Canada*. To the voice of hockey, Foster Hewitt. While the French Canadian priests were surely Canadiens fans at heart, the Habs games were only broadcast out west when they played the great Toronto Maple Leafs. It was the Leafs players, past and present, that the priests talked most about—including the legendary Charlie Conacher. He'd been a star player for the Leafs in the 1930s, a real goal scorer. We all wanted to be Charlie Conacher. We were so obsessed, we even began to refer to the water striders that skated across the lagoon as "Charlie Conachers."

The priests also taught us the basics of the game when we were out on ice. When I was about eleven, the newest priest, Father Roussel, took over hockey at St. Michael's.

When Father Roussel stepped out on the ice for the first time, everything that happened on that little rink changed. Father Roussel couldn't skate, but he really knew the game. And I think he must have understood the potential of a group of small, wiry boys who spent most of their days doing hard, physical labour. He wanted to make the older boys into a team. A team that could compete with high school and midget teams in the area.

So the first thing he did was find more used equipment. He'd drive all over the place—Prince Albert, Saskatoon—collecting donated skates, shin pads, gloves, and sticks. About that time, when I was around twelve, I earned my first pair of skates (and graduated from cleaning to working in the barns, milking two cows a day).

Eventually, Father Roussel managed to assemble enough battered equipment to outfit a whole team. He had the skates sharpened on an old stone that we used to hone the blades on the plows. And he had the girls at the school start making us hockey pants and knitting matching hockey sweaters.

Next he introduced real hockey practices instead of just games.

During the mid-afternoon and then again in the early evening, Father Roussel would get us older boys out onto the ice. We played for two or three hours a day, no matter how far the thermometer dropped. Sometimes it was so cold that Father Roussel's whistle would freeze up solid and not make a sound until he shook it long enough to get the little ball loose again.

The practices were rigorous. To strengthen our legs, Father Roussel would tie ropes to old tires and make us skate up and down the ice, dragging them behind us. He used to stand in the middle of the ice with a five-gallon pail of pucks at his feet. If you were coasting or not paying attention to the whistle, he'd fire one at you. It might be twenty or thirty degrees below zero, and those pucks were hard as rock, which we knew for a fact, because we didn't have any padding on. Sometimes he'd also use a stick to smack players on the rear end if he thought they were skating too slowly. When Father Roussel gave you a technique to practise, he'd stand next to you, watching you do it. If you didn't do it to his liking, he'd make you do it again. And again. And again. He wouldn't move on to the next player until he thought you'd got it right. And Father Roussel made *sure* he never had to tell you anything twice.

He was tough on us, and he knew it. He used to say, "Boys, you're gonna hate my guts, because I'm going to train you hard, get every bit of effort out of you. But at the end of the season, you're going to thank me."

Father Roussel wasn't wrong. A lot of the boys did hate his guts. But I didn't. I could tell he was a good coach. I was learning more from him than I did from anyone else at that damn school, and I didn't mind suffering a little—if it was on the ice and was making me a better player.

Father Roussel didn't let up on us when the weather warmed or the ice was bad. At those times, he had us out in the field, running. The school had some old roller skates, so we'd strap those on and skate in the playroom as well. We did gymnastics, bench work, and mat work there too, all to get conditioned for hockey.

As time went on, Father Roussel seemed to focus more and more on me. One afternoon, I'd finished my work in the barn a little early and had gone over to the rink to flood it for our evening practice. In the deep cold, it firmed up quickly, so I stepped out in my skates. I was concentrating so hard on shooting the puck around with my homemade hockey stick, I didn't notice Father Roussel was standing at the side of the ice.

"Frederick," he called, holding out a stick to me. I skated over. The stick was broken—it was just a shaft with no blade.

"Use this," he said.

I thought he was crazy. But he insisted.

"Learn to control the puck with this."

For two weeks, I practised manoeuvring the puck across the ice at the end of the broken stick. Then Father Roussel was at the side of the rink again. This time with a stick that had a blade.

"Now," he said, "practise the stickhandling you've learned without looking at the puck."

He told me to keep looking up, keep looking ahead, no matter what.

"You get hit with your head down, and you could be killed."

I worked at that too. Skating always with my eyes forward, focused on where I wanted to go, on what was happening on the ice around me. Feeling the puck on my blade but never glancing at it.

Not long after that, Father Roussel got me on the rink alone again. He came up behind me and put his hands on my shoulders, shook me a little.

"Frederick," he said, "you're stronger on your left than your right. I'm going to change you into a left-shooter."

We were short left-shooters on the team.

He went over to the end of the rink and nailed a coffee can to the boards. Then he told me to shoot at it, but only from the left. Man, I had a terrible time with that. But he wasn't going to let me off the hook. Every day, he made me practise. Every day, he stood outside in the cold and watched me take shot after shot. By the end of two weeks, I was shooting left almost as if it was the most natural thing for me.

And then I worked on my wrist shot. By this time, there were many days when I didn't sit in the classroom at all. I was working in the barns or fields and either playing hockey or doing hockey training. But I didn't mind. The priests used to tell us, "Work hard. Your wrists will become strong by pulling the teats on the cows." And I needed strong wrists for my shot.

Sticks were too expensive to replace, so we weren't allowed to ever raise them off the ice in case they broke when we brought them back down. The most you could do was try to make your snap shot and your wrist shot as powerful as you could. So that's what I focused on.

And I skated. I got out on the rink whenever I could. If didn't have work that needed to be done, I was on the ice when the younger kids were skating, so I could get in a little extra practice. I could sense myself getting faster and stronger. Some days, practising with the team, I felt as though I could skate through the whole lot of them without any effort at all.

Eventually, Father Roussel arranged for us to have games against the high school and midget teams from the little towns around us. The Mennonite college in Rosthern had a high school team. Waldheim and Laird had midget teams we could play. Midget hockey was supposed to be for boys fifteen to seventeen. But we didn't have enough players that age, so at thirteen or fourteen a number of us got to join the senior team at the school. I played forward. By that time, the girls had finished making our team uniforms. The hockey pants were unpadded, made out of heavy canvas. The sweaters had "SMS" over a huge flying duck across the chest. We were the St. Michael's Ducks. We felt like real hockey players.

To get to our games, we travelled in the back of the old tarp-covered truck that picked us up to take us to school every fall. But for these winter trips, Father Roussel had a little wood stove screwed into the floorboards in the back so we wouldn't freeze. For the longer trips, the girls in the kitchen would make us sandwiches to take with us. We never stopped for food or ate in cafés while we were away.

All of the small towns we played against had outdoor rinks, just like us. But they had a few extra luxuries. For one thing, beside the rinks there were often one or more cabooses. The kind of enclosed wooden trailers that were usually pulled by horses. In the cabooses were small wood stoves. That's where the players would go to put on their equipment or maybe get warmed up between periods. They were awfully small, so if they didn't have more than a couple, we would have to take turns. But they were a luxury we sure didn't have. And the white kids always seemed to have newer, better equipment than us. They even had bright store-bought hockey sweaters.

We also noticed that their ice was often a bit better than ours. I suspect they had more sophisticated equipment than we did. Back at the school, we made our own ice by flooding the rink with hoses and then trying to smooth the lumpy surface with scrapers we made in the wood shop out of old shovels. Before Father Roussel, you had to work to get across that ice without stumbling or catching a blade. But once he took over, he fussed at us until we got that ice as smooth as we possibly could.

The other thing we noticed about the town rinks was the lighting. When we played at the school during the day, visibility was good. But in the evenings, in the winter darkness, the rink was lit only by a weak spotlight perched on the roof of the school. It was easy for the puck to get lost in the shadows. You had to be razor-focused. Many of these small-town rinks had strings of lights overhead, so you could really see what was going on.

With the better rinks, never mind all the extra conditioning our team had, playing against these other teams should have been fairly easy. But it wasn't.

No matter where we went, we felt uncomfortable. We were welcomed only by hard stares from the white boys. They clearly didn't want to be playing us. Sometimes the players called us names. Sometimes those slurs came from people watching along the boards. And, of course, our team never had anyone rooting for us except for the priests. We didn't have parents, friends, or neighbours in the stands. The opposing team was always the home team. We were just the dark-skinned strangers trying to steal a victory from their boys.

A few times, however, the other teams played at St. Michael's. It was like the King had come for a visit. Father Roussel had us out flooding and scraping the ice—over and over—until it was as smooth as anyone could have possibly made it with the equipment we had. After the game, the school held a special lunch or dinner. The white team and their coaches would sit at a table with the priests and nuns. They never ate with the students. Our older girls would wait on them, bringing out their food and taking away their dirty plates. And while our meals were sometimes a bit nicer than usual, as if to show our visitors how well the kids at the school were treated, we could still tell that they were given treats we were never served. Creamy milk. Nice cuts of meat. Dessert.

The white teams were not the same as us. That's for sure. Yet when we met them on the ice, we were just as good as they were. We weren't big kids—none of us. And Father Roussel insisted we play a clean game. So we played smart, positional hockey. We were tough and tireless. Unlike the white kids, we didn't sit at desks for five or six hours a day. We worked. Or we practised. An hour on the ice was nothing to us.

In 1947–48, we had a hell of season. When we'd beaten all the teams from the little towns around us, Father Roussel decided to enter us into the provincial championships. We travelled to larger towns like Prince Albert, Flin Flon, and Saskatoon. The trips in the truck were long and exhausting, but when we arrived in these cities, the sight of them woke us right up. Big tall buildings, cars and trucks everywhere, and the streets lit up with electric lights.

When we got to their rinks, more shocks. They were *indoors*, in huge arenas as brightly lit as a prairie morning. And all around the ice were rows and rows of seats, filled with hundreds of fans.

The small-town teams had made us a bit self-conscious of our home-made sweaters, but these boys were something else. We imagined that this was what professional players must look like—shiny-bladed skates, bright crisp hockey sweaters, thick padded hockey pants, smooth leather gloves. Everything looked perfect. Everything looked brand new. It was intimidating, all that perfection.

And the ice. The ice was always so smooth, it was like you were floating along it. Skating was almost effortless. And then there was how it felt to take a shot on that hard, snow-free surface. The pucks just flew off our sticks.

We won game after game on the road, until we walked away with the northern Saskatchewan midget championship, which meant we would play the Weyburn Jaycees for the provincial title.

Weyburn was 280 miles from Duck Lake. I guess Father Roussel calculated we wouldn't be at our best if we'd been in the back of a truck on gravel roads for eight hours or so. Instead, he booked us train tickets for the trip south.

The train was incredibly exciting. None of us could sit still. But that wasn't the only wonder. When we got to Weyburn, we discovered we'd be staying in an actual motel. That was such a novelty that once we got into our shared rooms, we had to explore every inch. One of the boys in my room noticed the place was heated with a tiny radiator against one wall. We'd never seen one of these before. We were curious about it. One fellow found the knob at the side of the rad and decided to find out what would happen if you turned it. Well, what happens is that boiling hot water sprays out of the damn thing. All over us. All over the motel room. That produced lots of yelling, lots of commotion. We all ran out of the room. But we quickly realized that was no solution. We had to get that water off. When we got back into the room, we tried to get to the knob, but the water was too hot. Eventually, someone went to our hockey bags and got out a glove. He put it on and managed to turn the knob off. But everything, including our equipment bags, was already soaked.

Boy, oh, boy, we got hell from the motel owner. Father Roussel really told us off too. But the real punishment was later, when we tried to put our gloves on for the game. They were now dry, but the worn and absorbent leather had shrunk right up, and we could barely get our hands into the wood-stiff fingers.

We played two games in Weyburn. We lost the first—we were so tired from the train trip. But the second was a tight race. We ended up losing the championship game 7 to 6, Weyburn scoring with only seconds left on the clock.

It felt good to get so close to being the provincial champs, to proving we could meet and match all those white players. And we discovered that the people in the area had heard how good we were. The following season, Father Roussel told us that some of us had been asked to play in a senior tournament, for an Indian team from the Beardy's Duck Lake band, as they were short players.

The school dropped five of us off at Thomas Gardypie's house on the Beardy reserve to spend the night before the tournament. He was one of the Beardy players. At about five in the morning, a horse-drawn buggy pulled up in the dark in front of the place, and the five of us climbed into the tarp-covered trailer to make the trip to Laird, where the tournament was being held. It had been snowing heavily for a few days, and I guess the road must have been impassable. The driver drove over to the railroad tracks and then directed the horse onto them. They'd been cleared of snow, but the banks on either side were four or five feet high. He drove the whole twenty miles to Laird on those tracks. There was no way to get off if a train had been coming.

It wasn't just the idea that a train might barrel over us any minute that made the journey such an adventure. There was a little wood-burning stove in the trailer that was meant to keep us warm during the journey, but it wasn't really secured at the top, so as the caboose bounced along the rail ties, the stovepipe fell out of its fitting. In no time, the little cabin was filled with smoke, and we boys were shouting and yelling at the driver to stop. The pipe was too hot to wrestle back into place. Instead, the driver kicked it out of the caboose into the snow. When it cooled, he put it back in, and we started down the tracks again. We must have repeated that three or four times and didn't arrive in Laird until nine in the morning.

We spent the whole day playing in the tournament, with and against guys in their mid- and early twenties. I don't remember anything about the last game we played. But I do remember leaving the rink. I think the players on the winning team were mostly Ukrainians. And they were celebrating their victory with plenty of beer. As we climbed into the back of the buggy, one of them came over with five bottles in his hands.

"You did good," he said. Then he passed us the open bottles of beer.

None of us had ever had a drink before, and pretty soon we were having the time of our lives. During the long ride home, we weren't a bit worried about being on the train tracks or dying of smoke inhalation.

Not surprisingly, I guess, the good times ended as soon as we were deposited at St. Michael's. As we entered the school, one of the priests noticed the smell of beer on our breath. He took the strap to the palms of our hands, and we ate our next meal on the floor of the dining hall. Like every small taste of freedom and every brief moment of joy during those years at St. Michael's, our post-tournament happiness had ended swiftly.

The fall of 1948, some of our older players, including Alex Greyeyes, Harris Wichihin, and my cousin Herb Seeseequasis, had left the school, and we were so short-handed we couldn't form a midget team on our own. Father Roussel wasn't going to let that stop us from competing. He found two hockey-playing white boys who lived at an orphanage in Prince Albert and brought them onto the team. So a fellow named Slakinski and another named Ouellette joined me, Patrick Manitokan, Raphael Gamble, Albert Seenookeesick, John Sanderson, J-Harvey Ledoux, George Daniels, George Bird, Ivan Daniels, Narcisse Lafond, Azarie Bird, and Clarence Lafond.

The 1948–49 season was a repeat of the year before. We won game after game, until we beat out Flin Flon in the northern provincial championship with scores of 11–6 and 10–0 in the two games. I managed three goals in each game. The provincial championship would be in Regina, against the Regina Pats. It was a two-game, total-goals series.

This time, Father Roussel was not going to lose.

"We're going home as champions, boys," he told us. "We're going home with a trophy. That's it."

He benched the weaker players and made the best players stay on the ice as long as possible. I played at least forty-five minutes. More than once, he pointed at me, *You do it.* I knocked in one goal. Then another.

We played our hearts out, racking up a 5–2, then a 6–3 win. Years later, I would come across this description of the game in the *Saskatoon Star-Phoenix*: "While much smaller than the Regina squad, the Duck Lake team had the hockey know-how, skating ability, and shooting of a first class team, their drives from any angle had the Regina players somewhat baffled."

But we weren't baffled at all. We'd been told to win, and we did.

The train trip back to Duck Lake took us about eight hours. By the time our truck had got us from the station to the school, it was three in the morning. To our surprise, when we walked through the doors, the priests, the nuns, the kids, everyone in the school was awake, waiting for us. We all raced into the dining hall, where the tables were set up for dinner. The hockey team was told to sit at the raised table, where the nuns and priests usually ate. The only priest sitting in his regular place was Father Roussel. And then the food came out: beautiful cuts of beef, Jell-O, even Coca-Cola. It was the first time most of us had ever tasted a soft drink. What a feast. We'd never had anything like it. Our Christmas "celebration" was a nativity pageant and some carol singing. Christmas dinner, as well as Easter, was baloney and bread, eaten as quickly and quietly as any other meal. It wasn't just the food, however, that was different this night—the whole place seemed to have been transformed. The silent grey dining room was alive, filled with so much noisy chatter and laughing I felt almost giddy with the excitement of it. And then, about twenty minutes after the meal started, a priest noticed one of our players was missing. He disappeared to find the boy. But before the priest returned, the kid stumbled into the dining hall, a couple of gallon jugs of sacramental wine under his arms. He'd obviously already helped himself in the chapel. He was plenty drunk.

The priests got the wine off him and sat him down to eat, but there wasn't much they could do to straighten up the tipsy fourteen-year-old right then. I guess it's a pretty good measure of how happy and proud the priests and nuns were that all they did was laugh. And we continued with our party.

The next morning, we were roused out of bed at 6 A.M. as usual. We set about our chores and our school work as if it was just an ordinary day. But the feeling of accomplishment lingered. We were champions. With a trophy. A bunch of Indian kids had become the best players in Saskatchewan.

Father Roussel always said to the team, "I'm going to make champions out of you." Well, I guess he did. We won the provincials. But I don't think any of us were thinking beyond that. Sure, we talked about playing in the NHL one day, but none of us meant it. Not one. In the 1980s, Father Roussel was interviewed for an article about me and my hockey career. He said that I used to tell him I was going to play in the NHL. He said he told me that if I worked hard, I'd have a chance. But I don't recall any of that conversation. If I did make the boast, it was probably some kind of joke. Because I never thought about being a pro hockey player. I didn't believe that was possible for an Indian.

Even if Father Roussel really felt I might make it, I wouldn't have believed it if he'd told me. Nothing about my time at St. Michael's suggested there was a future for any of us in the white world. The nuns and priests wanted us to be white in every way that we could be. But that didn't mean we would ever really be the same as them. I don't remember anyone telling us that we could be doctors or lawyers or businessmen. At least not in the white world. I think they expected us to become "good Christian" farmers or labourers, or maybe even clergy or teachers who would share the white man's lessons on the reserves or in our own communities. I never heard the priests or nuns tell any of the kids they were proud of us. I never heard words of encouragement. Orders and corrections. That's all we ever got.

We loved the heroes' welcome we received when we returned to the school after the championship in Regina. We walked a little taller after that. But how could we really feel victorious in that place? Despite the few good times, the years at St. Michael's had covered us with scars. They had destroyed some part of us. They had made us realize we were poor. They had made us ashamed of being who we were. At the end of our days at St. Michael's, the only true victory was having made it through, was going home.

I couldn't wait.

5
kotak nīkihk
A SECOND HOME

I was back in Sandy Lake at last. For good.

Man, what a feeling. To be with my family. Peter came home for the summer. Little Leo had not yet been sent to St. Michael's. Clara was a cheerful toddler. The cabin was full of chatter and laughter. When Frank and I weren't working with my parents or out fishing, we'd take the younger kids for long walks. One of us would bundle Clara onto his back. The younger boys walked alongside us—the fear of bears and timber wolves keeping them close to their big brothers. Sometimes on the walks, we stopped to pick berries or gather the healing herbs and roots that our mother had taught us to identify. Other times, we simply explored the deep green woods of Ahtahkakoop's land.

Almost every evening in the warmer weather, my father would build a big fire outside the cabin, and my mother cooked bannock in a pan over its open flames. If my grandparents were visiting, my moosum Gaspar would bring out his drum, and he and my kokum Veronica would lead us in song.

In truth, every summer we spent nights under the stars like this. But now that residential school was no longer darkening my future, I felt I could really enjoy it. These people, this land, this was my whole world once again.

And then it was early fall. My parents, my brother Frank, and I were in Blue Heron, several hours away from the reserve, helping a white farmer stook his fields. We'd been at it for several hours when we saw dust rising from the dirt road and a car pulling up alongside the field. Two men got out of the sedan. One of them was wearing a long black cassock—he looked like Father Roussel. My stomach dropped. Just the glimpse of those flapping robes brought back memories I didn't want, fears I had hoped to leave behind. It *was* Father Roussel. What was he doing here? He had come in a car, not a grain truck, but why would a Catholic priest show up unless he was going to take you away?

The other man was a stranger to me. White, tall, wearing a hat and a long overcoat. I didn't recognize him. But if he was with a priest, I didn't want to talk to him either.

"I'm not going back to school," I said to Frank, before turning and hiking further into the field. Frank followed me.

When I looked over my shoulder, I could see the two men had approached my mother and father and they were talking. They were leaning towards my father, addressing him. Every few seconds, my dad would turn to my mother and speak. He must have been translating for her.

Then the men were standing straight, and my mother was yelling, "astam ōta nikosis." Come here, my son.

"She's calling you, Frank," I said. But he shook his head.

"toosaw," my mother called. "astam ōta, toosaw." Come here, Toosaw.

I walked back to them slowly, reluctantly. I didn't look at the white men.

"kikwaya nitaweyitakik māmā?" What do they want, Mom? I could feel tears welling in my eyes.

"ēh-penatskik." They've come to get you.

"Where am I going?" I asked my father in English.

"Moose Jaw," said Father Roussel. "We've come to take you to Moose Jaw."

Then the other man was introducing himself. His name was George Vogan, he said. He was the manager and club president of the Moose Jaw Canucks Junior A hockey team. They were part of the Western Canada Junior Hockey League. And their parent team was the Chicago Black Hawks. That meant any of their players might eventually be picked up by that NHL franchise. He'd seen me play during the midget championship, and he wanted me to try out for his team. The training camp was starting in a couple of days.

"How far away is Moose Jaw?" I asked.

Mr. Vogan told me it was about three hundred miles. That he would be driving me there, and putting me up in his house. I would get paid twenty-five cents a day while I was on the team, so I would have spending money.

All I could think about was the distance.

"nimāmā osam wāhyaw. asay oma ohpime kinwes ayiyayan," I told my mother. Mom, that's so far. I've been away so long already.

But she was saying, "niyah nikosis niyah." Go, my son, go.

And Dad echoed her. "misiweskamik astew kiya oci, toosaw." There's a world out there for you, Toosaw, he said. "miyopimatisowin oteh nikan." A better life. A future.

As I listened, I looked across the field. My middle-aged parents and my older brother would spend many more days this fall out here, their backs bent over, cutting and gathering wheat sheaves for a white farmer. The farmer treated us all well—he respected our hard work and paid us what he could. But there wasn't much money in farming, and at the end of each long day, my parents would go back to their tent with only a few dollars in their pocket. Their lives were hard.

I had no doubt that my father, who so loved to play soccer, would have jumped at the chance to play sports for a living. And my mother— after all her loneliness, what a comfort it might be for her to tell neighbours that Toosaw had been sought after by these white men. White men who wanted to help her boy make it in the môniyâwak world.

But then I looked down at my clothes. My knees were showing through my pants. Everything I had on was worn and ragged, even my shoes. I'd seen the white kids in all of those arenas, all of those towns. They didn't look like me. They didn't dress like me.

"I can't go," I said, relieved to have an excuse. Any excuse. "I have no clothes."

"We'll get you clothes, Frederick," said Father Roussel.

I finally looked at him. His expression was a mixture of pride and anxiety. This was what he had hoped for all along—for a player he had trained to make it in the wider hockey world. He desperately wanted me to take this opportunity. But I wasn't going to do it for him.

My parents pulled me aside. Talking softly, they urged me to go—at least for a while. I could hear the hope in their voices too. The belief that this was an opportunity I shouldn't ignore. I suppose they felt that all those years we had spent apart, the fact I now struggled to speak my mother tongue but had an "education," that should mean something. If those years resulted in an invitation to do something beyond what the Indian agent and Indian Affairs said we could do, well, then, we should do it. But I felt like I was being taken away again.

Yet I had to give my poor mother something. Some sign that I had at least tried.

"nīso-ispayiki." Two weeks, I said. "kasipwehtan maka kāwi-kapēwāyinīn." I'll go, but I'll be back in two weeks.

With that, I slowly followed Father Roussel and George Vogan to the car and slid into the back seat. As we bumped down the dirt road, I turned around, my heart like a weight in my chest. My parents and Frank were standing in the field of golden wheat, waving.

A short time later, George pulled the car up to St. Michael's Residential School. The sight of those grey walls filled me with dread—and sadness. Poor Peter was still here. Father Roussel hustled me inside, to the storeroom. There, he dug out a pair of pants, a shirt, a flat cap, and some shoes. They were used army surplus things. He took an old canvas duffle bag and filled it with more of the same types of clothes. Then I was back in the car with Mr. Vogan.

As we drove, George talked. He explained it had taken three days to find me out in Blue Heron. He talked about how the training camp would run, about what Moose Jaw was like, about how he would do what he could to make me comfortable at home and on the rink. His voice was gentle, and I sensed he was a kind man.

After about two and a half hours on the road, I asked him if we could stop so I could go to the bathroom. As I stood in the grass by the side of the road, I turned to look in the direction we'd come from, north. The sun was beginning to set, and in the distance the north sky seemed completely dark. I knew my home was somewhere out there, but I couldn't see a trace of it. It was like someone had pulled a heavy curtain in front of it.

By the time we arrived in Moose Jaw, it was night. The streets were lit up by lights. George pulled into the driveway of a big two-storey home on Ross Street. When we got through the front door, George introduced me to his wife, Flora, and their daughter, Phyllis, who was a year older than me, and her older brother, Don. Then someone led me upstairs to show me where the bathroom was and where I was to sleep.

It felt like another world. St. Michael's had indoor plumbing and electricity in the main building. But I'd never been in a family home that was heated by anything other than a wood stove, where the lights turned on with a switch on the wall. Where the floors were covered in soft carpet. And I had a bedroom all to myself. A whole room.

That night, I lay in my bed, unable to sleep. The mattress was downy, the sheets smooth. And the bed felt huge compared to the tiny metal cots of St. Michael's. But all that soft comfort didn't make up for the strangeness. I couldn't believe the noise. The sound of tires rolling along the street outside, car doors slamming, voices drifting up to the windows. And long after the sun had gone down, light from the street lamps continued to leak through the curtains. Compared to Sandy Lake, even to St. Michael's, this place seemed busy and alive, right into the depths of night.

I was still lying on my back, wide awake, when daylight began to shine into the room. I could hear footsteps up and down the hall and then a clatter of pots and pans coming from the floor below.

I wasn't sure what I was supposed to do. The thought of getting up and joining these strangers in the kitchen terrified me. I pulled the covers up to my chin and waited.

Eventually, there was a knock on the door. George's gentle voice.

"Time to get up, Freddy," he said. "Time to get dressed and come down to breakfast. It's almost ready."

I did as I was told. Walked into the kitchen, stiff and ill at ease. George, Phyllis, Flora, Don—they met me with smiles. George gestured to a chair. I sat. Flora put a plate in front of me. Pancakes with syrup, sausages. A glass of creamy whole milk. Like the breakfasts the priests and nuns had at St. Michael's.

It was strange. And yet wonderful at the same time.

Everyone at the Vogan home was as nice and welcoming as they could be. But things felt a little different at the hockey arena. When we got there the next day, George pointed me to a dressing room. I walked into the crowded room, in my army surplus clothes and my cap, and headed straight to a bench in the corner. Nobody said anything to me, and I didn't say anything to them. I felt ashamed. Ashamed that I was an Indian. I sat there with my head down, embarrassed and uncomfortable, until George came in, lugging a pile of hockey equipment. He helped me get dressed—thick shin pads, proper shoulder pads, padded hockey pants, and a real hockey sweater. The same equipment all the white kids had. Then he handed me a stick—a brand new stick—and gestured for me to get out onto the ice.

One hundred and thirty boys were competing for just twenty spots on the Moose Jaw team. We were broken into four groups, and practised in shifts. That first day, I skated about four hours. Out on the ice, I felt I could keep up with the other players, but the tension was thick. I could sense that everyone was looking for each other's weaknesses, hoping to knock someone out of the competition before they were knocked out themselves. I wasn't going to let another player get the better of me, but I knew I didn't want to be there as much as the other boys did.

At the end of the day, as George was driving me back to the house, he asked me what I thought of the training season.

"Take me home, George," I said. "I'm lonely. I want to go home."

"Freddy," he said, "keep going. You'll make it. I know you'll make it if you stick it out."

Every day for two weeks, I showed up at the rink in my odd-looking clothes, changed into my hockey gear, and headed out onto the ice without talking to anyone. Sometimes, when things got scrappy on the ice, I could hear other players spit out things like "f-ing Indian" as we raced for the puck. At one point, two brothers, Sandy and Fred Hucul, both came at me on the ice. I might have been smaller than a lot of the other players, but the Huculs didn't know how tough we Indian kids could be. I fought them off, and they didn't bother me again.

By the end of two weeks, the dressing room had really emptied out. One day, I asked another player where the friendly boy who'd been sitting next to me had gone.

"Oh, he got sent home. Not good enough," the other fellow said.

But I was still there. I couldn't figure it out. Why me? I was probably the only player who actually wanted to leave.

It wasn't that I didn't like playing hockey. It wasn't that the Vogans weren't trying hard to make me feel at home. I just couldn't see myself in this strange world.

Moose Jaw seemed so big to me. At the time, the population would have been about 24,000. When we had played in the midget finals in '48 and '49, we had travelled to some big cities, like Prince Albert and Regina. But we had never spent much time in those places—just sped past the big buildings and the people on the sidewalks on our way to the arena or perhaps the motel. But here, here I was living in the place, walking down busy city streets, past building after building that was as tall as St. Michael's school. Some taller. The Churchill Hotel. City Hall. The Metropolitan department store. Cafés, drugstores, clothes shops. Main Street was as wide as a river—one hundred feet across—with parked cars lining either side. Blocks and blocks of houses stretched past the downtown. The river ran along its southern edge. And people. Everywhere we went, people. And none of them looked like me. I was all alone in the vast strangeness.

In the dressing room, on the streets of the city, everywhere, I felt it. This was a white man's world. It was not a world made for me. I missed the trees and the water. The woodsmoke curling up the stovepipe. The rabbit-skin blankets warming me as I slept. The sound of Cree being spoken all around me. I missed my mom and dad, brothers and sister. My kokum and moosum Morin. I had lived too many years without these things. I didn't want to spend anymore time away.

One morning, when Flora and George had both left for work and Phyllis and Don had gone off to school, I went upstairs after breakfast and pulled the canvas duffle bag out of the closet. I stuffed all my clothes in it, threw it over my back, and walked back downstairs and out the door. I felt guilty not saying goodbye to George and his family. They'd been so nice to me. But I'd given the training camp two weeks like I had promised, and now I was ready to go. I walked out onto the street and looked north. I really had no idea of the route. I just knew I had to head in that direction. So I set off.

The terrain outside of Moose Jaw was so different than my home. There was no brush, no trees, no lakes. Just open grassland and farmers' fields that stretched for miles all around. It was different as well from the land I had travelled when Pete and I escaped from St. Michael's. But I couldn't help thinking about that earlier attempt to get home. This time, I wasn't hiding, I wasn't with a friend, I was not in pain. Yet the desperation to get home was just as strong.

After about three hours of walking, I started to get hungry. I managed to find a few chokecherry and saskatoon bushes along the side of the road. The berries were all shrivelled and dry, but I ate them anyway.

When I came across a small slough, I went down and drank from it to quench my thirst. Then I went back to walking.

I managed to get a few short rides as I moved down the road, but by late afternoon I was really tired. I put my bag down in the ditch by the side of the road and walked up a small hill. I sat down and looked north. I could see a couple of grain elevators a few miles off. That's where I need to get to, I thought. I guess I must have fallen asleep for a little while. When I woke, I went back down the hill, picked up my bag, and began to walk again.

I hadn't been on the road again for more than half an hour when a vehicle pulled up alongside me. I knew the car right away. I looked over and George was at the wheel, smiling at me.

"Where are you going, Freddy?"

"Two weeks, George," I said.

"Come on," he said. "Get in."

He got out of the car, took my bag from me, and put it in the trunk. "Are you hungry?" he asked.

I nodded.

He drove us into the little town I had seen from the top of the hill. Chamberlain was about thirty-five miles from Moose Jaw. I had a couple hundred miles to go. But I was glad to eat first.

George took me to a café. He told me to order whatever I liked. I'd never been in a restaurant before. When the food arrived, George started talking. I didn't have time to respond—I was too busy eating. George told me there were only thirty players left out of the 130 who had started. There was no doubt in his mind that I was going to make the team. And not just the Moose Jaw Canucks. He said he saw a long future in hockey ahead of me—maybe even the NHL. If only I would come back. If only I would give it a bit more time. He was almost begging. But what moved me wasn't his pleas—it was the way he spoke.

George was a dreamer. Maybe the biggest dreamer I ever met. He reminded me of my grandfather Alexan. My moosum saw something in me. George was the same.

In the years to come, George and I would sometimes go for walks along the streets of Moose Jaw. One day, we noticed a rainbow on the horizon. George pointed to it and said, "Freddy, you and I will walk to the end of that rainbow. And when we get there, we'll find the pot of gold." He looked down at me. "Do you know what that pot of gold is?"

I shook my head.

"That's you, Freddy."

I knew he wasn't talking about money. He was referring to my bright future, my good life. For a white man to talk this way to an Indian boy, it was almost beyond understanding.

He was speaking to me the same way in the café.

His words made me think of my grandpa. The way he seemed to have some vision of my future. And I felt his presence, as if he was sitting next to me, echoing George's words: *Don't quit, Toosaw, don't quit.*

By the time I had finished my sandwich, I knew I would keep walking—but now I would walk with George.

Not long after my day on the road, George took me shopping downtown. He bought me the same kinds of shoes and shirts and pants that all the other boys had. And about five days after I'd returned to Ross Street, the phone rang at the house. To my surprise it was my mother. She had kept track of the time. When I hadn't walked through the door after two weeks, the way I said I would, she had walked into Debden and used the phone at the café to call the Vogans.

She asked if I was going to stay. I told her that George kept telling me he was sure I was going to make the team. The sound of her voice made my heart ache, but I said if I didn't show up at home in the next couple of weeks, it meant I had earned a spot on the Canucks and would be staying put for the season. She was clearly delighted.

Around the time of my mother's phone call, George told me we were going to take a short road trip. In the car, he explained that he wanted me to see Notre Dame College, in Wilcox, a little town about an hour away. He told me it was a boarding school with an excellent sports program and top-notch academics. It'd been started by a priest named Athol Murray. Murray accepted kids not based on their ability to pay but on their desire to get a good education.

"If you don't stay with the Canucks, you could come here," George said. "Play hockey and finish high school. Get an education."

George believed strongly in education. Phyllis would go on to nursing school; Don would become an RCMP officer. But he had no idea what residential schools were really like. He didn't understand that we hadn't gone there willingly. And he sure didn't know how we had all been called savages and been beaten and abused. In those days, most of us didn't talk about our experiences—even to each other. And there certainly weren't any newspaper accounts or inquiries. I imagine that the white population accepted what the government and church told them— these places existed to help the Indian population. The only people who understood what *really* went on were the kids who suffered there and those who inflicted that pain in order to drive "the Indian" out of us.

So George just didn't get that, at fifteen or sixteen, I couldn't have gone into a white school and entered the same grade as all the other kids my age. I could read and I could write, but I had maybe a Grade Seven education—probably less. And I was lucky. Plenty of kids at the school never got that much. I tried to explain that part of my experience to him. And I told him I wasn't interested in going to the local Moose Jaw high school either, like the other players on the team did.

Yet George was driving all the way out to Wilcox with the best intentions. So I agreed to go into the school and meet Father Murray.

As soon as I crossed the threshold of the big brick building, I felt sick. It would take me years before I could walk into a Catholic school or any church without flinching. Once we entered Father Murray's office, I could see he was different than the men and women I knew at St. Michael's. The old curate sat smoking a cigar, with a bottle of whisky on the desk before him, as he talked. I couldn't believe he was a priest. But I didn't change my mind.

George didn't press the education issue after that.

Another two weeks passed, and everyone except the players who had made the team were sent home. I was still there.

When the final player list was announced, George came over to give me a hug. "What did I tell you, Freddy?" he said. And then, "How do you feel?"

"I feel good," I said. And I meant it.

Since I wasn't going to be in school during the day like the other players, George found me a couple of part-time jobs to keep me busy. In the mornings, I helped to deliver milk. The milkman drove the horse and the cart, where the milk was stored, and I'd run back and forth between the cart and the houses, leaving the bottles on the doorsteps. We'd cover eight to ten blocks in a couple of hours, and I'd be moving the whole time, getting in a little extra physical conditioning. In the afternoons, I worked at a local hardware store, moving stock and filling the shelves. By four o'clock, I'd be back at the house, where Flora or George would make me my pre-practice dinner.

On practice or game days, I usually ate by myself or with any other players who were staying at the house. Most often, I'd be served a piece of steak. George wanted me to have lots of protein to build my strength. It was a big change from the watery soups of residential school or the pemmican and rabbit stews of home. I never really thought of it at the time, but it must have been quite an expense for the Vogans. That might explain why one night, after I'd swallowed the last mouthful of meat, George asked me what I thought of the steak that night. When I said it was good, he chuckled and told me it was actually horsemeat, which he had got at a slaughterhouse. I wasn't too happy, but I'd already eaten the whole thing. Besides, complaining about anything seemed wrong—the Vogans were so generous to me.

Then we would leave for the rink.

On evenings we weren't on the ice, we still had practices. The team couldn't have the ice every day, as other teams and skaters needed it. So the coach, Roy Bentley, had us doing dryland training as well. We lifted weights, rode stationary bikes, or went for long runs outside. Sometimes the coaches would make us drag tires behind us as we sprinted—just like Father Roussel had.

Now that the team had been chosen, there was less tension between the players. But I was still aware of the importance of not backing down, of handling myself carefully on the ice and off. And I still felt out of place in the dressing room. Surrounded by all the white players, who seemed to belong without any trouble at all.

Gradually, however, that insecurity began to fade. Part of that was because of two other players.

Shortly after I arrived in Moose Jaw, another young man moved into the house. Dave Rusnell was from Wadena, Saskatchewan, where his parents ran a restaurant. Dave was a big guy, cheerful and friendly, much more at ease in his new home than I was. Unlike some of my other team-mates, he also seemed comfortable with me, seemed to accept me. He wanted to talk and to get to know me. One of the things we had in common was a love of music. Dave would often bring his guitar out in the evenings, and we would sing together.

For the next three years, until he moved on to the International Hockey League, Dave would be one of my closest friends and companions.

But while Dave's friendship was a blessing, it was another player who really changed how I felt in my new home.

A few months after Dave showed up, a fellow named Ray Leacock walked into the locker room. I couldn't believe my eyes. Ray was darker than I was. Much darker. I had never seen a Black person before. Both the Sandy Lake reserve and St. Michael's were little closed worlds. And, of course, we didn't have television at the time to bring the bigger population to us. I had grown up thinking there were really just two kinds of people—cowboys and Indians.

I had felt alone in Moose Jaw. Surrounded by people, sure, but not one of them like me. I could tell by the way Ray moved around the room and the cautious glances he gave the rest of the players that he was someone who struggled, like I did, with being different from everyone else. I noticed that the spot he picked on the bench was a little apart from the other players. After practice, I made sure to go over and speak with him. Ray and I became friends instantly.

In late October, early November, our hockey season started—and so did our travels. The other teams in the league were the Lethbridge Native Sons, the Calgary Buffaloes, the Regina Pats, the Medicine Hat Tigers, and the Crowsnest Pass Lions. Often we would be on the road for a whole week, or longer. Sometimes we hardly had a night off—we might play five games in seven days on the road.

The distances were long, and we travelled in an old bus the team had. On the bus, the guys would hash over the games we'd just played, play a few hands of cards, sleep. Most of the boys would also spend hours trying to get their homework done so they wouldn't fall behind in school. I, of course, didn't have any reading or school work to do. Ray and I spent a lot of time talking. I'd ask him about his life in Montreal, and he'd question me about the reservation. The other guys on the team were also interested in the Indian way of life. What did we eat? What kind of house did we have? Was there a town on the reserve? And they asked what I thought of their world. I was happy to answer their questions, but it did remind me how different my life was from theirs. And I didn't talk about the dark truths I carried with me. The horrors I had seen and experienced at St. Michael's. The oppression and discrimination of the Indian Act and all its rules. The way they made life almost unbearable for some. I didn't tell them about the men I'd heard of who had enlisted to fight in World War II, putting themselves at great risk, just to escape the damn Indian agent and life on the reserve for a little while. No matter how comfortable my teammates and I would become with each other, the secrets I carried would mean there was always a distance between us.

Often the team would have to sleep on the bus as we travelled through the night. But occasionally we'd stay in motels. Most of the times we stayed overnight in the towns, however, we were billeted with local families. Ray and I usually roomed together. We met some really nice people that way—the hosts were always welcoming. But no matter how friendly they were, I never liked the road trips. I missed the Vogan family and their cozy home. Being with the Vogans, I felt I was part of the family, and I loved that. The evening meals, my bedroom, listening to *Hockey Night in Canada* in the living room with everyone. I even missed the way Phyllis would bug me about making my bed or picking up my clothes. Phyllis was the older sister I never had.

Even their little bird made me feel at home. The Vogans had a budgie that became so fond of me after a few months, if I put my hand out he would fly right over and land on me whenever he was let out of the cage. At Christmas, I stayed in Moose Jaw, and there were just as many Christmas presents under the tree for me as there were for Phyllis and Don.

As busy as he was, George always had time for me. He realized that living in a city was an entirely new experience for me, so he showed me how to get around town and tried to teach me some street smarts. George warned against going to the pool hall alone—safety in numbers was always his advice. Sometimes he would take me to the movies. Or for a milkshake. Sometimes we'd just go for walks and talk. During my first months in Moose Jaw, George tried to help me be less self-conscious with the other players—I shouldn't worry so much about my English, he said. I was doing just fine.

I always felt that, more than anything, George wanted me to have a good future, even if it wasn't in hockey. So over the years, he gave me all sorts of advice about work, about marriage, about life—as well as about hockey. He also tried to bolster me when my spirits flagged. That first year, there were many times when homesickness would overcome me, when I'd think about packing it in. When George sensed my defeat, he'd give me a pep talk.

"You've already worked so hard, you can't give up. Just remember, there's no end to training. That's the only way you are going to make it to the big leagues."

Other times, he'd be less practical, more of the dreamer who'd won me over in the Chamberlain café.

Despite George's encouragement, I found it hard to believe there was really any future for me here. George might have welcomed me with open arms, and my teammates might have accepted me, but it was clear that not everyone who watched me during the games was happy that I was playing hockey.

On the ice, Ray would often protect me and the smaller players. He was over six feet tall, a muscled, towering defenceman. But he couldn't stop the name-calling and the jeering from the opposing players and their fans. I actually got it worse than Ray did. "You f-ing Indian." "Hey, squaw humper."

George always told me to ignore the taunts. "Don't retaliate," he'd say. "You have your whole future ahead of you. Don't throw it away."

Dave Rusnell used to say that the name-callers were trying to make me lose my focus, that they were only yelling those things because I was a threat on the ice. I should take the names as a compliment, he said. A lousy compliment, sure, but a compliment.

I appreciated George's and Dave's advice, but I also knew they could never really understand what it was like. How one moment you could feel like just another guy on the team and the next you'd be reminded you were an outsider. How one word could shatter your sense of belonging, could remind you that others did not see you as an equal. But Ray, Ray knew exactly how it felt to be targeted that way.

"Let it go," he would say. "Don't let them know they are getting to you. Besides, fighting back isn't going to make you feel better."

He wasn't always able to take his own advice. It was January 1951, and we were playing in Lethbridge when things started to get nasty. Ray was hit with a punishing cross-check, but it was the words the Lethbridge player flung at him that I think made him the angriest. Ray got up and went after the guy. Within seconds, other players joined in, as well as some of the fans. And then things began to rain down onto the ice. Candy wrappers, peanuts—and lumps of coal. Lots of pieces of coal. The game had to be stopped for ten minutes and the police were even called, the atmosphere in the rink was that heated.

It was an upsetting thing, that crowd's response. Sure, tempers often flared during a game, and people sometimes threw their garbage or uneaten snacks. But coal? You had to come to the game with that in your pocket. And you had to be bringing it for one purpose only.

Even when Ray and I weren't the target of slurs, the games were extremely physical. It was obvious that the fans liked it when players mixed it up. Not only that—we all somehow understood that the NHL wasn't going to look at anyone who couldn't take care of himself when the fists were flying. You had to show that you could absorb the hits and throw a few punches of your own. You had to prove you were tough. And that was okay with me. I was always more than ready to give as good as I got. I was a born fighter—or perhaps all that boxing at St. Michael's had just turned me into one.

That first year, our team struggled a bit. We didn't even make the play-offs. My love for the game never flagged, despite that. And the Vogans continued to work hard to make me feel at home. But I sure was ready to return to Sandy Lake when the season finished up. Before that could happen, George came home one evening excited to share some news with me. He'd managed to get me a job for the spring and summer working with the Kellogg construction company on the new pipeline just outside of town. It was full-time and good money. It wasn't what I had in mind, but then I thought of my parents. They'd been so hopeful when George told them about the Moose Jaw offer. They had told me they wanted me to take advantage of any opportunities I had to make it in the white world. I didn't think they'd be pleased to hear I had turned down a good job like this.

So I stayed in Moose Jaw.

Maybe, I thought, if I spent the summer in Moose Jaw it would all get a little easier. Maybe, if I put in more time in this place, I'd be able to see what my moosum had seen in my future, what George saw. But I wasn't sure about that. I couldn't seem to get rid of the sense of doubt and the lingering homesickness that sat in my heart like one of those pieces of coal.

6

peyakwahpitew sōniskwātahikēwinowak

THE TEAM

The second year I spent in Moose Jaw was easier than the first. By the third year, I was used to my new life—I'd say I was even enjoying it. My doubts had quieted. I found I was thinking less and less often about heading back to Sandy Lake. Part of that was probably because I knew I was getting better and better at the game.

The Canucks coaches sure did help me improve as a player. Each of the four years I was in Moose Jaw, the team had a different coach. Roy Bentley was there first. I always thought he looked a bit like me—a bit Indian. He had five hockey-playing brothers, and three of them—Doug, Max, and Reg—made it to the NHL. Roy had been a good hockey player, and word was he would have made it too, but responsibilities on the family farm kept him back.

Roy seemed to really like me, but then he was so dedicated to all the players. He spent a huge amount of time with us, always giving us unwavering support and great advice. He encouraged me to show what I could do.

"Don't just go through the motions, Freddy," he'd say. "Go out there and really play like I know you can."

Vic Myles was next. He was a big, rugged guy who had played for the New York Rangers. He seemed like a born fighter, and he loved a good rough game. After Myles, Ken Doraty took over. Doraty had had a colourful career with the Chicago Black Hawks, the Toronto Maples Leafs, *and* the Detroit Red Wings. He was the only NHL player ever to get a hat trick in overtime, and he had scored the tie-breaking goal in a semifinal game between the Leafs and the Bruins, ending what had been the longest game in NHL history at that point.

Ken was a real taskmaster, but, like Bentley, he was a finesse hockey player and focused on the finer points of the game. (He also ran Connaught Billiards, where the guys on the team would often go to shoot a few games and hang out.)

During my final season with the Canucks, Ab McDougall took over the coaching duties. McDougall was a good instructor who focused on skills, but he was also a mild, respectful man who treated his players like grown men instead of boys.

I was lucky to have four different coaches with four different approaches to training. I learned new things from each one. And then, of course, there was George. George would often come to the rink to watch our practices. He and I would sometimes go out onto the ice before or after the other players were there, and he'd give me little playing tips. The thing that George most wanted me to understand, however, was the power of believing in yourself. One day, when I skated out on the ice, he suggested that I practise jumping on my skates. He pointed to the arena lights overhead. "Jump up and touch those lights, Freddy."

I laughed. "That's a bit too high, George."

"Nothing's too high, Fred," he said. "If you put your mind to it, nothing's out of reach."

It would take a while for me to become infected with George's optimism, but even that first uncomfortable year, my game improved. Father Roussel had been right—I was stronger on my left side, and I now shot left most of the time. But I could still pivot to a right shot if needed to. And since I was finally playing with a good hockey stick, I didn't have to worry all the time about what might happen if I broke it. People say Bernie Geoffrion came up with the slapshot. Maybe he did, but I had never seen him. Even so, when I was playing on the Canucks, I began pulling my stick back, raising it behind me, turning my wrist shot (which was also getting stronger and more accurate) into a slapshot. My shots could be blazing now, and I started taking them further and further out from the net.

I also continued to work on my skating.

Early one morning, in my second year with the Canucks, I went down to the arena thinking the place would be empty and I might be able to get in a little extra time on the ice. I was surprised to hear the sound of skates. I walked into the rink and stood between the stands. There was a man on the ice. He was wearing a Moose Jaw Millers sweater—the local Saskatchewan senior hockey team. His name was George Hunchuk. And he was skating. Man, was he skating. I couldn't believe what I was seeing. Hunchuk was jumping—leaping left to right, right to left, backwards and forwards. Then he was running on the ice, the heels of his skate blades up, his toes digging into the ice as he flew. Whenever he stopped, a cloud of snow billowed around his skates and steam rose from his body, he was working so hard. I never saw anyone move that fast. I would have given anything to be able to skate like him.

Hunchuk must have guessed my thoughts. After a few minutes, he skated over to the boards where I was standing. "Hey, Chief. If you want to skate like me, be at the rink at 7 A.M. tomorrow."

I barely slept that night. Every time I closed my eyes, I saw Hunchuk's huge frame flying over the ice. I'd only ever listened to NHL games, but now I thought I knew how the players must look, flying across the rink. They must look like George Hunchuk.

Next morning, I jumped out of bed at 5:30 A.M. I was at the rink before 7. Hunchuk was already there. We skated non-stop for two hours.

Just like Father Roussel, Hunchuk stressed the importance of never looking at the puck. He encouraged me to visualize where I wanted to go on the ice, how I would make the play. In the end, however, he insisted it was all about balance. If you had balance, you could do anything on your skates.

"You've got to be able to dance on your skates, Freddy," he said. "You keep working on that, you learn how to dance, and you're going to hit the big time."

I took everything he taught me to heart. About a year later, I phoned him. "Come and see your student," I said.

When we got to the rink, I stepped on the ice and performed for him. I was jumping forwards, backwards, sideways, just like he did. I was running down the ice, barely letting my skates touch the surface, just like he did. I bet steam was coming off me too, just like him.

When I finished, Hunchuk came down to the ice. "Well, Freddy," he said. "You're better than I am!"

I don't know if that was true, but I could sense Hunchuk wanted it to be true, that he, like George, was in my corner.

George Hunchuk, George Vogan, Dave, Ray. They all made it a little easier to throw myself into hockey and to get used to the life I was now living. I still thought about home, of course. When I'd first arrived in Moose Jaw, George had driven me to a hill a couple of miles north of the city so I could get a good look at the surrounding country. One of my favourite things to do in the coming years when I had a little spare time was walk up to that hill. There, I could look north, towards Sandy Lake. I couldn't see it, but knowing it was there, just beyond my vision, made me feel closer to it. When I started doing this, George would get nervous.

"Where were you, Freddy?" he asked the first time I disappeared.

I had to assure him that I was just stretching my legs and thinking— I wasn't going to try to walk home again.

At one point, George came to me and said that the Lethbridge team wanted me to play for them. They were willing to send the Canucks two players in exchange. George said he wouldn't make me do anything I didn't want to do. I told him I was staying put.

"I started with you, George, and I'm going to be with you to the end." I meant it.

My second year with the Canucks, the team fared no better than we had the first year. Once again, we didn't make the playoffs. We lost some good players to injuries. We lost others in trades. New players arrived, and the coaches rebuilt. But one fellow left a huge hole, as far as I was concerned. By my third year with the Canucks, Ray Leacock had moved on.

But even though I missed Ray a lot, by the fall of 1952 I was finally feeling at home in Moose Jaw. The Vogans had become a second family—it wasn't just George who had taken me in. Phyllis seemed to have adopted me too. She told me how to dress and do my hair. She drove me to practices. She even gave me big hugs when I'd had a good game. Other players moved in with the Vogans—Dave Gordichuk, and later our goalie, Ray Ethier. I had my jobs and a good social life. I spent a lot of time down at the pool hall with Dave Rusnell, Dave Gordichuk, and some of the other players. When I walked down the streets in town, plenty of people nodded at me and said hi. That was one thing Ray and I discovered quickly—when you looked as different as we did, people started recognizing you pretty fast. Friends of the Vogans and Canuck fans tried to set me up with girls. I went on a few dates, but mostly I turned down the invitations. One older man even came up to me after a game and offered to take me fishing when the weather warmed up. He figured it was something I must be missing. And so I spent a number of spring and summer days sitting with a rod and reel out on Buffalo Pound Lake.

But perhaps the biggest change since George first brought me to the city was that I wanted to be there. Somehow, as my discomfort eased, ambition had taken its place. I began to dream like George did, like every player on that team did: I wanted to make it to the big time.

As the seasons went by, however, I could see that even the best players could have their careers ended in an instant. The games could be really rough. Bench-clearing brawls happened a lot. More than once, fans joined the fighting on the ice. More than once, the police had to be called in to break things up. During the dust-ups, fists and skate blades sliced open our faces. While the clock was running, the coaches would close the wounds with small metal clips. We had to wait until after the game to get stitches. But the cuts were really nothing. Other injuries were more dangerous. A hard check, dirty or not, could lay you out on the ice with a concussion. In one of our games, we scored the winning overtime goal while the other team's goalie was out cold in front of his net. In my second year, one of my teammates twisted his leg so badly that he was out for over half the season. My friend Dave Rusnell received a blow to his eye that required him to wear a patch on it for weeks. And worse yet, one of our best players, Emil Jurista, lost the sight in one eye after a hit. We had a benefit for him that third fall I was in Moose Jaw, but his time as a hockey player was over. Of course, there was no insurance, and we players were not compensated in any way. There were so many ways your future might be cut short. I counted myself lucky that all of my injuries could be fixed up with metal clamps and a bit of thread. Now that I was nursing a dream, I hoped my good luck would stay with me and that Tiny Thompson would notice how strong my shot had become, how fast my feet moved across the ice.

Cecil "Tiny" Thompson was a former NHL Vezina-winning goaltender for the Bruins and the Red Wings. He lived in Lethbridge now and was the Black Hawks scout for the area. Everyone would get nervous when Thompson showed up at the rink. When we spotted him in the stands, we'd try to skate a little harder, look a little sharper. We knew Thompson held our futures in his hands. In my first year or so in Moose Jaw, one of the Hucul brothers, Fred, got the nod from Thompson and headed down to Chicago. Moose Jaw had produced other NHLers in the past too. A few years earlier, Metro Prystai had left the Canucks for the Hawks and played for a few seasons in Chicago before being traded to Detroit. And the number of players who had come out of other teams in Saskatchewan—where to even start? Sid Abel, Al Rollins, Johnny Bower, Bryan Hextall, Glenn Hall, Gerry Couture, Bert Olmstead, and, of course, the amazing Gordie Howe, among so many others.

Even when Thompson wasn't in the stands, you never forgot that the other players, even your own teammates, were your competition for the pros. And the interleague games allowed you compare yourself to other juniors across the country too. By the time my third year with the Canucks was underway, I knew I could hold my own with any junior player. I'd begun to feel that George might just be right. Maybe I really did have a shot at the pros.

85

That idea helped give me a real sense of belonging, both on the team and in the league. A new player helped to make that even stronger.

During my third year, Jimmy Chow walked into our dressing room. Jimmy was a Moose Jaw native. He had been a star on his high school football team, and now he would play forward with me.

Over the course of the year, I got to know Jimmy's family. His father seemed to be a big fan of mine. He'd take my clothing off to his family's laundry and clean it for free. And he would often joke that he would hand over the business to me if only I'd marry his daughter.

Jimmy was a great guy, and I really enjoyed getting to know the Chows. But Jimmy's arrival meant more to me than just making a new friend. Having another player of colour on the team, that was really something. There'd been Ray, a Black man, on my right wing, and now there was Jimmy, a Chinese-Canadian guy, on my left. In an almost entirely white sport, our team was about as diverse as it got in those days.

Sitting next to Jimmy made me realize that, while I'd been ashamed of being an Indian when I first stepped into the locker room during that very first training camp, those feelings had faded away. Something else had taken their place. Something I got to celebrate a little later that season.

On February 10, 1953, we had a game in Edmonton. When the first period ended, I was told to stay on the ice after the other players had gone to the bench. The lights went down, and the arena grew quiet. Then the sound of drums and voices raised in song filled the air. I looked towards the end of the rink. About thirty Cree, from the local Hobbema nation, were walking out onto the ice. The men and women were wearing traditional Cree dress, their buckskin tunics, belts, and headbands decorated with beautiful beadwork. It made my heart swell to see them. When they got to me, one of them unfolded a huge ceremonial blanket and placed it over the ice. Chief Red Wing walked onto it, along with two women—Miss Rainbow and Miss Morningstar. One of them was holding a pipe and the other an exquisite feathered headdress. Before the Chief said anything, I knew what was about to happen. As a child, I'd heard about naming ceremonies. The presence of the sacred pipe symbolized the trust and truthfulness shared by the people present. The headdress was regalia signifying a great honour. It could only be worn by men who had earned that privilege through their behaviour and actions.

The Chief announced to the crowd that the Hobbema nation was making me an honorary Chief—Mekao Ru Apeseemose, Chief Running Deer—in recognition of my accomplishments in hockey. The name had been chosen to celebrate my skating speed. I knew Chief Red Wing would have thought about that name for days, and now, staring into my eyes, he was looking into my spirit, trying to see if his vision was correct. He held my gaze for a few moments and then nodded towards the ground.

I knelt down on the blanket, and one of the women placed the headdress on my head.

The singing resumed and a number of men and women began to perform a dance. The bells around their ankles rang to the beat of the drums and rattles. When they'd finished and began to file back out of the rink, the place exploded with thundering applause. I looked into the stands at the clapping, cheering crowd. There were tears in my eyes.

I'd later realize the event had been planned as a publicity stunt by the Edmonton Oil Kings manager. In *Edmonton Journal* articles about the upcoming event, the sportswriters didn't miss an opportunity to play up the clichés. One said it wasn't a bad idea "provided Sasakamoose doesn't go on a scalping party at the expense of the Kings."

Another mentioned the planned ceremony in an article about a recent win. "Kings Return with Scalps Dangling from Their Belts" was the headline of that piece. The Edmonton team even ran an ad in the paper the following season with a headshot of one of their star players and the lines "Will this man be scalped tomorrow night? Freddy Sasakamoose, Moose Jaw's Indian 'whiz kid,' is on the warpath as the Moose Jaw Canucks meet the Edmonton Oil Kings at the Gardens in another thrilling junior hockey engagement!"

But none of that would have mattered one bit to me, even if I'd been aware of it. Oh, man, to be nineteen years old, in that arena, hearing those drums. It was the greatest thrill of my life. I'd seen the look in Chief Red Wing's eyes. I'd seen the looks of the Hobbema members out on the ice and up in the stands. They were proud that one of their own was playing this game and showing everyone that we could be as good, that we could be *better*, than the white players. They were proud of me, and I was proud and honoured to be one of them. Looking at the magnificent headdress the Hobbema had made me, I understood the true significance of the gesture and the ceremony, even if the Edmonton manager didn't.

The way I felt about that ceremony echoes the way I feel about the term "Indian." It's how I still describe myself. I refuse to think of the word itself as something negative. And that grew out of my experiences in Moose Jaw. Sometime during my first three years there, I realized that the names people might shout from the stands said more about them than they did about me. If they called me an "Indian," I didn't have to accept it as a slur.

Even during the early months I was with George, I knew that the word itself could not insult me. At one point, George made some mention of my being "Native."

"Don't call me that," I said. "Call me Indian. That's the name white people gave us hundreds of years ago. You might as well keep using it."

"But I didn't want to hurt you, Freddy," he said.

"George," I said in return, "*you* could never hurt me."

I guess that's what I learned from George, Dave, and my other white friends on the team. The label didn't matter—it was how people treated you that did.

And as my junior years progressed, the fans, even those of the opposing teams, seemed to respond to me better. By my third year, they were cheering me most of the time instead of calling me names. One of those *Edmonton Journal* articles described me as "a great favourite with fans all around the seven-team WJHL." Other people commented on my speed, on my having a hard shot, and on my being a workhorse. And I could tell the fans liked to watch me play, particularly in places like Medicine Hat. Sometimes, as we exited the arena or waited at the canteen for an after-game snack, men from those other towns would come up to me to shake my hand and congratulate me.

"You played a wonderful game."

It was really something, hearing that from a person I didn't know— from a white person I didn't know. It helped me feel a future in the white world might just be possible.

At the end of my third season with the Canucks, we finally made it into the playoffs. We lost, however, in the semifinals to Lethbridge. It was disappointing, but I'd had a good year and ended up near the top of the leagues' goal scoring.

As I packed up my gear for the season, I realized I had only one more year in Moose Jaw. One more year of eligibility in the junior leagues. What was next? I wondered. What if there wasn't another team to move to? What if the pros weren't interested in me? Had I spent so many years away from home and the reserve for nothing? Was my new dream just a dream?

———

For the past two springs and summers, when I was working on that oil pipeline outside of Moose Jaw, I'd managed to get home for a few short visits. Those visits, as well as letters from my family and friends (including an exchange with a pretty young girl I had met named Loretta Isbister), kept me going. But after my third year away, I thought I'd return to Sandy Lake for the summer—to work with my father, logging around the reserve or maybe doing farm work. So I headed home.

When the train pulled into the Duck Lake station, I decided to make a short stop. I'd drop into St. Michael's to visit with my brothers Leo and Peter, who were still at the school, before getting on the next train north. (Father Roussel had left the school in the spring of 1950 or I would have wanted to say hi to him too.) When I got to St. Michael's, however, I found that my little sister Clara was now there as well as my brothers.

I was stunned.

She was tiny, only five or six, and she had already been at the school for a year. When I asked one of the nuns why she had been taken to the school so young, the woman just shrugged her shoulders.

When they brought Clara to me, I was even more shocked. She burst out crying when she saw me and couldn't stop. It was clear from the few words she said that terrible things had been happening to her. Leo and Peter couldn't help her because the boys and girls were always kept separate. I tried to comfort her the best I could. And then I went to find the principal to ask if I could take her home with me.

Father Chevrier, who had taken over from Father Latour, refused to let me take Clara from the school. Despite her young age, he insisted on following the rules: new students had to stay at the school for two full years before they could go home. Instead, he suggested that I could work at the school for the summer. Spending even another day at St. Michael's was not what I wanted, but I thought if I stayed there, I might be able to help Clara. I said yes.

I was given a bedroom of my own and was able to convince the school to let me put a cot in my room so Clara could spend the nights with me. That seemed to help her.

For the next three weeks or so, I did various jobs around the school. One afternoon, Father Chevrier told me he needed my help. He led me to the cloakroom where about thirty kids were lined up against the wall, trembling and sniffling. One of the lay brothers, a young man who was training to be a priest, was also there. I knew him from my time at St. Michael's—he had helped Father Roussel coach the hockey team. He was also part Mohawk, the only other Indian who had ever worked at the school, as far as I knew. Father Chevrier told me the children had been playing in the lagoon and had gotten their boots wet. They needed to be punished. He handed leather straps to the brother and me and told us to give each and every one of the little kids a whipping. I looked at the tear-stained faces—and I thought of Clara, my brothers, all my little friends. I turned to Father Chevrier and handed him the strap.

"What are you doing?" he said.

"I'm not hitting kids," I said. "I'm leaving."

I went back to my room, packed up my things, and walked to the train station.

The trip from Duck Lake to Prince Albert was a long, sad one. I was torn apart to be leaving little Clara behind. But I didn't feel I had a choice. I hadn't been able to do anything about the terrible things that happened when I had been at the school. I couldn't do anything now either. But I sure wasn't going to be a part of it. I wasn't going to be one of those men bringing a strap down across the backs of my own people.

———

Even with my worry about Clara, the summer at home was a good one. It was a comfort to spend time with my parents and the rest of the family. My father and Frank were working up north, in a lumber camp near Big River, and I decided to join them. It was heavy labour. After the trees were felled, we'd shave the bark off and let them sit for a few days to dry. Then we'd put big leather collars on—like the kind horses wear. They would be attached to the log with chains, and we'd drag those logs out of the bush to the saw mill. In my off-hours, I played baseball for the Big River team. When we went home to Sandy Lake for weekends or visits, we played soccer for the reservation team.

During one of the visits home, in mid-August, I got a message. Bill Tobin, the vice-president and general manager of the Chicago Black Hawks, had phoned the Debden store, leaving a phone number and asking that they tell me to call him back as soon as possible. (There were still no phones on the reservation.) When I did, he had exciting news. He wanted me to join a few other Canucks players at the Hawks training camp in Pembroke, Ontario.

"Listen, Fred," he said, "I'm letting you know now, because we expect all the players to arrive in shape. We don't have time to condition you. I don't know what you've been doing since the season ended, but you better spend the next month making sure you can play your best hockey."

I wondered if spending a summer pulling huge trees and running the bases and sprinting up and down a soccer pitch was enough.

I talked with George next. He said the other Canucks who'd been invited to the camp would be making their own way to Pembroke from their homes. But I should come down to Moose Jaw. He'd drive me to Pembroke. We'd go together.

I could hear it in his voice. He was pretty much as excited as I was.

7

ka-kochi

THE TRYOUTS

George decided that the three- or four-day drive from Moose Jaw to Pembroke, which was ninety miles northwest of Ottawa, would be easier if we went down through the States to get there. We cut across Manitoba, and northern Ontario, crossing into the US at Pigeon River. Then down through Minnesota and Wisconsin before getting into Illinois. The landscape began to change. No more fields and trees. No more farm communities and small towns. We were getting close to Chicago. We didn't go into the city. But I could tell it had to be huge—the highways around it were multi-laned and busy. I had just come from northern Saskatchewan, which was pretty much all gravel roads. And Sandy Lake, with its wagon trails. It was strange to see blacktop stretching out on either side, rows of traffic, cars pulling alongside of us, moving in the same direction. We crossed into Indiana, past the factories of Gary. Then we were heading north again, into the rolling green of Michigan. It was a relief to see all the trees again, to see the highways shrink in size.

"Grand Rapids" read a big sign by the side of the road.

"Is that the name of a town?" I asked George.

He nodded. I liked the sound of that. I wished we had time to stop and see the water the place was named for.

We came to Sault Ste. Marie several hours later and took a ferry to get to the Canadian side.

After about four days on the road, we arrived in Pembroke and the arena where the rookie camp would take place.

I was happy to see some familiar faces when I stepped out onto the ice for the first time. Fred and Sandy Hucul, and Wally Blaisdell, who had played with the Canucks in the 1951–52 season.

Camp for the 1953–54 season started on Saturday, September 12, at the local arena in Pembroke. First week was all the young hopefuls—thirty rookies who each wanted a shot at making the cut.

The pros didn't start until the next week, when most of the young players would be sent home. But it was still a thrill to hear the legendary player-coach Sid Abel call out instructions. And to catch sight of the dozen or so men up in the stands, heads bowed under fedoras, pens and clipboards in their hands. We knew they were making notes about everything they saw out on the ice, ranking and comparing us.

The level of play was a notch above what I had been experiencing in Moose Jaw—after all, these were some of the best juniors from across the country. The atmosphere on and off the ice was intense. I felt I was playing well, but I also knew it didn't matter so much how well I played. What mattered was that I play better than the other guys on the ice. Even on the Canucks, we were always aware that we had to work hard to keep our positions. That we could be bumped off the team if better players came along. But here, boy, it was dog eat dog. You could never let up. Day after day, I worked my heart out, all the time thinking about those guys in the stands. What were they writing down? What were they thinking? It was impossible to forget our future was being worked out on those clipboards.

Three days after the camp started, George told me we had to go down to an office in the arena. Bill Tobin wanted to talk with us. I could tell George was anxious and excited. My heart was pounding in my chest.

When we walked in the room, Tobin was sitting at a table, a single piece of paper in front of him. He slapped some money down beside it. It was an American hundred dollar bill. I had never seen one before. I had never seen that much money before in any form.

The paper was a C Form. It was an agreement with the Black Hawks organization.

"Sign that," Tobin said, "and you get the hundred dollars."

The agreement outlined the terms of a future contract with the club. I would get $500 right away if I was offered a full contract to play pro. I would get $3,000 if they assigned me to play in the Pacific Coast Hockey League or the Quebec Hockey League, and $3,500 if they sent me to the American Hockey League. The NHL would, of course, pay more than any of their farm teams—I would get $6,000 if I played a full season for the Black Hawks themselves. Not that I read through it for that kind of detail or asked about any of the specifics. My head was spinning. I was too overwhelmed to even know what to ask.

"This will make you Black Hawks property," Tobin said proudly.

This was what I had been hoping for.

"Go ahead," said George. I could hear the happiness in his voice.

I signed the paper. George, as my representative, did the same. Tobin pushed the hundred-dollar bill over to me and I picked it up.

"Now, Freddy," said Tobin. "Don't tell the other players that you've been signed. And don't tell anyone about the financial terms. You keep that to yourself."

As George and I left the office, George patted me on the back. He explained that the C Form meant I now officially belonged to the Chicago franchise. He wanted to make sure that I understood they could sign me to a contract any time—or, at the end of the year, they could renew the C Form. No other franchise or team could make me an offer unless Chicago released me first. I could tell from the way he was talking that he was thrilled. So was I. The C Form meant I really did have a shot at the big time.

It would be years before I thought back on that meeting with something other than pure excitement, before the word "property" began to have concerning echoes.

I had already been pumped to be at the camp. But now, with the C Form and everything it promised, I went back on the ice and threw everything I had into the hockey drills, the skating skills, the games.

At the end of the first week, there was a game between the eastern players and western players. Tiny Thompson coached our western team. It was a great match, and I managed to score a number of goals. At the end, I was named the first star of the game. Sid Abel seemed pleased with my performance, and George was beaming.

"You did just as good as Metro," he said. Metro Prystai, the Canucks player who had made it to the NHL. "Maybe better," George added.

Then he told me I was one of the lucky few who had been invited to stay for the second week—the main Hawks camp, when the team actually showed up. I would get a chance to share the ice with real NHL players. I couldn't believe my luck.

When the team training camp started, the rookie players joined the pros at the Pembroke military base for dryland work. The base had all sorts of fitness facilities—weights, machines, tracks. The routine during the second week was intense. We were all staying in a local motel. Our breakfast and dinners were brought to us in our rooms. We would get up at 6 A.M., eat in our rooms, and then be on the ice at the local arena by 8 A.M. We'd have two hours of skills training on the ice, followed by two hours of dryland training at the base. Then we'd break for lunch and have another four hours of ice and dryland work.

The coaches weighed us every day. I was told that at my height, five foot eight, my playing weight was 169 pounds—no more, no less.

The pros didn't really mingle with us kids. They had their own dressing room. Sat on their own bench. But a few of them reached out to the young players. Bill Mosienko was encouraging. And goalie Al Rollins took an interest in me. When I skated by him during practice games, he'd talk to me.

"Keep shooting, Chief, keep shooting. You've got a hard shot. Shoot it from the blue line. I'll make sure to let a few in. That'll get everyone's attention."

He also told me he had some Indian heritage. I got the sense he wanted me to make the team.

At the end of the camp, we had a number of exhibition games with local senior teams. We also had two games with the Detroit Red Wings training camp team.

Quite often, for these exhibitions, the veterans on the Hawks team didn't dress for the game. The management wanted to see the rookies perform. So I wasn't sure which NHL players would be on the ice for the Red Wings. There was one I was hoping would show up, of course.

When we pulled up to the arena that day, it looked like I was going to get my wish. A tall, muscular player was standing outside the entrance, talking to reporters. Everyone wanted to see him play, so I guess the management decided it was a good idea to put him on the ice.

My heart was beating pretty fast. I had been performing well when playing with and against other rookie players, but put me in front of Gordie Howe—that would be a completely different situation. Like me, Howe could shoot both left and right, but I wanted to play like him in every other way too. If there was one player I idolized, it was Howe.

Once the game started, I watched Gordie as much as I could when I was on the ice—and never took my eyes off him when I was on the bench. He was tall and wide, but with surprisingly sloped shoulders. He wasn't the very best skater I would ever see in the years to come. Nor the greatest finesse player. But he might have been the strongest. It seemed no effort for him to pick the puck up off someone's stick and just brush that player aside. And when he shot, it was like a bullet. I know a lot of us young players were studying him, hoping to learn from him, but what I realized watching Howe play was that I would have to approach the game differently. To play like Gordie Howe, you had to have that extraordinary strength. And not many of us did. He was something special.

I wasn't Gordie Howe good, but when I got a few shifts during those exhibition games against the Red Wings, I felt I did well.

By the time George and I packed our bags and got into his car for the long ride home, we were both pretty happy about the training camp. George was sure I was going to get called up. He continued to talk me up once we were back in Saskatchewan. He even told a reporter for the *Lethbridge Herald* that while Sid Abel had positive things to say about the other Canucks at the training camp, I had been the star at the Hawks drills. It was a lot to live up to. But I sure was going to try.

When we got to Moose Jaw, I was surprised at how good it felt to be back. My performance at the training camp had created a little buzz on the team and around town. Everyone seemed excited for me. I was even named team captain. That meant a lot to me—the management always announced the appointment, but usually the players recommended someone for the position. It also reminded me of the challenges of the white world. I had confidence that I could lead the team on the ice, but, oh, boy, the pep talks in the dressing room and on the bench? The chatty advice and words of guidance? I just didn't have enough faith in my English skills to put those sentences together. Luckily, the team didn't seem to mind having a quiet captain.

Shortly after I was named captain, George had another bit of good news for me. The Canucks organization had bought me a second-hand car so I could get around on my own. A 1946 two-seater Chevy coupe.

And then one evening, George came home from work more animated than usual. He had just heard that the Hawks wanted me to come down to Chicago for a couple of tryout games in a few days' time. I could hardly take in what he was telling me. Not a training camp. A real NHL game, playing on a real NHL team. The Black Hawks. I felt a strange mix of anxiety and joy. This was my chance.

Unfortunately, George couldn't take time off to go with me. Tiny Thompson would take me down. There was no question of me travelling alone. The Indian Act prohibited any Indian nineteen or younger from leaving the country unescorted. During the two world wars, plenty of my people (including my mother's father and brother) had gone off to fight in Europe, many of them when they were only eighteen—but I guess that didn't count for anything. It was an insult, sure, but I wasn't unhappy about having the company for such a big trip.

Tiny drove. The trip took us two days.

We followed pretty much the same route I had driven with George a few months earlier. But this time, once we hit Illinois, we let the huge highways take us right through the suburbs of Chicago, through stretches of houses and more houses, until we were in the midst of a mass of grey concrete and towering buildings.

Edmonton and Calgary were "big city" to me. A few hundred thousand people. How would that compare to the millions of Chicago? That became clear pretty quickly.

To me, Chicago was pure chaos. The streets were choked with cars. Horns honked every minute. The sidewalks were crammed with people—who walked within inches of each other even though they were perfect strangers. A lot of people looked like Ray. And the buildings. Some of them were so big, they filled a whole city block. And many were so tall they turned the streets into narrow canyons.

Overhead, what a sight. Trains rattled by on iron scaffolding that reached up to the second-storey windows of the buildings around them. It was crazy.

It wasn't just the buildings and all the people that made the city feel different than anywhere I had been before. The air itself was foreign—grey and heavy with soot. It smelled of car exhaust and something else I didn't recognize. The winds off the huge lake were damp and cold like I had never felt before. And the sky. It was so small compared to the wide blue prairie skies of home. Just patches of grey. The only place you could see the horizon was if you were by the lake, looking east. And that lake. It appeared to have no end. As if there wasn't another shore to it.

Yet the city was amazing.

When we got to our hotel, the Piccadilly, on Hyde Park Boulevard, we were given rooms on the seventh floor. We had to take an elevator up. When I entered my room, I went straight to the window and stared out. The city stretched as far as I could see. I looked down—people appeared like tiny animals scurrying up and down the sidewalks. I couldn't move away. I was trying to take it all in.

———

When we arrived at the arena for the pre-game warm-up, it was no less strange. Tiny had played here when he was with the Bruins and the Red Wings. He was excited to show the place to me.

Chicago Stadium was huge. The seats around the rink rose up and up, in three tiers. The ceiling looked as if it was several storeys high. Tiny said the place could seat about 16,000 people for a hockey game with room for about 2,000 more to stand. And the ice was actually a little shorter than most NHL rinks—only 185 feet instead of 200. But it sure didn't look small to me. The surprising thing, though, was for all that space, the dressing rooms were not on the main floor but under the ice itself. The narrow flight of stairs that led into this basement had a ceiling so low that some of the taller players actually had to duck so they wouldn't hit their heads. And the dressing rooms were about as dank and unpleasant as you'd imagine dressing rooms in a concrete basement would be. It was such a strange contrast—all this space and all these seats for spectators, yet the players themselves stashed away in the basement.

After checking out the arena, Tiny and I went back to the hotel. Tiny wanted me to rest. But how could I? When I lay down on the bed and closed my eyes, all I could see was that ice, all I could feel were my skates cutting into it. And I could hear George's voice. "Freddy, you are going to make it. You're going to make it to the big leagues."

We returned to the arena in the early evening. It was November 20, 1953. A match against the Boston Bruins.

My first game as a professional hockey player.

Of course, I'd seen most of the Hawks players when I was at the training camp, but the majority had kept to themselves, so I hadn't actually met or talked to many of them. It was a strange, overwhelming feeling to walk into that dressing room. I spotted Fred Hucul right away. Fred gave me a quick smile. It was a relief to see someone I had known for so many years. Bill Mosienko also greeted me.

Other than that, no one spoke to me as I sat on the hard bench, getting dressed for my first skate in the big leagues. Looking around the dressing room, it struck me how old many of the Chicago players were. I hadn't really noticed that at the training camp, probably because there was a bunch of us young hopefuls there. But now it was clear that this team was full of veterans. And they all seemed a bit glum.

Since I was just trying out, there was no Black Hawks sweater for me—just a red and black vest. But that was enough. To wear the Hawks colours.

And then I was walking up the steep stairs with the rest of the team. Before stepping onto the ice, I looked up in the stands. I was surprised. The seats were mostly empty. The night I had got named Chief Running Deer, in Edmonton, more than 4,000 fans were watching. One of our other Edmonton games drew 5,500. There couldn't have been more than 6,000 fans here, in one of the biggest arenas in the country. No wonder everyone in the dressing room was so quiet.

As soon as my skates touched the ice, that thought, and the nervousness I'd felt for days, just fell away. I began circling around, faster and faster, warming up with all of the players. Skating with the Black Hawks and the Bruins. It seemed unreal.

After my second or third pass around the ice, I noticed something. The organist was playing that drum beat they always played in the movies whenever "Indians" were on the screen.

And then I thought of home. No one from Sandy Lake knew I was playing in Chicago. The notice to come down to the tryouts had been so quick. There was no chance to get a message to my mother, father, or Frank. Yet I felt somehow Alexan must know what was happening, must be watching, in his way. I wondered if he had foreseen something like this. Imagined his grandson in this world.

Being on this ice, playing with these players. It was a dream. A dream shared by every Canuck player. Every junior player I had played against for the last three years. But how long would I be here? Was it possible that Sid Abel and Bill Tobin would like what they saw and invite me back? Was it possible that I would one day wear a real Black Hawks sweater?

Then I could feel my skates on my feet again, my blades slicing along the ice. I joined the rest of the players heading to the bench, getting ready for the first faceoff, for the game to start. And all I wanted to do was play.

Despite the relatively small crowd watching, the energy in the place was thunderous. Tiny Thompson had warned me about the level of sound in the building. The organ was huge. Over 3,600 pipes. When the organist, Al Melgard, began pounding out the notes, it was so loud the boards, the benches, everything, seemed to vibrate. That's why people called the arena the "Madhouse on Madison," according to Tiny. Didn't matter how many people were in the stands. When the organ started to play, the place felt full.

I got my first shift in the big leagues on a line with rookie Murray Costello and Pete Conacher. Pete was the son of Charlie Conacher—who I'd heard so much about at St. Michael's. Oh, man, who could have imagined that?

The action was rugged and rough. In the juniors, we played a kind of freewheeling game. It was pretty easy for someone who was a powerful skater like me to dart through other players, to break away and get in position to shoot. The games we had played at the Hawks training camp were just a more skilled version of that style. Now that the team was playing regular season hockey, however, things were different. It was disciplined man-on-man hockey. The huge Bruins defencemen really covered the forwards. I received punishing hits from men much larger and stronger than me, and while I didn't mind mixing it up or taking the blows, I felt I could barely move out from under the Bruins guard. I managed to get off a couple of shots, but I could never work myself into a position that allowed me to put the puck in the net.

We ended up losing that game 2–0, the club's fifteenth loss of the season, but I couldn't be upset. Never mind the challenges or the loss, I'd felt great on the ice. Like I belonged out there. The man-on-man playing style would take some getting used to, but I could tell I was fast enough and nimble enough to pivot from the defencemen. I just had to change my own style of play a bit. After the game, Tiny said I'd done a good job. And the next day, the *Chicago Tribune* mentioned that I'd given "a spirited account" of myself. It also noted that I "displayed a pleasing willingness to rough it up, and got off two or three good shots."

The next game was two days later. I'd been excited about my first game in the pros, but this game—I could barely wait. We would be playing the Toronto Maple Leafs.

The Leafs were coming off a pretty poor season from the previous year. But that didn't dampen my enthusiasm for them. Today, Toronto has its diehard followers, sure, but with so many teams in the league, the Leafs have a lot of competition for fans. In 1953, there were only two Canadian teams—Toronto and Montreal—and only one whose games were broadcast out west. This was the team we cheered on, sitting on the hard concrete floor in the playroom at St. Michael's. This was the team that drew us all into the Vogans' living room every Saturday night. These were the players I had followed so closely, who were larger than life in my imagination—Tim Horton, Ted Kennedy,

George Armstrong, Harry Lumley, Howie Meeker. I had heard about their moves for years. Now I would see them for myself.

This time, I was on a line with Bill Mosienko and George Gee.

What do I remember of that game?

I remember Tim Horton. I knew he was big, but, boy, there was nothing like seeing him standing there, towering over you. His neck was as wide as his head, and the rest was just pure muscle. Despite his hulking size, that man could move.

Ted Kennedy wasn't nearly so big, but what a player. I'd heard people say he wasn't a great skater. That was true, but it didn't seem to matter. When he barrelled down the ice, it looked like he was going to run right over you. He sure wasn't slower than a lot of the other players. And he was great with his stick, tough as hell to beat on a faceoff.

Most of all, I remember my first sight of George Armstrong. George's mother was Ojibway and his father was white. He wasn't a treaty Indian, but he was thought at the time to be the first player with an Indigenous background to score a goal in the league. He had only been playing for the Leafs for two years, but I knew how important he was to Indian hockey fans. When I first caught a glimpse of him, skating onto the ice, a little shiver went down my spine. His complexion. Not as dark as me, but not white either. And such a great hockey player. It was a wonderful thing to see him speed around the ice.

The Black Hawks struggled in that game. The Leafs scored goal after goal, and we only managed to put one in their net. Then, in the last period of the game, Bill Mosienko fired a shot that seem to go in. The goal judge ruled that it didn't. The crowd (which seemed slightly bigger than the previous night) roared in disapproval and threw bits of paper on the rink. The organ blasted out "Three Blind Mice." That made me smile.

But the fans' anger didn't matter. We lost 5–1.

The next day, Tiny and I got in his car and started the long drive home. Tiny seemed as pumped up by our time in Chicago as I was.

"You did good, Freddy," he said. "I think they are going to call you back. I think you are going to make it." He talked like that the whole way home.

When we got to Moose Jaw, I was itching to get on the ice again. To help my team and show my stuff. My Chicago experience had me feeling upbeat. The team had been struggling a bit, and I felt I could really make a difference.

Now that I was back on the Canucks, Coach Ab McDougall began to put me on defence. He figured it would give our team a bit of an edge during power plays, because I could hit my top speed in two or three strides and manoeuvre into a scoring position before the penalty killers could cover me.

Yes, even on defence, I was scoring plenty of goals.

The only shouts from the stands these days were positive ones. When I fired off a slapshot or scored on a big breakaway or put a puck in the net from fifteen feet out, it sounded like everyone in the stands was cheering. In Medicine Hat, I actually got a standing ovation from the crowd—from the opposing fans—for my penalty killing.

It felt good.

In January, George and Ab were talking to Bill Tobin again. The Black Hawks had been having a bad year. Not just a bad year—a terrible year. They seemed on track to have the worst season in franchise history. Years later, I would learn that a lot of Chicago fans blamed this on Tobin and the Norris family. When the previous team owner had died, in 1944, Tobin became the head of a syndicate that bought the club. It was an open secret, however, that the money had come from the Norris family, who owned both Chicago Stadium *and* the Detroit Red Wings. Many people felt Tobin and the Norrises had built up the Wings at the expense of the Hawks—all trades seemed to be in Detroit's favour. During the 1953–54 season, that practice appeared to be really catching up with the Chicago franchise. And then they got hit by a bunch of player injuries. Things didn't look good.

George said Tobin wanted me to come back down to Chicago. Ab, however, was not having it. The Canucks were doing better this season than we had in many years. It seemed as if we would make the playoffs, and we had a good chance to win it all.

"Freddy," Ab explained, "I need you here for the playoffs. If you go down to Chicago, that's it. Three games in the NHL and you're considered a professional. You can't play junior anymore."

George agreed. It was a gamble. I might go down, play one more game, and then be sent packing. If that happened, I wouldn't be able to join the Canucks if they made it to the playoffs. I might have to go to one of Chicago's farm teams. Or nowhere at all. I might not be able to finish the hockey season anywhere.

"Next year, Freddy," Ab said. "Next year, you'll be with Chicago. This year, you'll stay here and help us win."

The choice was not mine to make—Ab made that clear. I was disappointed. The next season seemed a long way away. Anything, anything at all, could happen before then.

What if I'd finally gotten my chance and missed it?

In the middle of February, the Canucks started a seven-game quarterfinal run against the Regina Pats. We tied the first two games, then lost the next two. With four games already played, we had to win the next one to stay in the playoffs. We were in Regina, where 3,700 fans packed the stands. That game was a struggle, to say the least. Our goalie had injured his eye in game three, and now his eyelid had to be taped to keep his eye open. Defenceman Sandy Hucul was kneed in the first period and injured his leg. Another of our players was knocked unconscious in the third period. The Pats got an early lead on us. I scored in the second period to tie it up, but they came back with another couple goals soon after. Wally Blaisdell scored twice in the third period, but we couldn't match the Pats' five goals. We were out.

The mood in the dressing room was sombre. No one was talking. We had come so far to be knocked out in such a disappointing way. As I took off my equipment, it hit me that my junior career was over. I'd had a good season, with 57 points in thirty-four games, but I'd played four years and my eligibility was done. At the end of my third year, George had mentioned that the Moose Jaw Millers, the senior team, was interested in adding me to their roster when I was finished with junior hockey. At the time, that sounded like a good option. The idea of staying in Moose Jaw, where I could get my job back with Kellogg, and where I finally felt comfortable, had been pretty appealing. But now, now that I'd had a taste of the pros, I wasn't so certain. Maybe this is the end, I thought. Time to finally go home.

Just then, George Vogan walked into the dressing room. With him were six women from Moose Jaw. Two of them were carrying large suitcases.

George was beaming—a bit strange, since we had just been knocked out of the playoffs. He was holding a piece of paper.

"I've got a telegram to read," he announced.

"'Fred Sasakamoose. Report immediately to the Chicago Black Hawks.'"

There was a moment of stunned silence, and then the guys on the team were cheering, calling out to me, excitement bouncing around the room.

But Ray, Ray Leacock, he was the most proud and pleased.

Of course, Ray was long gone, playing out east somewhere, by the time I was sitting in that dressing room, listening to that telegram being read out. But still, I can see him clearly, right beside me. Looking at me with tears in his eyes.

"Freddy, you made it. You made it," he is saying.

When you get to be an old man, sometimes your mind plays tricks on you. But this memory doesn't feel like that. It feels like the truth. The truth was Ray was there beside me. And he was as happy as if he was going to play for the Hawks himself.

8

kici-sōniskwātahikēwinikamikok

THE BIG LEAGUES

George knew about the Chicago call-up before we started that final game, but he didn't want me to be distracted, so he'd kept quiet. But he had told some of the supporters of the team. Together, they organized everything I would need for my life in the pros, in the big city.

Just like today, all professional hockey players had to show up for games dressed in a suit. In those big leather cases were several new suits. A good supply of crisp shirts. There were also pairs of dress shoes, a snappy overcoat, tie pins, handkerchiefs, socks, a hat, a watch.

Oh, boy, Freddy, I thought. You are going to look good!

And then, before I knew it, I was on a train to Toronto, where the Hawks would be playing the Leafs.

It took over two days to cut across the country to get to Toronto. I had a sleeper berth, but it was no use. I was so excited, I could barely close my eyes. Sure, I'd already played two games with the Hawks in Chicago. But to a Canadian kid, Toronto, Montreal, those cities *were* hockey. The places you dreamed of playing.

I wasn't the only one who was excited. The first day on the train, I had gone up to the domed seating area to look at the land passing us by. Someone asked where I was headed. When I mentioned that I was on my way to Toronto to play with the Chicago Black Hawks, the fellow sat up straight and began to pepper me with questions. After that, word seemed to get around the train. People started coming up to me to introduce themselves whenever I moved about.

I spent most of the night on the train sitting by the window in my berth and staring out at the endless night sky. The next morning, I went looking for the porter.

"Can you help me?" I asked.

I knew I had to show up at the Gardens dressed in a suit. George had gotten the ladies to shop for me, but he hadn't had time to show me how to wear the clothes. I had no idea what to do with the tie.

The porter was a kind fellow. He came into my berth and patiently instructed me, showing me how to make the loops and tighten the knot. Then he helped me into my suit jacket. By the time we were done and I was slicking my hair back in the bathroom mirror, I looked like a new man entirely.

The train finally pulled into Union Station at about two o'clock on Saturday afternoon. As I stepped onto the crowded platform, I looked about. There was a man standing a few yards off holding a big sign. It said "Sasakamoose." I headed over.

The fellow was the Hawks trainer, Walter Humeniuk, or, as everyone called him, Gunzo.

"They want you at the rink right now," he said. "You've been on the train for so long, you need to skate and loosen up before tonight's game."

When we walked outside the station, I looked across the street to a tall grey building with a beautiful pale green roof. It looked like how I imagined a palace might look. Whoa, I thought. Where the heck am I?

"What's that?" I asked Gunzo.

"The Royal York Hotel." He didn't seem to think anything of it.

Then we were in a car, and before I knew it I was standing outside a *real* palace, the place I hear some refer to as "Puckingham Palace"— Maple Leaf Gardens. Home of hockey royalty. I was in a daze as I followed Gunzo inside. Down a corridor, through a door. And then I was in the middle of the Black Hawks' dressing room. It was already set for that night's game. Each stall had a sweater hanging up in it and equipment lined up on the shelves above. I looked at the names on the back of each stall. Rollins, Gadsby, Mosienko, Fogolin, Dewsbury, Wharram . . . *Sasakamoose* #21. I was going to be number 21. It was almost more than I could take in.

I walked over to my stall and looked at what was laid out for me. Oh, boy, what beautiful stuff. For each player, the equipment manager had prepared about twenty sticks—the brand you wanted and just the length you liked them. And the pads and gloves were the best that money could buy. When I first started with the Canucks, I had hated the stiff leather of the hockey gloves, so unlike the soft, worn-out stuff we'd had at St. Michael's. Eventually, I'd sent a pair of gloves to my mother. She had repalmed them with deer hide and stitched them back together with moose sinew. ("What's that smell?" some of my Canucks teammates had asked when I put on my refashioned gloves. "Woodsmoke," I told them. The gloves smelled like home.) The suppleness of the deer hide allowed me to feel my stick and control it with more precision. But the gloves the pros used didn't need that kind of alteration—the leather on the palms was as flexible as buckskin.

Gunzo interrupted my inspection.

"Just your skates, Chief," he said.

After I'd changed out of my new suit and into clothes to skate in, I sat down on the bench and Gunzo handed me my blades. But before I put them on, I pulled a couple of packs of skate laces from my pocket. I'd grabbed them from the Canucks' dressing room before I left. Kept them safe in my jacket the whole trip east. One pair was black and the other yellow. I took one lace from each pair and started to thread them through the eyelets. Gunzo looked at me with a question on his face.

"To remember a couple of good friends," I said.

The yellow lace was for Jimmy Chow. The black one was for Ray. Playing with those guys in Moose Jaw had meant the world to me. I wanted to honour them here in the big leagues. I wanted to represent my people, but also theirs. I wore those black and yellow laces for every game I played in the pros.

When I'd finished putting on my skates, I walked out of the dressing room and down the short corridor to the rink. As I stepped out onto the ice, I looked up into the stands. Bill Tobin and some of the other Chicago executives were sitting up there watching. I spotted the gondola, from where Foster Hewitt's voice made its way right across the Prairies. I skated out to centre ice. I tilted my head back, peered up. There above me, maybe seventy feet up in the air, were the lights. Bright, bright lights. I thought back to that afternoon in Moose Jaw when George had told me to jump and touch the lights. *This* was what he was talking about. George was sure I could do it. I hadn't felt that way. But I was here now, at the highest point a young player could be. Skating where the greatest hockey players who ever lived had played. I was touching the light.

I began to skate. It was the most wonderful feeling in the world.

After my skate, Gunzo brought me a bowl of soup, and then he took me back to our hotel, where I could rest for a while. I'd only had about four hours of sleep the night before, but even so, I didn't drift off when I stretched out on the hotel bed. I was too excited.

And then, finally, it was game time.

In Chicago, we'd gotten to the arena several hours before each game time and the place had been pretty quiet. Here in Toronto, however, as soon as I joined my teammates walking through the front doors, I heard the shouts of fans. In the lobby, on either side of the entrance, were gold ropes that led towards the dressing room. And standing behind those ropes were people who had arrived early to catch a glimpse of their favourite players. As I followed my teammates, I could see several of them glancing at me with curiosity. I wondered if they had ever seen a full-blooded Indian before.

And then Black Hawks' dressing room door was before me. I took a deep breath and squared my shoulders. I followed the others in, trying to walk as if it was the most natural thing in the world, to be here.

Now that I was actually a member of the team, the players greeted me as I headed to my stall. A few nodded, a few said, "Hi, Chief." I sat down on the bench where my sweater was. Bill Mosienko sat to my left. George Gee to my right. After I'd got dressed, Bill Gadsby, the captain, came over to me.

"How'ya feeling, Chief?" he said.

"Nervous. How many people out there?"

"About thirteen thousand. And they're waiting for you. Your name has been all over the place. First Native and all."

That didn't make me feel any less nervous. But Bill kept talking to me, calm and encouraging.

And then we were all lined up and walking out of the dressing room. Even before I got to the stands, I could feel the electricity. The Gardens could hold fewer people than Chicago Stadium, but that didn't matter when there was a fan in every seat. You could tell the place was jam-packed just by the rumble of voices that hit you as soon as you got anywhere near the stands. The Madhouse on Madison felt loud and alive because of that crazy organ. The Gardens felt loud and alive because of the crowd.

As I walked through the entrance to the rink, I could see people in the stands at each side of the walkway—it looked like there were so many they might spill out over the railings. And every face was turned to us as we marched out.

As I circled the rink during the warm-up, Bill Gadsby came up and told me someone wanted to talk to me on the phone. He pointed to the penalty box, where the phone was. I skated over. When I picked up the receiver, a man was on the other end of the line.

"How the hell do you pronounce your damn name?" he said. "Is it Sas-ka-moose?"

"Who am I talking to?" I said.

"Foster Hewitt!" said the voice.

I couldn't believe it. Foster Hewitt. I had spent so many nights at St. Michael's, at the Vogans', listening to this man. To this legend.

I gave him my correct name, and then it was time to get to the bench for the beginning of the game.

Since I'd played the Leafs in Chicago in the fall, I knew what to expect out on the ice from them. And it was a rough, hard game. But I found my own team's style of play just as challenging. The guys didn't pass very often. Everyone seemed to work in their own little bubble. If you couldn't get the puck off the stick of an opposing player or intercept the other team's pass, you weren't going to get it.

Just like in the games I had played in the fall in Chicago, the defence-men were on me whenever I got the puck. But I got off at least one shot that came close to disappearing into the net. And I managed to swing around and get passes away—although several times my wingers weren't able to pick them up. And then, before I knew it, the horn was sounding and we had lost the game 4–2. I hadn't managed to score, but my first game as an official Hawk had been a thrill.

In the dressing room, the trainers and other Black Hawks staff took our equipment from us as we shed each piece. The pros didn't take care of their own equipment. They didn't carry their own bags. Instead, it was all whisked away, cleaned, dried, repaired, and made ready for the next game. But for now it would be packed up. We had a train to catch.

We slept overnight in the little bunk beds of the sleeper to Chicago. We would meet the Leafs again, the very next night, on home turf.

When we got in to Chicago, we went immediately to the arena for a practice and then were sent home to rest. A bunch of us were driven to the Midwest Athletic Club, where I would be living, along with some of the newer players on the team.

The Athletic Club was a thirteen-storey hotel-like building on Hamlin Avenue, in the West Garfield Park neighbourhood of Chicago. It had a number of floors of housekeeping units. On the lower levels were a ballroom, a pool, handball courts, billiard rooms, as well as a gym and other exercise rooms. In the basement was a huge boxing ring, where training matches took place and some fights were held.

I'd been given a big room, with a bed, a living area, and a little kitchenette. I'd be on my own for the first time. I didn't have much chance to get used to the idea or settle in before I had to head back to the arena for the game.

My appearance this time at the Madhouse on Madison was very different than when I'd showed up in the fall. I was now a real member of the team, and the papers had been making a fair bit of fuss about the arrival of the "full-blooded Indian center."

As I got out on the ice and my name was announced, the song "Indian Love Call" began pounding out of the organ. I could feel the eyes of everyone in the arena on me.

A lot of people ask me if I was offended by that—to be serenaded by a Broadway tune that pretended to have something to do with Indigenous traditions. Or if it bothered me to play for a team that had an Indian head as its logo. And my answer is always no. I didn't feel like anyone was making fun of me. I felt like they were trying to honour me, in their way. Just like in Edmonton, I felt only pride. Proud of being identified as an Indian. The fact that the white audience didn't really understand who I was or where I came from, the fact that they didn't understand the significance of the symbols they were using, well, that didn't diminish my pride one damn bit.

And, oh, man, was I proud. Stepping out on home ice as a Black Hawk, the Indian on my chest as well as in my heart, the music telling everyone in the arena that this was something special. As I skated around to the melody, I felt like I wasn't on the ice any longer. Instead, I was floating above the rink watching Freddy Sasakamoose skate. Then I was on the slough, the willow stick in my hands, my moosum sitting in the distance. I was back there, where it all started. With my family. I wished that my mother and father, my moosum, could see what I was seeing. That they were here with me.

And then the music stopped. The whistle blew. And my first home game as a real Black Hawk player began.

Like the match in Toronto, it was a close game. During the first period, a fellow named Jerry Toppazzini scored the first goal for us. Shortly after, Lee Fogolin, one of our defencemen, crashed into the Leafs net, injuring his arm so badly he had to leave the ice and head to the hospital. The Leafs tied it up in the second period, and then we scored again in the third.

It seemed to be over almost as soon as it started. Before I knew it, the horn was sounding and we leaving the ice having broken a six-game losing streak. I still hadn't managed to score, but I felt confident out there.

After the game, reporters were waiting in the dressing room to interview me. I was a little uncomfortable with all the attention. I could see a few of the other players grinning at me—but I wasn't sure if they were smiles or smirks.

After we had all finished cleaning up and dressing, Bill Tobin came in and told us to hurry up and get outside. There were fans wanting autographs. "They're the ones who pay your salaries, so you better not keep them waiting much longer."

I followed the rest of the team out one of the side doors that opened onto an alley, not quite understanding what we were being asked to do. In the alley stood a long line of people. Each was holding a piece of paper. I remembered the people waving pieces of paper at us when we walked into the arena in Toronto. I realized that these fans, like the Toronto crowd, wanted us to sign our names. The only things I'd ever signed were my hockey stick, so everyone knew it was mine, and that C Form. It seemed like a strange ritual, but I was happy to go along with it, if that's what you did as a pro.

Our next game wasn't going to be for four days, so now I had a little time to settle into my new home and this new city.

The Midwest Athletic Club was a lively place. Gunzo would meet us there each day and take us down to the basement for workouts and training sessions. In the evenings, the hockey players staying there liked to party. These could be really rowdy evenings, with bathtubs full of ice and bottles of beer. I didn't drink at the time, but guys kept shoving bottles at me even when I said no. At the beginning of one of these evenings, someone announced that they were getting "a girl" sent up. I didn't want to have anything to do with that, so I left right away and tended to avoid the parties from then on.

I think I might have gotten lonely, or felt a little uncomfortable with my new living arrangements, if it wasn't for my next-door neighbour, Jerry Toppazzini. Jerry had been traded from Boston halfway through the season, so he was new to the Hawks too. For some reason, he took a shine to me and decided he would be my unofficial chaperone.

I was happy about that. As much as I wanted to see the city, I wasn't too keen to go about on my own. It wasn't just that Chicago was so big. It was also a dangerous place. My teammates at the Athletic Club all talked about the city's reputation for violence—and how organized crime was still a big deal. When I went downstairs to the boxing ring, there was always a bunch of tough-looking guys in flashy suits, smoking cigars, watching and betting on the boxers. I didn't know who they were, but I knew that I didn't *want* to know.

Jerry, however, was eager to take advantage of everything the city had to offer. When he discovered I was a fan of Louis Armstrong, he got excited.

"You want to see Louis Armstrong? He's in town!"

So one evening, we made our way to the Blue Note, on Madison Street. The place was packed.

When Satchmo walked out on stage, the room rang with applause. But when he lifted his trumpet to his lips, you could have heard a pin drop. It was amazing to see him standing there, not twenty feet in front of me. His cheeks ballooned and then a blast of perfect sound filled the air. "St. Louis Blues," "West End Blues," "Potato Head Blues." His trumpet playing was great, but when he sang, his voice just rumbled through the space. It felt as if you were surrounded by each note, surrounded by him. Like he *was* the blues. I sat in awe.

Our next game was also in Chicago. A tie this time, to the New York Rangers, on March 5.

A day later, we headed out on a road trip. We would be in Boston, New York, Detroit, and Montreal—four cities and four games in less than a week.

I don't remember much about Boston. It seemed like we arrived at the arena and left again without seeing any of the town. I didn't even get a glimpse of the sea.

Perhaps I don't remember much about Boston because New York City takes up all the space.

Oh, man, was I excited to see that place. I'd heard about it for years. The nuns and priests had not taught us much about the world when I was at St. Michael's, but for some reason they talked a lot about New York. They told us about the majestic Empire State Building, the symbolic Statue of Liberty—and Madison Square Garden, the home of some of the greatest sporting events in the world. They had always made the city sound like a magical place. And now the team would have a day or two there and I would actually get to see it myself.

Jerry once again acted as my tour guide. He suggested we head straight for the Empire State Building to get a sense of the size and shape of the city. As we approached it, I craned my neck back—the skyscraper shot up and up, dwarfing everything around it. The needle at the top looked like it could poke through the clouds. At the time, the Empire State Building, at 102 storeys, was the tallest building in the world. The elevator ride up to the eighty-sixth-floor observation deck seemed to last forever.

We stepped out in the cool March air, over 1,000 feet above ground level. The cars below us looked like fleas. Jerry read a sign that said the building was designed to sway eighteen inches. We could see the Brooklyn Bridge, Central Park, Times Square, the East River, and the Hudson. Jerry pointed out binoculars on metal stands. We each put a nickel in and I swivelled mine to get a closer look at the Statue of Liberty.

It was hard to really take it all in.

We walked and walked the streets of Manhattan. Jerry wanted to take me to see Madison Square Garden before we had to play there. This was the old Garden, on Eighth Avenue, between Forty-Ninth and Fiftieth Streets. (It was torn down in 1968.) Of course, I knew it was the home of the Rangers, but I had heard about it more often when people talked about famous boxing matches. It was an impressive-looking place.

As we were leaving, Jerry turned to me and said, "Hey, do you want to meet Jack Dempsey?"

Dempsey was one of the sports heroes the priests talked about whenever they had us boxing in the playroom. He had been the hugely popular world heavyweight champion for seven years in the 1920s. I guess he'd taken advantage of that fame to open a restaurant right across the street from the Garden. It had now moved to Broadway and Fiftieth, so Jerry and I walked over. When we got there, Dempsey was actually standing in the doorway, chomping on a cigar, greeting people. We introduced ourselves and told him we were in town to play against the Rangers. That caught his attention. He ushered us into the restaurant and found us a table. He told us to order anything we wanted, on the house.

We thanked him but couldn't take him up on his generous offer. Bill Tobin and Sid Abel were extremely strict about what we ate and when we ate it. Specially planned meals were always sent up to our hotel rooms. On game days, dinner would be as early as 4 P.M. If Tobin found out you'd be eating or drinking anything else, he'd tear a strip off you.

Dempsey had lots of questions for us. He seemed particularly fascinated that I was an Indian, from Saskatchewan. One of Dempsey's nicknames was "Kid Blackie." And he was dark. I thought he might be Black or half Black. I would later learn he was part Cherokee. No wonder he was so interested in me.

We talked a little about Dempsey's extraordinary career, and then Dempsey turned and pointed to a large screen at the front of the restaurant.

"Hey, do you want to watch the fight?"

Dempsey got someone to start up a film of his famous 1927 comeback title match against Gene Tunney. It had been a huge event at the time, bringing in millions of dollars at the gate. Al Capone had tried and failed to fix the fight. Dempsey had managed to knock out Tunney midway through. A controversial call had allowed Tunney time to recover and get up, so the bout was prevented from being called in Dempsey's favour. We boys at St. Michael's had heard all about it. As the grainy black-and-white footage began to play on the screen, it didn't seem quite real that I was actually seeing this piece of boxing history—and in the company of the great fighter himself.

After visiting with Dempsey, we went back to the hotel. But there was no time for me to rest. A car was coming to take me to a local television station before the game.

I was being interviewed along with Sky Hi Lee, a Canadian pro wrestler who was in town. His real name was Robert Leedy, but his stage name was perfect. He was huge—six foot seven and rippling with muscle. In fact, he was the tallest professional wrestler in the world at that time, and he was going to be in the ring at the Garden the next day.

When the interviewer turned his attention to me, I told my story—the slough, St. Michael's hockey, Moose Jaw. Then he asked me to say something in "Indian." So I said, "nanaskomon ē-nakiskawakik ayisiyinowak ōta ōtēnaw New York City. anohc tipiskaki niwi-metawan Madison Square Garden. ni-pakoseyihtān kamamihcihakik nīci-nēhiyawak." It's been a pleasure meeting the people of New York City. I am playing tonight at Madison Square Garden. I hope to make my people proud.

After the interview, the producer thanked me and gave me a box of cigars and a transistor radio. Transistor radios had just come on the market that year, and I had never seen anything like it. The producer opened the back and explained to me about the tiny disposable batteries. The radio we had at St. Michael's and the one at the Vogans' house were huge vacuum tube models that had to be plugged in. The portable one my parents had managed to acquire to listen to my games was big and bulky and needed a battery the size of a pound of butter. This radio was so small you could put it in your pocket. I couldn't wait to show my parents this precious new thing.

When we finally got onto the ice to face the Rangers, I was in high spirits from all of my adventures. I felt full of energy, eager to show what I could do. At one point late in the game, I got the puck at the blue line. With no clear shot, I decided to send it into the corner, where I could pick it up again. A huge New York defenceman was on me, but I figured I was fast enough to beat him to the puck. And I did. In my enthusiasm, however, I forgot a few things. I no sooner got the puck on my stick than I felt something come crashing into me. After that, only black.

I woke up lying on my back, in a place I didn't recognize.

"Where am I?" I asked.

Bill Mosienko was leaning over me.

"You're in the dressing room."

I realized I was on some sort of table.

"Chief," Bill was saying, "you gotta keep your head up. You're fast, but you're going get yourself killed playing like that."

It was a head-throbbing reminder that in the pros, the players hit hard—and all my fancy footwork wasn't going to help me escape them.

We lost our game to the Rangers. Despite that, and my aches and pains, I'd had the time of my life in the Big Apple.

The very next night, we played in Detroit.

We went straight from the train station to the arena for a pre-game skate. After the skate, I was leaving the dressing room when I heard someone call "Freddy!"

I had to do a double-take when I saw the fellow. How could this be? It was Albert Seenookeesick. My old teammate from the St. Michael's Ducks.

"Albert," I said, "what in the hell are you doing here?"

"I came to see you play."

Albert had hitchhiked all the way from Saskatchewan, from his home on the One Arrow reserve, just north of Duck Lake. It had taken him over a week to get to Detroit. He had slept in Catholic churches along the way. The priests had given him meals from time to time.

I shook my head in amazement as he explained it all.

Just then, Gordie Howe came out of the Red Wings' dressing room and walked towards us. I think he recognized me from the exhibition game we had played after training camp. Of course, I knew who *he* was, but he introduced himself anyway and asked Albert where he was from. Gordie grew up in Saskatchewan. He knew Duck Lake.

Maybe because Gordie was being so easygoing and friendly, Albert started to get a little cocky.

"After I watch the game tonight, I'm going to try out for Jack Adams," he said to Gordie. Jack Adams was the general manager of the Red Wings. Perhaps Albert was making a joke, but he said it seriously. Gordie looked at him, but he didn't laugh or dismiss him. He just nodded, and we exchanged a few more words before Gordie said goodbye to us. Once he'd left, I began to ask Albert more about his plans.

"After this, I'm going down to Florida. If I don't make this team, I have a chance to make the farm team down there."

He didn't have any hockey equipment with him as far as I could see.

"Are you going to hitchhike to Florida too?" I said.

"Yeah," he replied.

Of course, if he really did have a tryout, the club would have paid for his travel.

"It's a long way home from there," I said. "You should take the train back." I gave him some cash for the ticket and food.

Then I had to go. I'm not sure if he actually saw the game. Or whether he made it down to Florida. When I saw him next, years later, I forgot to ask about that.

That night, the Red Wings handed us another loss. But it didn't come as a surprise. They were the league leaders, on their way to a Stanley Cup win at the end of the year. And they had Gordie Howe.

It was great to face Howe on the ice again. But it was Ted Lindsay who really caught my attention that night. Lindsay wasn't a big guy (he was actually a little shorter than me), but he didn't seem to know that. He was like a damn warrior, his face covered in so many scars it looked like a road map. He would fight anybody, and he didn't seem to know how to quit once he started. When I found out a few years later he had started the players' union and taken on the team owners and management to get fair compensation, I wasn't one bit surprised. If anyone was up for that fight, it was Ted Lindsay.

Two days later, we made our final stop—Montreal. The Forum. I had played in Maple Leaf Gardens. And now I would be skating in that other cathedral of hockey.

Maybe because playing in Montreal, against the Canadiens, was such a big deal for me, I have more vivid memories of that game than I do of many of the others.

Like watching Boom Boom Geoffrion wind up for his slapshot. By this time, I'd heard a lot about his technique, but I was surprised to realize he lifted his stick less than I did, that my windup was actually more extreme than his. But then he was so strong. I guess he didn't have to raise his stick as high to get the power in his shot.

And Doug Harvey. Everyone talked about his defensive skills, but to watch him skate backwards with such strength and speed. Boy, that was really something. Like watching George Hunchuk skate—but backwards. I could forget about trying to go around him. One Montreal sports columnist later wrote that I was skating that night as if I had "outboard motors" on my blades. But when Doug Harvey covered me, I was trapped. He did, however, give me the opportunity for a good verbal shot.

When we first skated onto the ice, he looked at me and said, in that Western movie Indian-talk kind of way, "How!"

The word had barely passed his lips when I shot back, "I'm not Howe. He plays for Detroit." Harvey laughed out loud.

Turns out this was a joke that would come up more than once in my playing days.

Jean Béliveau was on the ice that night too. He was just two years older than me, playing his first full season with the Canadiens. But already there was so much excitement about him. And I could see why. If only I could play with that kind of talent, I found myself wishing after the first period. And then I thought, I will. I will come back next year, and I'll work to be that good.

But what I remember most clearly about my games against the Canadiens was Maurice Richard. I'd heard so much about him, and he was more impressive than I could have imagined. Where Gordie Howe seemed to hold all his power in his height and long, loose limbs, Richard was like a block of concrete. But it was more than just his build that was intimidating. The thing about Richard was that he was all business. If you tried to catch his eye or connect, he wouldn't respond in any way. Even sitting on the bench between periods, he never smiled, never chatted with his teammates. You could tell that when he was on the ice, he didn't have friends—he didn't *want* friends. Ted Lindsay has always said that about himself, that everyone on the ice was an enemy. But Richard was different. He wasn't mean or aggressive. Just hard and steely. Which made him even more fearsome. And his glare! Standing in front of him during a faceoff, I looked up into his face. His eyes were black, but they were shooting fire. It felt like they were cutting right through me. I found it hard not to be unnerved.

And then there was the adulation that followed Richard on the ice— that was something to witness. At one point in the play, Bill Gadsby crushed the Rocket with a powerful hit. The second Gadsby touched Richard, the entire Forum erupted in a blast of boos so loud I thought Gadsby was going to get blown out of the rink. Montreal adored Richard, and they were beside themselves at the thought he might get hurt or removed from the game. (In fact, it was almost exactly a year later that the city's streets would fill with rioters, enraged that Richard had been suspended for the season after a fight.)

Afterwards, on the bench, Bill Gadsby said to me, "Yeah, it's never a good idea to hit Richard in Montreal. Maybe back in Chicago, but here . . . you're taking your life in your hands."

We ended our road trip with that 4–0 loss to Montreal.

I was lucky to have come away with so many great memories from that trip. I imagine I was one of the few players who did. We didn't win one game we played on the road. After our defeat in New York, the headline in the *Chicago Tribune* was "Hawks Beaten: Now Losingest Team of All." After our drubbing in Detroit: "Hawks Do It! Absorb 50th Defeat, 6 to 0."

And then we came home and lost again to the Canadiens. The morale on the team was at rock bottom, and it must have been really tough for the older players. The Hawks had been bringing in new blood over the last couple of years—Ken Wharram, Pete Conacher, Larry Wilson, Larry Zeidel, Murray Costello, Fred Hucul, me—but it wasn't enough. It was pretty obvious that this would indeed be the worst season in club history. There were even rumours swirling around that the franchise might close after this year.

And then there was a little light.

On March 19, we faced the Bruins in Chicago Stadium and won 7–0. Pete Conacher got a hat trick. Ken Wharram got his first NHL goal. Boy, I envied them. But to win a game, and to win with that kind of margin, was still a great feeling. The mood in the locker room was a lot cheerier after that.

I can't remember why we played so much better that game than any of the others, but I think it might have had something to do with the milestone the club was celebrating that night. It was Bill Mosienko's last game in front of a hometown crowd. He was retiring from the Hawks, ending his NHL career with this season. Everyone knew it was coming, but now that his last game was here, it really hit me. Bill was such a generous guy, and he had been so kind to me. He had made me feel welcome as soon as I'd arrived. I couldn't quite imagine returning to the team without him. And his retirement was the end to an extraordinary career. (Although Bill would come out of retirement the following year.)

Bill was from Winnipeg, one of fourteen kids born to Ukrainian immigrant parents. He joined the Hawks organization when he was eighteen and had played fourteen seasons with them. Like me, he was small. He took a lot of hits over the years, but he was tough as nails. He had a reputation as a gentlemanly player and rarely took penalties. And he hit the record books too. Just two years before, in the third period of a game against the Rangers, he scored the fastest hat trick ever in NHL history—three goals in twenty-one seconds. It's a record that still stands.

Bill and his wife were brought out to centre ice after the game. There were presented with all sorts of gifts. Speeches were made. That arena was huge, but, oh, man, the emotion in the place just then made it feel as small as a living room. You could see what it all meant to Bill. Hockey was his life. It was his love. He hated to say goodbye to it. But age was creeping up on him, and he felt he had to leave before he was hurt or shown the door. Giving up hockey. I couldn't imagine how that felt. There were plenty of tears falling on the ice that evening. Even mine.

After that great victory over Boston, we returned to their hometown and got beat 9–5 to end the season on a pretty low note. I was a bit frustrated that I'd played a dozen pro games but hadn't managed to put one in the net the whole time. Yet I couldn't help looking forward with excitement. Now that I'd broken into the big leagues and knew the ropes, next year would be better. The thought of returning to show what I could really do crowded out any disappointment.

Once back in Chicago, guys began talking about their end-of-season plans. Bill Gadsby, Bill Mosienko, Jim McFadden, and Lee Fogolin were planning a vacation in Los Angeles before heading home.

"Hey, Chief," one of them said, "want to join us?"

It was a great surprise, to be included like that. Jerry Toppazzini had become a friend—Bill Mosienko and Bill Gadsby had always been welcoming. But it was tough to know what the rest of them thought of me. I sometimes wondered if some of the players resented all the attention I'd been getting. After every game on the recent road trip, reporters had been waiting for me in the dressing room. It seemed that everyone was curious about this full-blooded Indian who was playing hockey. (Interest, however, wasn't the same as acceptance. I was always aware of that.) But even if my teammates weren't bothered by the media attention I was getting, that didn't mean they considered me one of them. During my entire time with the team, not one player ever called me Fred or Freddy or even Sasakamoose. To a man, they called me Chief. Some meant it as a friendly nickname, I'm sure. But I sometimes suspected others were using it to make fun of me. After all, the two Bills, Jerry, Kenny Wharram, those were the only guys who ever really talked to me. And then there was my experience on the ice. The fact that so few passes seemed to come my way. Was that because I was a rookie, or was something else going on?

I had tried not to dwell on what others might be thinking. I tried to fit in.

———

My doubts made me a bit nervous about the car trip, with this small group of fellows who knew each other so well. Yet I was glad to be invited along. And the trip would get me out of a bit of a jam.

After one of our early home games, I'd been in the lobby signing autographs when a beautiful girl came up to me and introduced herself. Her name was Helen. She was a fashion model, and a Cherokee.

"What are you doing tomorrow?" she asked. "Do you want to meet for breakfast?"

I took her up on the invitation.

We got along well. She was from Oklahoma. About a hundred years earlier, her people had relocated there after being forced out of the American southeast as part of the Trail of Tears. Some of the members of her band, however, were relatively lucky—they found oil on the land where they were settled. She had grown up with all sorts of luxuries. Her father, she told me, was a rich man. When she described her life at home, it was very different from the reservation life I knew.

Whenever I was in town, we would go out for coffee or meals. She had a car, so she would sometimes pick me up at my apartment and drive me to my practices.

As the season drew to a close, she began to talk about our future. We'd known each other for less than a month. I tried to explain that I was just starting out. I wasn't in any position to make plans. She didn't care. Her father would build us a house, she said. We wouldn't have to worry about anything. But first she wanted to go home with me. She wanted to see Sandy Lake and meet my family.

Oh, boy, I thought. That's not going to work.

For one thing, I knew that showing up at my mother's house with a girlfriend was a bad idea. During my visits home in the last few years, my mother made sure I knew her rules when it came to relationships.

"Don't bring a woman home unless you're married," she warned me.

But that didn't mean she was giving me permission to marry.

"You're not your own boss until you're twenty-one," she used to say. "And even after that, when it comes to marriage, I've got a say."

But even if I had thought my mother would welcome this young woman with open arms, I didn't want her coming back with me. My family still lived in the same one-room log house. We had no power. No running water. We used an outhouse. I was too embarrassed for her to see that. Too embarrassed even to explain it to her. I hated being ashamed of my home, but I was.

I told Helen I couldn't take her to Sandy Lake because I was heading to the coast with some of my teammates. She gave me a photograph of herself. I didn't give her my address. Or make any promises about the following year. I kind of figured that she would forget about me—that someone better would come along for her. (When I got back to Moose Jaw, I showed Phyllis the photograph. "Wow, Freddy," she said, in her very sister-like way. "You may have played in the big leagues, but this girl is out of your league!")

So the five of us piled into Lee Fogolin's car and drove across the country, through the plains and then over mountains, past the desert, and under the swaying palm trees of Los Angeles. To be honest, most of the trip was spent in nightclubs, although I still didn't really drink. The sun and sand? We didn't see much of either. In fact, we never went to the beach.

We did make it out onto the hill where the big Hollywood sign stood, and then into Hollywood itself.

Bill Gadsby had arranged for us to have a private tour of one of the movie studios. I can't remember which one. I was amazed by the huge domed buildings that hid elaborate sets inside. More amazed to be walking through the vast lot, catching glimpses of Rock Hudson and

Jimmy Stewart. My favourite part of the tour, however, was the outdoor set for the Western movies that were so popular back then. The wooden storefronts, the saloon, the horse rails along each side of the dusty main street. All looking so real. All completely make-believe. Like the actors playing cowboys and Indians. But perhaps the most amazing thing about our private tour was the way Bill had pulled it all off. I don't know if he was able to arrange it because of his self-confidence or because the studio knew he was a star hockey player. Either way, I felt pretty good spending time with a guy as accomplished and respected as he was—as well as with Lee, Jim, and Bill Mosienko.

Perhaps I was tired from all our evenings out, but I don't remember anything of the drive up the coast until we hit the redwood forests of northern California, Oregon, and Washington State. I thought I'd seen trees before, but nothing like these giants. I wondered what my father, the logger, would have thought of them.

Once we hit Seattle, we started east. When we got to Bismarck, North Dakota, Lee Fogolin told me they were going to drive straight from there to Winnipeg, to drop Bill Mosienko off. They didn't want to make a detour to Moose Jaw.

"You're not taking me home?" I asked, a bit surprised.

"It's too far," Lee said.

I didn't know what to make of that. I thought the trip had gone well. Was it just their eagerness to get home? Or had I misjudged their friendship or acceptance?

These uncomfortable thoughts bounced around in my head as I stood alone, in an empty bus station in North Dakota, trying to figure out where I should be heading. I dropped my luggage at my feet and began to dig around in my wallet for the fare. Home seemed very far away. How long, I wondered, was it now going to take me to get there?

9

ka-pe-kiwet

HOMECOMING

When I got to Moose Jaw, George gave me a huge hug. He told me that while I'd been on my California road trip, I'd been named MVP for the Western Canada Junior Hockey League and would be awarded the Ed Bruchet Trophy. The selection had been made by the sportswriters and announcers in the west. What a year, I thought.

And then he wanted to hear all about my time with the Hawks. I spent the evening with him, Flora, and Phyllis, telling them stories. When I was finished, I thanked George for everything he'd done for me. He shook his head.

"No, you did this yourself, Freddy," he said. "Now go home and keep working all summer. Keep yourself in shape and get ready for the training camp in September."

The next morning, as I was preparing to leave, George handed me some cash. During all my time in Moose Jaw, he'd always kept my money for me. Now he gave me the balance of what he still had and a cheque the Black Hawks had mailed to Moose Jaw for me. Then he nodded his head towards the driveway, where my '46 Chevy coupe was parked.

"Time to go?" he asked.

"Yeah," I said.

We walked to the front door together. When I got to the stoop, I hesitated. I felt sorry for George, standing in the doorway, looking at me sadly. And I was finding it hard to say goodbye as well.

"This is your home too, Freddy," George said. "Anytime you want, you come home." There were tears in his eyes.

He was right. His place felt like home. He had treated me like a son, and I thought of him as a father. He had believed in me. His confidence had allowed me to dream. And he had given me everything I needed to make that dream come true. The lump in my throat stopped me from saying anything.

I think George must have seen the emotion on my face.

"No goodbyes, Freddy. Don't look back. Just go to your car. We'll see you again!"

He waved me off, and I slid behind the wheel of the Chevy.

Once I hit the road, the excitement of returning to Sandy Lake and seeing my family pushed all the sadness from me. I couldn't believe I had walked this road four years ago, so desperate to get home. Now I was returning in my own car, as an NHL player. I was living my dream. Playing in a league that had only 120 spots for all the hockey-crazed guys in Canada and the US. And I was seeing the world at the same time.

Just past Chamberlain, the car started to thump against the blacktop— a flat tire. I pulled over to change it. After I was done, I got back into the car and kept going to Humboldt. I planned to stop there and say hi to a girl, a former St. Michael's classmate who I had been in touch with since moving to Moose Jaw. She had been going to nursing school in Humboldt, and we had written to each other and occasionally gotten together over the years. But when I went into a café to use the pay phone to call her, I realized I had lost my wallet. I'd had it when I gassed up in Chamberlain. The only place I could have lost it was when I was changing the tire.

I dug a nickel out of my pocket and called George in a panic.

"Don't worry," he said. "I'll phone the radio station and they can make an announcement about it. Just wait there for a while to see if anyone phones in to say they found it."

My friend joined me in the café, and we waited and waited. After an hour or two, the pay phone rang. It was George. Someone had found my wallet.

"But he didn't want to give it to me," said George. "He wanted to deliver it to you in person. He's on his way to Humboldt. Just sit tight a little longer."

It seemed like an odd thing, someone insisting on making that trip instead of getting George to pick up the wallet. The reason became clear about two hours later, when a middle-aged man and a couple of children entered the café.

"I looked in the wallet, and I saw that cheque from the Chicago Black Hawks, and I thought, Hey, I've got to meet this guy. My kids wanted to meet you too."

The fellow insisted on buying us lunch before he went on his way again. His attention was flattering, but it also made me a bit uncomfortable.

I guess that was a sign of things to come.

After the man from Chamberlain and his kids had gone, and as I was standing to leave the café, another guy walked over to me. He must have overheard the conversation I'd had over lunch.

"Come outside," he said. "I have something to show you."

He walked me across the street to a car lot and pointed to a big silver-grey DeSoto. The car was a beauty, covered in chrome details—hubcaps, headlights, door handles, bumpers, side trim. The whole thing sparkled in the sun.

The fellow opened the door to show me the push-button start, but it didn't matter. I was already sold. He wanted $3,900. I had a wallet full of cash and my cheque from the Black Hawks. But I didn't want to spend everything I had, so even with that and the Chevy as a trade-in, I still had to finance a good portion of the car. But as soon as I put my foot on the gas and started gliding down the road, all thought of money was left behind.

The miles just flew by.

Once I hit Prince Albert, I turned onto the smaller road that leads northwest to Sandy Lake. Before I headed into the reserve, I stopped at the general store in Debden. I wondered if my parents would even be home—they could be visiting or working off the reserve. I asked the store owner if they had been in recently. He didn't recognize me, so he wasn't sure who my parents were. I told him I was Fred Sasakamoose. Before I knew it, I was surrounded by people. I have no idea where they all came from—the store hadn't seemed overly busy when I walked in. But now there were a bunch of people in front of me, and every one of them wanted my autograph. I signed about fifteen scraps of paper and then explained I had to go. I wanted to see my parents.

Once I got onto the reserve, my fancy city car had a hard time. There were still no real roads in Sandy Lake—just wagon trails and a few raised mud stretches. I bumped slowly along until I pulled up outside my parents' log cabin.

My mother came out and stood on the steps. "mōniyās, mōniyās," she called back through the doorway. White man, white man.

I stepped out of the DeSoto as my father appeared in the doorway.

My mother let out a cry. "nikosis!" My son!

She ran towards me and threw her arms around me, her shoulders heaving with sobs.

The day after I got home, I told my mom and dad to get ready to go out. I was taking them into Prince Albert to go shopping. We stopped at a grocery store and filled the car with supplies, as well as a pair of new rubber boots for my father. Then I took them to a women's clothing shop. There were several dresses hanging in the window. One was apple red, with flowers. I knew how much my mother loved bright colours.

"eoko ekwanima kiya, nikāwiy." That's the one for you, Mother, I said.

"moya, toosaw." No, Toosaw, she replied. "nikosihtamason, nita-weyitān senipanekin, kīkway ka-wāsihkwak." I make my own. I want cloth. Silk. Something that sparkles.

So we went to a department store, and she picked out a bolt of bright fabric and some thread.

A few days later, I told my dad I wanted to get him a team of horses and a buggy.

"tanteh maka eh-wiymiskaman ekoni?" he asked. Where're you going to find that?

I'd heard of a farmer in Blaine Lake who was looking to sell a couple of horses. We drove out to the farm to check them out. They were beautiful big grey Clydesdales, in great shape. And the farmer also had a wagon and harnesses he was willing to sell with them. I paid $800 for everything. My dad drove the team home. I think he was pleased. I sure was happy about doing that for him. It made me feel that my parents had been right. The môniyâwak world could provide a better life for me—provide a better life for all of us.

I planned to spend the summer much like I'd spent it the year before—logging with Dad and Frank, playing soccer and baseball, doing a bit of socializing. But right from my first days back, it was clear my time with the NHL had shifted everything around me. Of course, my parents were proud of me—especially my mother. Everyone told me about how she would hunker down in front of the radio every Saturday night in late February and March. If anyone got near, she'd shoo them away.

"kawiya samina kitohcikan kā-natohtamihk. e-wiynatohtaman *Hockey Night in Canada*. nikosis oma e-metatawet." Don't touch the radio. I'm going to listen to *Hockey Night in Canada*. My son is playing. And then she'd spend the evening waiting to hear my name.

People outside my family seemed proud too, but also a bit in awe. I'd become something of a celebrity in northern Saskatchewan. My cousin Ken Cameron remembers an evening when I arrived at a dance hall in Mont Nebo. He says as soon as I walked through the doors, the place went quiet. I guess my arrival was a bit of a shock. I was no longer the Freddy Sasakamoose who had been hauling logs and playing ball the summer before. I was wearing a suit, a dress shirt, a long wool overcoat, and penny loafers. I had on a flashy watch and my hair was slicked back. This was how I had been dressing since I took the train to Toronto two months or so earlier. To be honest, I was just getting used to it myself. In Chicago, in New York, if I caught a reflection of myself in a mirror or store window, I'd do a double-take. I didn't look like me. And I guess I didn't look like too many of the guys in the Mont Nebo hall that night either.

Apparently, I walked over to the prettiest girl in the room and asked her to dance. We were the only ones on the floor—everyone else stood around and watched.

I remember a similar night, but it was a wedding—the same day I had driven my parents into Prince Albert. The day after I arrived back at the reserve. I got all dressed up and drove over to the hall in the DeSoto. When I walked into the room, the Chief, Allan Ahenakew, was playing the piano. His son was playing the fiddle. I could feel people staring at me, but I don't think anyone recognized me. Then Allan looked my way. When he spotted me, he stopped playing, stood up, and walked over. He asked me how I was and when had I got back. And then he told me to join him on the little stage. There, he spoke in Cree, introducing me as a son of the community and now a member of the Chicago Black Hawks team. He described me as the first Indian ever in the NHL. People often said that, that I was the first—I never knew if it was true or not. Allan said he was proud of me and my achievement—that the whole of Sandy Lake felt the same. The next thing I knew, I was surrounded by people, all shaking my hand and wanting to talk. Boy, that felt good. I was honoured to be recognized by our Chief, but it was more than that. I had spent so much of my life living away from the reserve that I often felt like a stranger there. Even though I played sports on the Sandy Lake teams in the summers when I was home, there were so many people in my community I didn't know and who didn't know me. This introduction by Allan made me feel like I was closing that gap. Like I was becoming closer with my people and my home.

My fame drew people to me when I was out and about, and it also brought lots of people to our little cabin. All summer long, visitors dropped in on my parents. Often they came with gifts. Sometimes they brought their daughters. A lot of the time, I wasn't at home, and my mother wasn't interested in marrying me off quite yet, so most of the people went away disappointed.

In fact, my mother was quite clear that she didn't think any sort of serious romance was a good idea for me at this point. All summer long, I took my shiny car to dances and get-togethers in just about every little town in the area. I loved the music and I loved to dance. I had no trouble finding partners to twirl on the dance floor. I went on dates with some of the girls, and I started seeing one of them, Christina Ledoux, regularly. But when we'd been going out about a month, my mother put her foot down.

"osam kitoskāyiwin, toosaw." You're too young to get serious, Toosaw, she said. "poko ka-poniwicewat." You have to break up with her.

I guess part of me agreed, so I stopped seeing Christina.

But I sure didn't slow down. I was working in the bush and playing a few sports. I was also spending a huge amount of time in the local bars and halls. I hadn't been a drinker while with the Hawks, but now I was developing quite a taste for it. For one thing, a steady supply was on offer everywhere I went. It was still illegal in Saskatchewan for Indians to be served alcohol in a bar or restaurant. But that didn't seem to apply to me. Unlike my Indian friends, I could walk into any place in the area and order a drink. Or I could buy alcohol and bring it back home to share with friends. Lots of things made me feel special that summer, and that was one of them.

Another thing that drew me to drink was simply comfort. While I'd been offered beer and drinks all the time I'd been with the Hawks, my self-consciousness kept me from cutting loose. Now I was home, surrounded by friends and family, feeling at ease, and I was ready to celebrate.

My mother's stepfather, my moosum Gaspar Morin, didn't approve of the good times I was having.

"All this drinking is no good for you," he warned. "You're going to ruin yourself."

I just laughed him off. I was young and strong and I deserved to have a little fun.

He was also concerned with my poor DeSoto.

"Stop driving that car around the reserve," he said. "These old trails are destroying it."

And he was right. The muffler was knocked off in no time. After about three months, the undercarriage was falling apart, and I was shedding bits and pieces of chrome everywhere I drove. By the end of the summer, the whole thing was a wreck.

But I didn't care.

"Don't worry, Grandpa. I'll buy another car next year. I'll buy ten cars!" I boasted.

"Not the way you're going," he muttered.

At the beginning of September, I said my goodbyes to Mom, Dad, Frank, and the rest of my family and got on a train for the long journey to Pembroke. This year, I was going by myself, but I didn't mind. My nervousness was largely gone. I was excited about starting a new season, seeing old teammates, getting my skates on again.

When I got to the camp, one of the very first things they did was weigh me. I had gained about five pounds. Tommy Ivan had taken over from Bill Tobin as general manager and Frank Eddolls was the new coach. Neither was happy with me. We were all supposed to show up at camp at our playing weight. (Of course, I didn't have a scale at home, so there had been no way to check.)

"You're going to work that off right away," Frank said.

On the first day of training and drills, Gunzo made me put on a rubber suit. The thing covered my whole body—cinched at my ankles and wrists and tied close around my neck. And then he told me to do all the drills and skate up and down the ice in the damn thing. Within about half an hour, the suit was filled with sweat, but Gunzo made me slosh around in it for the whole three hours. It was terrible, yet when I took the suit off, I had lost the five pounds.

To keep the weight off, they also put me on a diet. But even back at 169 pounds, I wasn't where I was four months ago. It wasn't just the DeSoto I had abused all summer. The drinking, the late nights, the big meals. They had all taken a toll on my body. That made me pretty anxious, but each day at camp I got a little more energetic, a little stronger. By the end of the second week, I felt like I was back in top form. Once the exhibition games started, my speed had returned and I was scoring goals again.

When the camp finished up at the beginning of October, the final pruning all done, I was still on the team, and Gunzo was packing my equipment to put on the train to Montreal for our first game.

I was thrilled to be back, excited to play again in the Forum, anxious to get out on the ice with Maurice Richard, Bernie Geoffrion, and Jean Béliveau.

When I entered the dressing room at the Forum for our practice skate, I looked over at the wall. There was my sweater: number 21. I went over to the bench and took off my jacket, began to loosen the knot in my tie. Suddenly Tommy Ivan was next to me.

He was shaking his head.

"No, Fred, stop."

I looked at him. What was going on?

"Change of plans. We're not going to dress you tonight. We've decided to send you to the Buffalo Bisons instead."

I felt like I had been knocked headfirst into the boards. My mouth wasn't making any words. I stood there with my jaw hanging open, my face burning, my hands curled into fists. When the numbness cleared a bit, I stormed out of the dressing room. Gunzo was standing outside the door. I stopped when I saw him. We exchanged words, but I can't remember what we said. I imagine he was trying to calm me down and reassure me. I didn't stay for the practice—I took a cab back to the hotel instead.

To be honest, I don't know if it ever occurred to me that I might not make the team again. Or if I just wouldn't let myself think about that possibility. But even if I had been worried, once I was on that train to Montreal with the rest of the team, I'd felt secure in my spot. Tommy Ivan's words blindsided me. Completely. Ken Wharram was starting the season with Buffalo too. But at this point, that didn't comfort me at all.

That night, when my disbelief and anger subsided for a spell, I tried to imagine what it might be like to play in the American Hockey League, in Buffalo. But I couldn't picture myself living in that kind of limbo. Not having my family nearby. Not having George Vogan. Although Jerry Toppazzini's friendship had helped, being all on my own last year, the only Indian player surrounded by people who didn't really understand me, had been tough. Going to Buffalo would mean I'd be even more adrift than I had been in Chicago. I would be in a strange city, miles away from home and miles away from my NHL dream.

The next morning, when Ivan called me down to his room to talk, I was blunt.

"I don't want to go to Buffalo," I told Ivan. "Send me someplace closer to home."

Ivan looked surprised. And not particularly happy.

"New Westminster has been wanting you on their team," he said. The New Westminster Royals, in British Columbia, were a Hawks affiliate in the Western Hockey League. While the Calgary Stampeders were another Hawks-associated team in that league, the BC team was apparently all that was on offer. That was still a thousand miles from Sandy Lake, but closer than Buffalo, and in Canada. It would have to do.

I went back to my room and packed my bags.

The New Westminster team was owned and managed by a man named Kenny MacKenzie. He seemed excited to have me join his roster, going as far as to tell the local papers that I was going to "give goalies an ugly time of it."

The Western Hockey League had a reputation for good, tough play. A large number of its players had come down from the NHL. Some were older guys whose NHL days were over, like Bud Poile, Max Bentley, Max McNab, and my Hawks teammate Gerry Couture. Many, like Johnny Bower, Norm Ullman, Glenn Hall, Val Fonteyne, and Johnny Bucyk, were about to start their long NHL careers. Others, like Fred Hucul, who was playing on the Calgary Stampeders with his brother Sandy, were like me—players who'd had a number of games in the big league and were hoping to bounce back up.

It was no doubt a great place for me to improve my game. Unfortunately, it didn't really work out that way.

Almost as soon as I'd arrived in New Westminster, another player, Jim Zarie, invited me to share an apartment with him. Jim had a house rule—no alcohol in the place and no parties. He wanted us both to take care of ourselves. After the summer I'd had, I was willing to agree.

Jim was a great guy, and we quickly became friends. I also became close with another player, Gordon Fashoway, who had played thirteen games for the Hawks during the 1950–51 season. Those two made my transition to the new team easier than I might have expected. Jim, like Jerry Toppazzini, was a born tour guide. And despite his no-alcohol rule for the house, he was quite happy to go out to parties or to drive down into the States, where the beer was inexpensive. In our off-hours, the three of us travelled all over the Lower Mainland and down into Washington State. I don't know how many hours we spent hunched over the pinball machines in the huge arcades there, knocking back cheap beer.

But despite the friends I made and the strengths of the league, I couldn't get over my disappointment at not being in Chicago. As soon as I started with the new team, the reality of my choice struck me. The WHL was minor professional hockey, like the AHL. But the AHL was more prestigious and was considered closer to the big leagues. I had dropped down not one level but two. Further than ever from returning to the Hawks.

Tommy Ivan had told me, when I was sent down, that he would be in touch, that he would phone soon. But if he talked to anyone, it was Kenny MacKenzie. And I didn't hear a word from either of them about my prospects. I was frustrated to be left in the dark like that. And I was frustrated to have lost my chance. What am I doing here? I thought.

And all of that showed in my game. MacKenzie had brought me onto the team expecting me to run up the scores. But I wasn't playing well, and I sure wasn't putting many pucks in the net. Gordon showed me how he shaved sticks down to give the straight blade a bit of a curve and make them lighter. (This was a decade before Stan Mikita was shaping his blade with a blowtorch, and long before manufacturers were making curved-blade hockey sticks.) I didn't want to curve my blade—that would have meant I could no longer switch my shot— but I did thin it out. While that helped, I still wasn't scoring like I should've been.

In early December, I had to sit out a couple of games with a charley horse I'd got after a hard check on the ice. A week or two after I got back on the ice, MacKenzie hit me with another blow. He had released me back to Chicago, and they were sending me to the Chicoutimi Sagueneens, of the Quebec Hockey League, in the new year. There wasn't going to be any discussion. The decision had been made.

Tommy Ivan then called with some reassurance.

"Go to Chicoutimi," he said. "We may need you in the new year, and Chicoutimi is closer than New Westminster."

That was exactly what I needed to hear.

I stayed in New Westminster and spent Christmas with Jim and the other hockey players who were stuck there over the holidays. Then I boarded a train for another long, long ride across the country.

As soon as I got to Chicoutimi in early January, I recognized what I had lost with the move from New Westminster. I had surprised myself with how much I actually liked it on the West Coast. Chicago was damp, but that was nothing compared to the constant rain of southern BC. It took me quite a while to get used to the grey skies and being soaked every time I stepped out the door. Yet, aside from the wet, the place and the people had quickly grown on me. I could tell things would be different in Quebec.

For one thing, there was no cozy apartment to move into. I would be living in a roadside motel, along with a few of the other players on the team. If we wanted something to eat and were tired of cold baloney sandwiches eaten in our rooms, we had to go out in the waist-high snow and sub-zero temperature to the local diner.

And then there was the language barrier. Suddenly I was back in a world where I didn't understand a single word. Everyone in town spoke only French. And many of the players spoke little or no English. A good deal of the coaching was in French.

Of course, I'd heard French spoken by Métis and French Canadians in the little towns of northern Saskatchewan. My mother spoke a bit of French. But this was different. I felt as if I was back at St. Michael's.

There were no nuns here who slapped you for not answering a question you didn't understand, or priests who whipped you for speaking your own language. And yet, every time a person addressed me in French, or I couldn't respond to someone, a bit of that old fear would return. (I guess it didn't help that the most French I had ever heard was when the nuns and priests talked to each other, especially when they were angry.)

One of the other players who lived at the motel was a French speaker named Léo Gravelle. Léo was quite a lot older than me, and he had played a number of seasons with the Canadiens before being sent down to the minors. He was bilingual—he spoke to me in English. I tried to join him whenever he went to the café for a meal. He would look at the menu and order in French. When the waitress turned to me, I always said, "*La même chose*." The same thing. (It was about the only thing I knew how to say in French.)

One day, when the waitress placed my meal in front of me, I threw my hands up.

"Goddamn, Léo! Can't you order something else?" I said. "I'm sick of rabbit!"

I enjoyed spending time with Léo, but I soon came to understand that my social life in Chicoutimi would be limited. One evening, early in my time there, Léo invited me to join him and the other English-speaking players at the local bar. I was happy for the opportunity to spend an evening listening to conversation I could understand.

At the bar, beer was served in quarts, and after a bottle or two I had to go to the washroom. As I walked in, a huge man followed me. He said something to me in French. I had no idea what he meant, but I understood the next word out of his mouth: "*Sauvage*!"

The next thing I knew, I was on the ground, blood pouring from my forehead.

My teammates must have heard something. They rushed into the washroom and picked me up. A few disappeared to look for my attacker.

They tried to get me back to the table for another drink, but I wasn't interested. I left the bar and never went back again.

The incident left me feeling shaken and vulnerable, like a residential school child, always waiting for the next blow. As much as I was proud to be Indian, the attack was yet another reminder (as if I needed one) that it could bring intense pain too. That people could use words like "*sauvage*" and "Indian" as weapons. And now my difference was keeping me from the only company I had in the evenings. My loneliness grew intense.

The single positive thing to come from the assault in the bar was that it forced me to more or less stop drinking. Just about every day we didn't have a game, the other players would head to the tavern and begin downing those quarts of beer. I heard that by four o'clock, everyone would be drunk. But I wasn't abusing my body like that, and perhaps not surprisingly, with nothing else to do but focus on hockey, my playing improved—the slump I had been experiencing in New Westminster slipped away, and I began scoring goals.

Still, the weeks and months in Chicoutimi just inched by. The team wasn't having a terrible year, and we made it to the best-of-nine semifinals. In early April, we were knocked out in the seventh game. It was finally time to go home.

When I'd first heard about Chicoutimi, I had really hoped that the move might mean I would be returning to Chicago. After all, that's what Tommy Ivan seemed to suggest. I hoped that since I hadn't been playing my best in New Westminster, this change might give me a boost. But Tommy Ivan never called me. Never talked to me after the move. I felt more discouraged than ever. Sure, the Western Hockey League and the Quebec Hockey League were full of players bouncing back and forth between the minors and the majors. But they were also full of people, like my friend Gordon, who'd played for part of an NHL season and then spent years in the minors without being invited back up. Was I going to be one of those guys?

I talked with George Vogan on the phone from time to time. He was, as always, encouraging, but the calls couldn't lift my spirits for long. I just didn't know how to improve my odds and restart my NHL career.

I couldn't help thinking back to the training camp. I hadn't gotten off to the best start, but I'd rallied quickly, and I'd performed well in the final exhibition games. On top of that, Sid Abel, Tiny Thompson, Bill Tobin—they had all said very positive things about my playing while I was in Chicago a year ago. Was I ever going to be able to play better than that if I wasn't playing in the big leagues? If I couldn't convince them with that calibre of play, what were my odds of ever getting a second shot? It made me wonder if I'd ever really had a chance. If there hadn't always been lumps of coal in the way of my skates.

By the middle of April, I was on my way back to Sandy Lake, plagued with doubts and questions—and more than ready to put a miserable hockey season behind me.

10

tipiyawēwihowin

PROPERTY

My return home in the spring of 1955 was quieter than it'd been the previous year. But people were still excited to see me. And there was one person in particular I was anxious to see.

I'd met Loretta Isbister years earlier, at the beginning of my time with the Canucks. I knew her brothers, Ralph and Myron. The family lived about sixty miles north of Sandy Lake, at a place called Winter Lake, near Bodmin. But the boys came down to watch hockey games and play soccer—we had crossed paths a number of times. I guess one of the brothers had moved a little further south, to Eldred, and one summer day Loretta had come down to visit him and gone to a local dance with her siblings.

That's where I first spotted her. I asked her to take a turn on the floor. She was two years younger than me, quiet, maybe a bit shy, but a beautiful girl. I danced with her a few times, and we talked briefly. I danced with a number of other girls too, and before I knew it the evening was over and Loretta had gone home. But I didn't forget about her. When

I got back to Moose Jaw, I started to send her cards and letters from time to time.

Sometime in 1954, Loretta's father had moved the whole family to Eldred so two of Loretta's younger siblings could go to high school. Eldred is only about twenty miles from Sandy Lake, so I'd seen Loretta a couple of times after I broke up with Christina and before I'd left for training camp that fall. One of those times, my friend Charlie Knife and I had just come down from logging up north and dropped in at someone's house for a visit. Loretta was there. She made a pot of coffee for us and brought it to the table with two mugs. I watched the way she moved across the kitchen, the way she lifted the pot, the way her fingers uncurled from the cup as she handed it to me. It was the most beautiful thing in the world. As we were leaving the house, I turned to my friend.

"Charlie, I think I'm going to marry that girl."

As soon as I got back to Sandy Lake, I got in touch with Loretta. By the time a month or two had passed, I was more certain than ever that she was the woman for me. Luckily, she seemed to feel the same way. And my mother, who still maintained her right to help choose a wife for me, liked Loretta as soon as she met her. Loretta was quiet around my parents—out of shyness, sure, but also because her first language was English, not Cree. It wasn't so easy for her to make conversation. Of course, since my father didn't talk much, they got to know each other slowly. But my mother didn't let the language barrier stand for long. Loretta couldn't resist my mother's chattiness and warmth. Anytime they were together, my mother had Loretta laughing within minutes.

We decided we wanted to get married sometime in the summer. But first I had to ask her father for her hand. That terrified me. Loretta and

I had had very different childhoods, and I wondered what her father would think of me.

Loretta's family was Anglican, and they were Métis, so they had not had to send their children away to residential school. She had thirteen brothers and sisters, and she was one of the older girls. The family had lived in the bush, a fair distance away from their neighbours and two and a half miles from the closest school. They had a big garden, grew their own vegetables, raised chickens for eggs, had their own cows for milk and butter. Her dad was a carpenter, but he also provided for the family by hunting and fishing. Her mother canned vegetables and berries to get them through the winter.

When Loretta was fourteen, her mother died in childbirth and everything changed. Loretta and her sister Pansy had to stay home from school to watch the baby and the younger children. Her father moved the family into their big two-storey house in Eldred, and then took work further from home to provide for them.

I knew that Loretta was like a mother to her younger siblings, and that her dad, Miles, depended on her. And I'd never met Miles. I didn't want to go alone to ask if I could take his daughter away, so Loretta's brother-in-law, Johnny, went with me. I put on my best clothes and made sure my hair was slicked back.

We'd been told that Loretta and her dad were out working on their old property, what they called "the farm." So Johnny and I drove up there. When we pulled up alongside the field, I could see Loretta out in the garden, pulling weeds. There was a tall older man beside her. I didn't want to get out of the car.

Johnny looked over at me. "Come on, Freddy. It's time to go ask," he said. When I didn't move: "It's not me getting married, Fred. It's you!"

I could see that Loretta's dad had spotted us and was heading over. I had to get out of the car.

When I got close to Mr. Isbister, his face was unsmiling. He didn't say hello, or even nod. I introduced myself. He still said nothing. I began to shuffle my feet.

Finally, I said, "I want to talk to you."

"What do you want to talk to me about?"

"I want to marry your daughter."

"Which one?"

"Loretta."

"You want to take part of my life away? You want me to give you the daughter who is helping me raise my kids?"

I didn't know what to say to that.

"And how are you going to provide for her? Are you working?"

"No, but I will be," I said.

"What do you do?"

"I've been logging. And I play hockey."

Mr. Isbister snorted.

"How much money can that be? Maybe you work for a month or two and then it's over."

By this time, Loretta had come over to stand near her dad.

"Etta, is this what you want?"

Loretta gave her shoulders a little shrug. I knew she felt bad about the idea of leaving her two youngest siblings, Jean and Doreen. They weren't yet in school. There were older children at home, but it was hard for Loretta to imagine how the family would function without her.

"If this is what you want, Etta, I'll let you go," her father said. "But don't bother me with how you are getting along once you're gone. This man who is coming to ask for you is going to have to look after you. Feed you, supply you with what you need. A house. Somewhere to live."

Loretta nodded.

"Okay," Miles said to me. "You have her hand. You have my blessing."

Then we all drove back to the house in Eldred to celebrate over tea.

Loretta and her sister Ethel, Johnny's wife, made all the arrangements for the wedding. On the morning of July 22, 1955, we were married in the Catholic church on Whitefish Reserve by Father Paquette. After, about forty or fifty of our friends and family gathered at Ethel and Johnny's house for the party. The meal was a group effort—mountains of chicken, potatoes, vegetables, desserts. It was a beautiful sunny day and clear crisp evening. We celebrated well into the night.

After the wedding, Loretta and I went back to Sandy Lake. Frank, his wife, Madeline, and their two children were already living there in the cabin with Mom and Dad, Clara, Leo, and Peter. The place was crowded.

Even if Loretta and I could have squeezed into the cabin, I wouldn't have moved in. I wanted to start off my married life with a bit of privacy. I also wanted at least a bit of distance from Frank.

Since I had been in Moose Jaw, the times I'd spent at home with Frank had been both good and bad. I loved my brother, that's for damn sure. And I knew he loved me. We were still best friends. But our lives had been moving in different directions for a while, and now tension had crept in between us. Sometimes I found myself envious of his closeness to Mom and Dad. Sometimes it seemed like he was jealous of my hockey success and the attention I got out in the community. More and more often, we would spar with each other.

So instead of joining everyone in the cabin, I opted to move Loretta and me into a little granary that my dad had built nearby. It was a rough structure, no more than ten feet by ten, but it would have to do.

I had, of course, grown up sleeping on the floor. Everyone in my family was used to that. Mom said she actually preferred sleeping on the ground to being in a bed. Frank's wife, Madeline, had spent a lot of her youth travelling around with her family and sleeping in tents. She claimed to be most comfortable close to the earth as well. But poor Loretta had always had a proper bed to sleep in—hell, she'd always had an actual bedroom. In a house with a kitchen and other conveniences. I managed to find a mattress somewhere and dragged it into the granary for us, but the thing was so thin and worn its springs left marks on our skin. Sleeping in the granary, and life on the reserve, must have been a big adjustment for my new wife. Loretta, however, never once complained or even commented on the change.

For the last few summers, I'd been logging on the reserve, clearing land that I could now start to farm. Since getting engaged, I had been imagining a future for Loretta and me in Sandy Lake. Building our own home. Raising a family. I would hunt, fish, and plant the fields. It would not be the bright lights of Chicago or New York, but it would be a good life. That's what I was focusing on. Sure, I was running as well as doing physical labour, keeping in shape, but as the summer days wound down, I really wasn't thinking about the Black Hawks. And given how little I had heard from them during the previous season, I was pretty sure they weren't thinking about me.

But in early September, someone came to say a phone message had been left for me at the general store in Debden. "Call Dick Irvin." Irvin was the new coach for the Black Hawks. He had been appointed in the spring. I drove into town and dialled the number he'd left.

"Fred," he said, "why aren't you on your way to training camp?"

I told him I wasn't sure I was going to make it.

"No, no, we need you here. We want you back. Get on down here as soon as you can." He sounded upbeat and insistent. I thought I heard a promise in his voice.

I remembered the last training camp. I felt conflicted. I knew it was foolish to get my hopes up. The previous season had been so crushing. But I was just twenty-one years old. Still young enough to dream. And I could feel those dreams coming to life again. The coach of the Black Hawks wanted me to come to training camp. Who was I to turn him down?

Loretta was one of the few people who didn't seem to care if I played in the NHL or not. I knew my mother wanted me to keep playing, to make it back to the big leagues. But since I was married, she'd told Loretta I was her problem now—my mom was not going to tell us what to do. I didn't ask either of them what they thought. Instead, I went home and told Loretta and my family I was going to take another stab at an NHL career. I could tell my mother was pleased. I wasn't sure how Loretta felt.

The next day, I said goodbye to Loretta and my family and boarded a train to Niagara Falls, Ontario. The camp was being held in nearby Welland that year.

I arrived a day late, but no one seemed to mind. The last hockey season had been a rough one for me, but it felt great to be sitting on the bench, chatting again to Ken Wharram, Al Rollins, Lee Fogolin. Then someone nudged me in the ribs. Two young players had just walked through the door. One was blond, with a brush cut and a tight white T-shirt. The other, smaller and darker.

"Who're they?" I asked.

Chicago was still trying to rebuild. They had traded a number of new players from the Red Wings. Metro Prystai, who'd played with the Moose Jaw Canucks before me, was now on the team. But they were also bringing in a lot of newer players to the camp. These two fellows, Bobby Hull and Stan Mikita, were just fifteen or sixteen years old, junior players with the St. Catharines Teepees. They were still considered too young for the NHL, but apparently they had so much potential that the Hawks had invited them to skate with the team for a day.

No wonder. Stan Mikita was not a big guy. It wasn't until he got on the ice that you could see he was one hell of a player. But Bobby Hull. The moment Bobby Hull walked in the dressing room, you knew he was exceptional. He was a hardworking farm boy built of solid muscle. His legs were so damn wide, he had to pull his pant legs down one at a time, peeling the fabric away from his thighs, just to get the things off. And when Hull was on the ice, every time he took a shot, his stick cracked like rifle shot. I was kind of glad he was so young—I didn't need the extra competition for a spot on the team.

The camp got off to a much better start than it had the previous year. I was at my target weight, I hadn't been drinking as much during the summer. I was ready to play.

During intra-squad games, I was scoring goals, just the way I had in previous years. I felt I could compete with the best players, the NHLers, that my game was pretty much as good as any other forward. The camp was restoring my confidence and my spirits were high when I was on the ice.

Off the ice, it was another thing. Before I'd left for camp, Loretta and I had talked about the future. Loretta told me that if I made the Chicago team again, she would be fine with me being away during the hockey season. But she didn't want to move to Chicago. In fact, while I was gone, she was going to move back in with her father in Eldred. I was disappointed—I'd assumed she would follow me anywhere.

But I figured that when the time came, I'd be able to convince her, so I shrugged it off. Once I got to Welland, however, I began to worry.

Every day, when we came back from practice, I'd go down to the motel office to see if there were any messages or letters for me. But the front desk clerk just shook his head. Why wasn't Loretta writing? I had written several times. What was she thinking? Was she angry that I left? Was she trying to tell me I would have to pick between her and the team?

It turned out I wasn't going to have to make a choice.

It was about ten days into the camp. I was in the dressing room, taking off my equipment after one of our games, when Tommy Ivan appeared before me.

"Fred," he said, "we're going to send you to the Buffalo Bisons this year."

I stopped what I was doing and stared at him in shock. *The same thing as last year.*

"The hell you are," I said.

There was a moment of silence. But I wasn't thinking about my options or what I should say next. I wasn't thinking about anything. I was just trying to control my anger. Ivan didn't say a word.

Finally, I said, "I've got a wife now. If I'm not making this damn team, I'm going home."

"Fred," Ivan replied coolly, "your wife comes second. The NHL comes first."

I glared at him.

"Well, Calgary is interested in you," Ivan said, stuffing his hands in his pockets. "We'll send you there instead. You can join the others leaving for the Stampeders training camp tomorrow."

———

Back in the motel room that night, I paced the room in a fury.

The first time Ivan had told me he wanted me to go to Buffalo, that I wasn't going to start the season with the Hawks, it had come as an enormous shock. And I'd been angry. But when that passed, I realized I was most upset with myself. I'd been overconfident and hadn't gone to Pembroke in top form. I should have known better. My twelve games with the Hawks had taught me that the management was always on the lookout for mistakes. And they weren't in the business of forgiveness, not with all those other guys fighting to take your place. Last training camp, I hadn't shown my best stuff right from the start. And because of that I might have spoiled an opportunity.

But this time I came in shape, and I was playing well. I'd been scoring goals and making plays in every game. And I'd done all of that in a haze of worry and homesickness.

The truth was I had been homesick my whole damn life. I had been willing to put up with that if I was going to play pro. But to be in the same position I was in last year? To be all alone, away from home, with my dream no closer than it was a year ago?

I thought about that nickname, Chief. The silence that sometimes greeted me in the dressing rooms or on the train trips. Was part of this because I was Indian? Were they telling me I would have to be twice as good as any white rookie if I was going to get a spot?

I was so frustrated. And I couldn't help thinking of that first meeting I'd had with Bill Tobin, two years before, at my first training camp in Pembroke. Signing that C Form. I now wondered about how quickly I had agreed, how few questions I had asked. We Indians trusted in the *word* of a man—we had never fared well when môniyâwak insisted we sign papers with them.

———

I'd never considered money when I thought about the possibility of playing hockey. None of the young players did. We just wanted to play. And we followed Tobin's instructions. We never talked about how much we'd been given or how much we'd been promised. I had no idea if other players were being paid more or less than me. I was beginning to see that all that secrecy probably didn't do us any good.

Yet now, sitting there with a half-packed suitcase, I knew it wasn't the money that was troubling me. It was that word Tobin had used.

"You're Black Hawks property."

St. Michael's had considered me property too. They told me what to do, where to go, when I could leave them. When I had to come back. They thought I was theirs, that I no longer belonged to my parents, my family, my community. And now I apparently belonged to the Hawks. I'd traded in number 437 for number 21. The Hawks were moving me about like some residential school kid.

It seemed like my whole life was just whistles, whistles, whistles. The whistles the nuns blew in mornings at school. The whistles Father Roussel blew on the ice. The whistles the refs blew at us during the games.

Of course, players at the beginning of their careers often moved back and forth between farm teams and the NHL. I knew that. But being called to this camp just to be turned away again made it impossible for me to trust in the system any longer. Or to accept it. I hated the way the coaches and managers talked to each other but told you nothing. The way they gave you instructions but no explanations. They parcelled out information as if it was in short supply. They kept your hopes up, strung you along, made you feel like you belonged, just in case they needed you later. They threw you promises like you might throw scraps to a dog. I got the feeling they were never going to be honest with me, that I would never know where I really stood, until it was too late, until they closed the door on me completely. If someone had told me that my

NHL dream was completely pointless, that the whole thing was over for good—it would have been hard. A terrible blow. But this process, having my hope dashed over and over, this was unbearable.

Perhaps I could have handled it if I wasn't so worried about Loretta. But people had been taking me away from home, moving me away from the family I loved, ever since I was seven. I was tired of that. Tired of being told what to do at every turn.

I was aware of it again. The feeling I had when I first walked into the Moose Jaw dressing room. The white world was not made for me. And I was not made for the white world.

Two days later, I got on a train with the three other players heading for the Stampeders: Sandy Hucul, Milan Marcetta, and Barrie Ross. There is a picture of the four of us, dressed in fancy overcoats and hats, looking professional and pleased. But I was anything but happy. I would go to Calgary. Loretta and I would return to Sandy Lake for the summer. But I no longer envisioned the two of us in Chicago, me with a shining career in the NHL. I felt as if my dream had slipped out of my grasp.

Sandy, Milan, Barrie, and I arrived at the Stampeders training camp in time for an intra-squad game, followed by a couple of exhibition games against the New York Rangers. Then we had a few days off before the regular season started. The Calgary Stampeders management told me they'd provide a house for me and Loretta to live in during the season, but when I phoned her, Loretta said she was going to stay put.

It wore on me—thinking about living so far away from Loretta. Especially considering that to be closer to home I had agreed to be sent to Calgary instead of Buffalo. Nothing Loretta had ever said or done had led me to doubt her. But she was so beautiful and kind, I couldn't help imagining how other men might see what I saw, might want to take my place.

There were plenty of familiar faces on the Stampeders team. Gerry Couture was there. Jim McFadden. Both Sandy and Fred Hucul. Goalie Ray Frederick who I knew from the Hawks training camps. But I couldn't relax and enjoy the company of the veterans or the hopefulness of the newer players. My heart wasn't in the game.

I no longer had a vehicle, so I'd arranged for a local taxi driver to pick me up at my motel each day to take me to practice. One day, he told me he wouldn't be available for a few days. He was driving to Saskatoon for some reason.

"Then I'm going with you!" I said.

Maybe if I could talk to Loretta in person I could change her mind.

"Can you wait until I've finished practice?"

"Don't you need to check with someone first?" he asked. "Get permission?"

"To hell with that," I said.

I went into the arena and joined the team for practice. But before I could exit the building, someone told me that the head coach, Frank Currie, wanted to see me in his office.

Frank had my contract for me to sign. Three thousand dollars for the year. After I signed, I figured I should tell him where I was going.

"Wait until tomorrow," he said. "We'll get train tickets for you and your wife."

"I've got a taxi waiting outside," I told him. "I can't wait. And by the way, you're paying for the cab."

The cab driver was going to Saskatoon anyway. He was going to charge me a reasonable price for the trip. But I didn't tell Frank that.

I went outside and got in the car.

It was a long, long drive to Saskatoon. By the time we got there, it was night. The cab driver dropped me off someplace, and I found a pay phone. I called Rene Savard. Rene lived in Debden. He had the only taxi anywhere near Sandy Lake or Eldred.

When he picked up, I said, "Rene, it's Fred Sasakamoose. I'm in Saskatoon. Come and get me."

Rene and I drove through the night, pulling up in front of Loretta's father's place in the early morning. The sun was just peeking over the horizon. I got out of the car.

"Rene, wait here for me, okay?"

"Sure," he said.

I knocked on the Isbisters' front door. A few seconds later, Loretta opened the window of her second-storey bedroom. She leaned out.

"What are you doing here?" she asked. She wasn't smiling.

Then her father was opening the door, telling me to come in.

As we sat down at the kitchen table, he asked if anything was wrong. I told him I had come to get my wife. He nodded.

When I had asked for Loretta's hand, Miles hadn't been pleased at the thought of losing his daughter. But now I think he saw in me a man who could provide a good future for her. He seemed to have developed some respect for me.

He put a mug of tea in front of me, and we sat there for about fifteen minutes before Loretta came downstairs.

When she did, I made my pitch.

"Loretta, I got a contract for big money. And a house for us. All we have to pay for is electricity and groceries. Come back with me, Loretta. Come to Calgary."

"I'm not going anyplace," she said. "I told you already."

Loretta had opened a cupboard, was searching for something. I started talking again. I was hoping to wear her down.

But when she turned around, I could see a look of annoyance and frustration on her face. She had an apple in her hand. She chucked it at me.

I had my answer.

I walked back to Rene and the cab with my head low.

"Take me to Sandy Lake," I told Rene. "To my mom and dad's place."

When I got to the cabin, my parents were happy to see me but surprised too. I told them my troubles. I told them I thought I was losing my wife.

My mom loved Loretta. But I was her son. Her priority.

"kawi-wayinīy Calgary, toosaw." Go back to Calgary, Toosaw, she said. "āhkamimetawey, kihtwam kochi NHL. misawac wanihaci Loretta . . ." Play hockey, try for the NHL again. If you lose Loretta . . . My mother patted my hand. "oskāyawiyin oma. misawac mihcet oskinīkiskwēsisak ayawak." You're young. There are lots of girls out there.

"moya maka niya oci." Not for me, I said glumly. "moya taskoc Loretta." Not like Loretta.

I stayed overnight with my folks, and the next day I made my way back to Calgary.

At the time, I have to admit it, I was really frustrated, even angry.

I knew Loretta didn't care if I played professional hockey or not, but I had imagined us living together either way. And I had come back to Calgary instead of heading to Buffalo so we'd be closer to home. I hadn't expected that such a quiet, gentle woman would have such an iron backbone. But Loretta clearly wasn't budging.

I was a young man, not yet twenty-two, wrapped up in my own world. Unable to understand my even-younger wife's point of view. Now, so many years later, I can appreciate her reluctance. If she moved to Calgary, she wouldn't be able to help her father with her younger siblings. But it was more than that. Loretta had never been anywhere outside of northern Saskatchewan. Calgary was a big city, hundreds of times larger than any place she had ever visited. If she joined me, she would have to live in this huge, strange place all alone. She would know no one other than me. And I would not have been such a reliable companion. I would be at practices and games for long stretches of the day. I would be on road trips too, gone for a week or more at a time. And when I was home, I was likely to be with my teammates in the evenings instead of sitting quietly in the house with my wife. My years away from home had given me a taste for socializing and partying. I liked to be out on the town. But Loretta was not a drinker. She was a homebody. And she came from a family of fifteen people. I bet she'd never had even one hour by herself. In Calgary, most of her time would be spent with no company whatsoever. She knew that. She understood it. I just couldn't see it.

A few weeks later, the Stampeders had an away game against the Saskatoon Quakers. I heard from my parents that a number of people from the reserve were going to hire a truck to bring them to the game. Mom and Dad were joining them, and they would bring Loretta.

I was excited that both my mother and Loretta would be seeing me play hockey for the first time.

When I stepped onto the ice that night, I scanned the crowd. I spotted a group of Indians sitting together in one section of the stands. I thought I picked out my mother's face, but I couldn't find Loretta. All through the game, I kept peering up into the stands, but I couldn't see her.

After the game, I rushed out to the lobby. My mother and father were there. My mom had a huge smile on her face. My dad had a twinkle in his eye. They were both so proud. My mom had brought me a beautiful beaded buckskin jacket she had just made for me. But I could hardly appreciate it.

All I wanted to know was where Loretta was.

"moya pe-takohtew." She didn't come, said my mom.

"tanekih?" Why?

Years later, I would realize that Loretta, who was pregnant at the time, had been battling terrible morning sickness. She never enjoyed car travel. A long ride in the unheated bed of an old tarp-covered truck, hours bouncing along on the hard wooden benches—it would have been too much for her. But I guess my mother, so excited to see me play, didn't really understand that. She just shook her head.

After my parents got back on the road again, I returned to the hotel room I was sharing with my teammate Sid Finney. The rest of the team had gone out drinking, but I had other things to do.

Sid came in while I was stuffing my clothes into my suitcase.

"What are you doing?" he asked.

"I'm going home," I told him.

"You can't do that!" said Sid. "You'll get suspended."

I shrugged my shoulders. Sid bolted from the room. A few minutes later, he came back with another player, Gus Kyle. Gus repeated what Sid had said. About me being suspended. He reminded me I was still Chicago property. That I was supposed to play where they told me to play. If I left, I couldn't play for another minor professional team. I'd never again earn a paycheque for playing hockey.

"Goodbye, Gus" was all I said to him.

Then, with Sid and Gus standing there in shock, I walked out of the room. In the lobby, I called for a cab. When it showed up, I hoisted my bag into the trunk and climbed into the back seat. Then Saskatoon was disappearing in the rear-view mirror. And with it my NHL career.

II

pahkisimōtāhk

OUT WEST

When people write my story, this is usually where they end it. They say I came back to live on the reserve and be with my family. That's true. But of course, it was more complicated than that.

It was the end of October when the taxi dropped me off in Eldred again. I drove into Sandy Lake not long after my return to tell my parents I was back. The sight of Lonesome Pine Hill made my heart hammer—like when I was a boy, coming back in the summer in that damn truck. But now the air was chilly and the trees were almost bare. You could tell that winter was not far away. That the snow would soon begin to fall, and the fields and hills would turn white.

It struck me. This was going to be the first winter I'd spend at home since that terrible fall day fourteen years ago. My first birthday and my first Christmas with my parents since I was six. The first time I could set my skate blades down on the old slough since my moosum's passing. The weight of all that time swept over me, almost knocking me down. And then I felt lighter.

When I'd driven away with George all those years ago, it was like a curtain had dropped down over my world. It disappeared. I'd been back home many summers since then, but this was the first time I felt like the curtain had been raised. Like the place was mine again, open to me. I had my home back. Nothing was pulling me away, telling me that my return was only temporary. During the cab ride from Saskatoon, I'd worried about how I'd explain my decision to my parents. But the sight of Lonesome Pine Hill wiped that thought away. I'd made a choice for myself. The first real decision I ever made in my life was marrying Loretta. This choice felt just as important—maybe more. Because it meant I was making that first decision real. I was truly taking charge of my life. My future was now in my own hands. I was finally free. Man, that felt good.

My professional hockey life was over. That's what I thought. I'd play for fun, but that would be it. Turned out, however, that hockey wasn't done with me yet.

When I got back to Eldred, Loretta was cautiously optimistic about starting our new life together. We rented a house from the local shopkeeper. We'd be close to her family—and in a real house of our own for the very first time. We hadn't been there long when the manager of the senior men's hockey team from Debden came to see me. Debden is about six miles from Eldred, fifteen miles from Sandy Lake. It was the small town where my moosum Alexan used to go to watch hockey games. The Debden Rockets played in a little league called the Big V against teams from Shellbrook, Leask, Blaine Lake, and Canwood. And they wanted me to play for the team—and coach, teach skills, and manage the local kids' teams. They'd pay me per game, and there was a nice house in Debden that Loretta and I could live in for free.

I couldn't play in any league that had an association with the NHL—or was even on their radar—if I was being paid. But the Big V was literally a bush league, too small for anyone in the Hawks organization to pay attention to. It seemed like the perfect way to earn good money over the winter. Loretta and I packed up our stuff and moved down the road to Debden.

I was so excited to finally have a Christmas with my family. I can't remember if I said this to the manager of the Debden team or whether he just figured it out. But he came up to me shortly before Christmas with a cheque.

"Christmas bonus," he said. "Drive to Prince Albert and buy some presents for your family."

I'd barely begun to play for the team. I sure didn't expect a bonus. But I accepted the cheque with thanks and went shopping right away for gifts for Mom and Dad, Loretta, and Frank and his family.

Christmas didn't disappoint. Loretta and I spent the day in Sandy Lake with my family, exchanging presents, eating, laughing. And then we drove to Eldred, where another big meal was spread out: moose, deer, elk, potatoes, vegetables . . . the feast seemed to go on and on. And to finish, a traditional Métis dessert: *pouchine au sac*. A sweet suet pudding with raisins and currants, which Loretta and her sisters boiled up in a lady's stocking and served with a rich sauce. When we'd finished eating, we all headed to the local hall for the annual Christmas dance. When I walked through the doors and heard the fiddlers playing and saw the dancers doing a jig, my breath caught in my throat. It reminded me so much of that magical Christmas when my mother had danced with the mysterious beaded trapper. The last Christmas I'd celebrated at home.

———

After Christmas, in the early new year, I played my first game at Debden's brand new rink. Debden loved its hockey and was willing to work for it. In the late fall, the locals had decided they needed a covered rink. Almost everyone pitched in to build it—men went out into the bush to cut trees. They planed the logs and then hauled the timber into town. The guys worked around the clock, and by the time January arrived, the team had a brand new arena that could seat 1,200 fans.

It was a long, brutal winter in the north that year, but hockey fans didn't seem put off. The attendance for the league was apparently the best it'd been in years. Despite the fact that the population of Debden was only a few hundred people, their rink was usually filled far past capacity, with folks standing in every spare corner of the place. And it seemed like I had something to do with that.

My NHL games had made me a celebrity in northern Saskatchewan, and now that people had the opportunity to see me play, their curiosity brought them to the Big V games. Before the games, teams of horses would pull up outside the arenas, depositing wagon after wagon of local spectators. People from further away—North Battleford, Prince Albert, even Saskatoon—hired buses to bring them to the little arenas of the north. For the Debden games, folks from Sandy Lake and the Big River reserve would come by horse and wagon or hired truck. And sometimes even on foot. Jerry Rabbitskin, the trapper who'd danced with my mother that Christmas so many years ago, came to just about every Debden game. One game day, we were hit with such a heavy snowfall that roads from miles around were pretty much impassable. That night, about the only fans who could make it were ones who lived in town. Then Jerry walked through the doors of the arena. Surprised, I went up to him and asked how he managed to get all the way over from Sandy Lake in the deep snow.

"I snowshoed, of course," he said.

I've been blessed with many riches in my life, none of which would have been possible without my parents and grandparents. At the top is Alexan, my moosum, who saw a future in me, and Julia Sasakamoose, along with their youngest son Roderick (my father), and their eldest grandson Gilbert (my cousin), in Sandy Lake, 1914. The photo to the right is my mother, Sugil, and my father, Roderick, in the 1940s. And below are my mother's parents, Gaspar Morin and Veronica Bear, posing with their great-grandchildren in the 1960s. The children are a mix of mine and Frank's; Frank is sitting next to our grandma, and standing behind Veronica is Chucky. Garth is sitting between Gaspar and Veronica, and the young girl on the left of Gaspar with her arm on his knee is Phyllis.

I've been married to this wonderful lady for over 66 years now. The above photo was taken shortly after we were married, and the second photo is of our growing family in the sixties. With Loretta and me are Debbie, Phyllis, Garth, Derrick, and Chucky.

Northern Saskatchewan Midget Hockey Champions 1947-48

L. Prosper,   H. Seeseequasis,   I. Daniels   A. Seenookisich

F. Sasakamoose,   G. Bird,   J. H. Ledoux,   P. Monitokan,   A. Bird,   N. Lafond,

Rev. Fr. G. M. Latour, o.m.i.   H. Wichihin,   R. Mike,   A. Greyeyes,   Rev. Fr. G. L. Roussel, o.m.i

In 2019, my son Neil put on a viewing of the only known full-game footage of me in a Black Hawks jersey. Before we watched the game, Neil surprised my cousin Herb Seeseequasis (seen with me in both photos) and me by having Father Roussel's surviving family members present us with the 1949 Saskatchewan Midget Championship trophy, the one we won playing for the St. Michael's Ducks. Roussel's family had found the trophy after he passed away.

Moose Jaw Canucks, 1952–53. Back row, farthest left is Dave Rusnell. Sandy Hucul is in the back row, second from the end on the right. Jimmy Chow wears the "C" in the front row, and I am to the right of him. George Vogan is in the middle of the front row, with the fur collar.

Billy McNeill
Starry Oil
King Winger

Will
This Man
Be

SCALPED
TOMORROW NIGHT?

Freddy Sasakamoose
MOOSE JAW'S INDIAN "WHIZ KID"
is on the warpath as the

MOOSE JAW CANUCKS
Meet the
EDMONTON OIL KINGS
At the GARDENS
in another thrilling

JUNIOR
HOCKEY
ENGAGEMENT !

● See Sasakamoose, the Sensation of the Chicago
Black Hawks' Training Camp.
● Enjoy Pre-Game and Between-Period
Entertainment.

GAME TIME 8:30 P.M.

Tickets on Sale Today and Tomorrow at
MIKE'S NEWSSTAND
Box Office Opens 7:30 a.m. Game Time 8:30 p.m.
TICKETS $1.00 and 75c
Students 50c

Back then, being a full Treaty Indigenous hockey player was an oddity. Some teams liked to use this fact in their marketing, like in the advertisement you see here. This is my hockey card, originally produced by Parkhurst. I don't have any memory of this photo being taken, or of being told that a hockey card was being made of me. In fact, I didn't even realize I had a hockey card until someone showed one to me years after I had left the Black Hawks.

Advertisement originally published in
The Edmonton Journal,
a Division of Postmedia Network Inc

Fred Haas Takes Lead

FOUR FELLOWS WHO HOPE to make Stampeder hockey coach Frank Currie sit up and take notice within the next few days is the contingent above. Milan Marcetta, Barrie Ross, Fred Sasakamoose and Sandy Hucul detrained off the "Dominion" this morning and promptly headed for Victoria Arena where the Stamps are conducting their fall drills. The four arrived from Welland where they attended the Chicago Black Hawk camp.

Mr. Turf Tossed Into Stakes Tes

Originally published in *The Calgary Herald*, a division of Postmedia Network Inc

Though I didn't enjoy that playing hockey kept me away from my family, I ended up making good friends and travelling to places I never would have gone otherwise. The newspaper clipping is from when I was sent to Calgary to play for the Stampeders. Below is from my time in Kamloops, when we grew to be great friends with the Gottfriedsons.

Heap Big Whoop-Up At Gardens Last Night

Fred Sasakamoose, 19-year-old Cree, was made an honorary chief of the Indian tribe last night at a Western Junior Hockey League game at the Gardens. Sasakamoose, a member of Moose Jaw Canucks, is shown here kneeling on ceremonial blankets while Miss Morning Star adjusts a feathered war bonnet, Chief Red Wing of Hobbema, on the left, reads his address while Miss Rainbow in the background, holds a peace pipe. However Sasakamoose, named Running Deer, failed to get a point when Edmonton Oil Kings whipped Canucks 5-1.

Originally published in *The Edmonton Journal*,
a Division of Postmedia Network Inc

© Alexis Christensen

In Junior, the Hobbema nation named me Chief Running Deer. Chief Gottfriedson of the Kamloops band named me Chief Thunderstick. Later on, I served as Chief of Ahtahkakoop Cree Nation. You can see me here, shaking hands with NHL Commissioner Gary Bettman in 2019, in front of the Stanley Cup Trophy.

My siblings: Leo, Peter, Clara, Frank, and me, in 1992. Below is my parents' log cabin, the one I grew up in, until the priests took me away. It is no longer standing but I still am—mamihcihiwêw, a proud Cree man.

People might've come out of curiosity to see the Indian guy play, but I made sure they got a good show too. There were some strong players in that league, but I had been playing for the last couple of years with NHLers and others who were very close to making it to the pros. It didn't take much for me to skate through the Big V defencemen, to score on breakaways, or to fire a shot in from the blue line. And, boy, would that puck move on those little rinks. I was still shaving my stick down, the way Gordon Fashoway taught me. But that wasn't the only thing that sped my shot.

Many of the rinks were open to the air, but even the ones that were covered, like Debden's, didn't have heat or artificial ice. Like I said, the winter of 1955–56 was extremely cold. The temperatures inside and out were often thirty degrees below zero. In that cold, the pucks froze up so hard they were like little chunks of marble. And they flew across the rock-hard ice like missiles. I bet my shots reached one hundred miles an hour. In fact, not long after the new arena was finished, one of my slapshots missed the net and ended up embedded in the boards.

But you can't play like that and have an entertaining, competitive game. A couple of slapshots into a game, and the opposition would either freeze up as soon as they saw me near the puck or move out of my way. So I began to hold back, playing defence, and passing more often than shooting. When our team needed the goals, I'd move forward and put enough pucks in the net that we won. But I made sure the Rockets didn't run up the score too much. Even so, the Debden team won game after game, taking the championship and making a clean sweep of the league awards. I received the Chalifour Trophy for highest score in the league, with 100 points.

I had fun playing without the pressure of NHL scrutiny or wondering if I was going to be called up or not. There were always folks waiting to talk to me outside the dressing room or take me for a drink in whatever town we were in. When I wasn't playing, I was down at the rink with the local kids, teaching them everything I knew about the game. On my days off, I went trapping or ice fishing. And every night I came home to Loretta.

Just a short time after the Debden Rockets had wrapped up the season, on April 26, 1956, Loretta and I had our first child. A big, healthy boy. We named him Algin, but found ourselves calling him "Chucky" most of the time. I now had not just a home but my own family too.

It sure was a year of big changes. It was a good feeling that so many people were excited to see me play, that my people felt pride in what I'd done. But sometimes I got other reactions. When I'd told my mother and father that I'd decided to quit pro hockey for good, I knew they were both disappointed. My father said nothing, but my mother had urged me to change my mind. To go back. I bowed my head and didn't reply.

My mother wasn't the only one who was shocked and disappointed by my decision. For months and months after my return, it seemed as if every time I was at the arena, doing errands in town, or at a bar for a drink, someone would come up to me and ask me why I'd returned.

"What was so important to bring you back?" they might say. Or, "Geez, Freddy. What're you doing here? You had a future."

Some were even more blunt. I remember one fellow shaking his head and saying, "Damn it, Freddy, you disappointed me. Why'd you come back? There's nothing here for you. I've lived here my whole life, and there's nothing here."

Another cut right through me with his words: "We thought you were going to lead our people. Do things for us. Break a trail. You're not a role model anymore—you're just another bush league player."

I didn't respond to any of these guys.

I couldn't explain to them how hard it had been to live in that world. To always hide some important part of you, to keep so much of your past a secret from the only people you could call friends. To wonder if people thought differently about you because you were an Indian. To have no one to talk to who might have understood how it felt when someone made a hurtful or insensitive comment. To be powerless in a system that made you feel like a checker piece being moved around on a huge, unfamiliar board.

And yet each time someone voiced their surprise and disapproval, I felt a pang of doubt. Had I stopped too soon? Thrown something precious away? Failed my people? And then, as the years passed, and memories of those twelve NHL games became a bit shadowy, I'd find myself wondering, Even if I'd stayed, would I have made it? Was I ever really good enough?

But mostly, in those early months back home, I pushed those thoughts from my mind. I focused on enjoying my freedom and a winter up north, living and working surrounded by the deep quiet of the snow-covered trees.

Once the hockey season was over, I went back to logging and fishing. But since it seemed as if playing hockey might actually be a good way to put food on the table in the winter, I made sure I kept myself in shape. Occasionally, I even strapped on the leather harnesses we used to haul logs from the bush and pulled tires down the road.

But before I could start on a new season with the Debden Rockets, I got another invitation. Kenny MacKenzie, the owner and manager of the New Westminster Royals when I had been there, had left that organization and purchased a team in the Okanagan Senior Amateur Hockey League: the Kamloops Chiefs. During the summer, he tracked me down, and we had a conversation on the phone.

"I want the Chiefs to win the Allan Cup," he told me. "I need you here, Fred. I need you on my team."

The Okanagan league was called "amateur," but all the players were being paid and the salary was pretty good. The league probably wasn't small enough to escape the notice of the NHL. But Kenny told me not to worry about my suspension or my contract with the Hawks. He figured, since I hadn't played any league-associated hockey in a whole year, I should be free to play. And if the NHL objected, he knew the management from his time with the New Westminster team. He'd talk with them and buy me out of my contract if I'd agree to come out west and play for him.

I told him I'd made a decision. I was going to stay put.

But he called me again and again. His insistence began to make me rethink.

Perhaps it was all those people who were disappointed in me for playing in a bush league. Not living up to my hockey potential. Perhaps it was the idea that the Okanagan league would be a step up from the Big V, that there might still be a little hockey glory left for me. Perhaps it was just curiosity. Despite my homesickness, I'd enjoyed all the travel I'd been able to do in my short time in the big leagues. While some of my destinations were disappointing, I looked forward to finding out what a new town was like. What I hadn't enjoyed was being forced to relocate—and not knowing how long I'd stay in any one place. But the move to Kamloops would be my choice. If Loretta and Chucky were with me, I might really be able to enjoy the experience. And if we didn't like it, we could simply come back.

I decided to talk to Loretta about moving.

When I told her about Kenny's offer, she didn't say no right away. That was a good sign. I told her that I'd liked what I had seen of BC. That it was a beautiful place, with mild weather. And that, according to Kenny, Kamloops was a small city—much, much smaller than even Prince Albert, which Loretta had visited. This would be nothing like moving to Calgary.

While Loretta didn't say anything right away, I noticed my mother's eyes light up when I told her about the opportunity in Kamloops. I could tell she wanted Loretta and me to go.

When my mother had first encouraged me to follow George Vogan to Moose Jaw, I'd been confused. I'd just got back home after so many years at school. Why did she want to send me away again? Why did she want me to live so far from her? But over time, I'd come to appreciate her ambition for me.

When the priests took her children—me, Frank, Peter, Leo, Clara— they told her it was for our own good. They would teach us the ways of the white man so we could have a better life. My mother never complained about life on the reserve. She found comfort and strength in nēhiyaw ways and beliefs. She loved the land. But those priests and the Indian agent had been so insistent, she'd been convinced that there must be more for her children. That there was some sort of better life for them out in the mōniyâw world. And she still needed to believe that. If not, what was the point of all those years of separation? What was the point of the suffering we'd all undergone—her and my father and us kids? The NHL might not be in my future anymore, but she seemed to think the better life for me was still in the bigger, white hockey leagues. And the spark in my eyes must have confirmed this for her. She could see I was getting excited by the opportunity.

Over the next few days, my mother spent time with Loretta, talking quietly with her. Then Loretta was telling me she thought we should give it a try. She and Chucky would join me in Kamloops.

———

In late September, we were in a sleeping berth on the train to Kamloops. My seventeen-year-old brother, Peter, had a seat on the train too. I'd convinced him to join us.

Peter was a gifted athlete. Like me, he had played on the St. Michael's Ducks, but he also excelled in soccer and baseball. In fact, four years earlier, he'd won the Tom Longboat Award for Saskatchewan. At the time, Peter had no idea who Tom Longboat was. Neither did I. Longboat's story wasn't the kind of thing they taught you at St. Michael's. Many years later, we would both learn that Longboat, whose Iroquois name was Cogwagee, was an Onondaga from the Six Nations reserve, near Brantford, Ontario. He was a long-distance runner who won the Boston Marathon in 1907, breaking the record by almost five minutes. He also participated in the 1908 Olympics before becoming professional and setting many more world speed records. During World War I, he was a dispatch runner and was twice injured in action. He was a residential school Survivor. In 1951, the Department of Indian Affairs and the Amateur Athletic Union of Canada started an award in his name to honour Indigenous athletes in Canada. And in 1952, at the age of fourteen, Peter won the regional prize that carried Longboat's name. (At the time, all we knew was it was an honour. But I think if we'd known about Longboat, we might have found it curious that the very department that was shipping us off to residential schools to beat the Indian out of us was giving an award celebrating our accomplishments as Indians.)

After Peter had left St. Michael's, he spent a year in Moose Jaw with the Canucks. He was a finesse hockey player, but he wasn't performing quite well enough to stay on the team. (I think his damaged eye, the one that had been hurt by the blow at St. Michael's, interfered with his playing skill. He could turn in one direction but had difficulty turning in the other.) When he was cut from the team, he'd come home to

Sandy Lake. Now I thought he should try out for the Kamloops Chiefs. Even if he didn't make it, the trip would be a good adventure.

As we travelled through the mountains on the train, we passed through areas of pure white. At one point, I was surprised to see a little chimney sticking out from a snowdrift, smoke puffing up through the air. Somewhere underneath it must have been a small cabin, but I couldn't make it out.

When we got to Kamloops, there wasn't a spot of snow on the ground. In fact, apples, pears, and plums still clung to the trees. Loretta and I were amazed by the greenness of the valley and the low mountains that surrounded it. Loretta was less impressed with day after day of rain. And the accommodations. Kenny had put us all up in a roadside motel in town.

As soon as I started skating with the Chiefs, it became clear that Kenny had been hoping he could drum up a bit more interest in the club by highlighting his newest player. The local paper did a big write-up about the Indian hockey player from Saskatchewan who was going to join the Chiefs that season. And after every game, people came up to meet me. I soon came to realize that across the river from the town was a sizable Shuswap (Secwépemc) community, living on the Kamloops (Tk'emlúps) reserve. They all seemed excited and proud to see an Indian player—and none of them was disappointed that I wasn't still an NHLer.

Peter didn't make the Kamloops Chiefs, but he settled in town, getting a job with the provincial department of highways. Not long after he arrived, he met a young Shuswap man named Bob Gottfriedson in a local pool hall. Peter mentioned that we were new to Kamloops. Bob immediately invited all of us to join him and his family for Thanksgiving dinner. He also introduced Peter to his sister Muriel.

And that was that. Peter and Muriel would get married less than a year later.

Muriel later told me that her mother, Mildred, was delighted to welcome a family of newcomers to their Thanksgiving meal. But when she discovered that Peter's last name was Sasakamoose, and his brother was the hockey player she'd heard so much about, she went on a huge cleaning and cooking blitz before we arrived. The whole family was awestruck that evening, not just by having me in the house. They thought Loretta, slim and beautiful, wearing a bright red dress, looked just like a movie star. They were all too nervous to talk much, and it was the most awkward Thanksgiving Muriel ever recalls.

Loretta and I don't remember it like that at all. We found the Gottfriedson family warm and welcoming. They put out a huge feast—we ate like kings. Loretta was touched by the fuss Mildred made over Chucky. And we were honoured to be included. We discovered that Bob's father, Gus, was the Chief of the Kamloops band. It was something to have been invited to join them for the holiday, and even more special that the whole family made us feel we had a home away from home.

I enjoyed myself that fall, playing in the Okanagan league. The hockey was good and challenging, and I discovered that there were lots of Indian fans in many of the towns we played against—Vernon, Penticton, Kelowna. It was a little harder for Loretta. She hated staying alone with the baby in the cramped motel room. And she missed her family.

Christmas was especially tough. I was so used to spending Christmases away from home that I thought nothing of it. Besides, the Gottfriedson family, who we'd been seeing a lot of, invited us to join them. But poor Loretta. She'd never been away from her many siblings or her father at Christmas. The shock of being so distant took some of the joy out of our celebrations.

And then, when the new year started, things got bumpy for me as well.

It turned out that my eligibility wasn't quite as straightforward as Kenny had hoped. The Black Hawks weren't making a stink, but the other teams in the Okanagan Senior Amateur Hockey League were. The league had a rule that you could have only two previously professional hockey players on any team, and they said the Chiefs had three: the player-coach Bob Dawes, who had been with the Toronto Maple Leafs; Gerry Prince, who had played for the Hawks affiliate the New Westminster Royals; and me. The other team managers wanted me out. In January, the league suspended me. But Kenny wasn't going to accept that, and he kept putting me back on the ice. Eventually, however, he accepted defeat and benched me.

By early February, Loretta, Chucky, and I were back in Sandy Lake. I finished off the season with the Debden Rockets. But Kenny promised me he'd have his roster straightened out by the following fall, and he expected me to return to the team in September.

The only place for us to stay was my parents' old log cabin. They'd built a new house, just up the rise from the old place. It was nice to have a house of our own on the reserve instead of being in the granary, but the old cabin had been sitting empty for a time, and the elements had been hard on it. It wasn't in good shape. The floors were rough, and there were gaps between the logs. It still had no power or running water—luxuries that Loretta and I had gotten used to in Debden and Kamloops. But we made do. I went back to work logging. And planning for the farm we'd have on the reserve one day.

The spring and summer were busy. In May, Peter returned to the reserve with Muriel to get married. Loretta was pregnant again and had her hands full making a home in the old house. I played soccer and baseball on the Sandy Lake teams. And then the close of summer brought a great gift. On September 8, 1957, our first girl was born. We named her Phyllis, after Phyllis Vogan, the woman I'd long considered my sister. Phyllis cried when I phoned her with the news.

When Phyllis was only a few weeks old, we were on the train out west once again. I'd been assured by Kenny MacKenzie that I'd be able to play a whole season with the Chiefs this time. And Loretta had been willing to give Kamloops another shot because of the Gottfriedsons. We were both excited to introduce the baby to Muriel's parents, who we had asked to be her godparents.

When we got to Kamloops, Gus Gottfriedson and some of his councillors invited me and Loretta to a big feast. They had great news for us. A house was sitting vacant on the Kamloops reserve, and the band council wanted us to have it. Loretta and I were thrilled. It felt good to be part of an Indigenous community again. Sure, the band spoke Shuswap (Secwepemctsín), not Cree, and had slightly different customs, but it was a world that still felt familiar and reassuring. A place where we didn't have to explain ourselves. Where everyone understood each others' histories, beliefs, and wounds without sharing a word. And where we recognized the divide between our world and the môniyâw one.

Loretta began to feel more at home. When the Chiefs played in town, she'd often get a babysitter and come to the games to watch me. She was disappointed, however, to discover that she was expected to sit with the wives of the other players and not with the Gottfriedsons and our other new friends from the reserve.

Sometime in the late fall, Bob Dawes, the Chiefs coach, went to talk with Chief Gottfriedson. The attendance at the games was too low for the team to pay its bills. Dawes said that he and the Chiefs management wondered if Gus and other Elders might help them encourage more Indigenous people from Kamloops and the surrounding area to come to the games. He suggested they find a way to draw attention to my presence on the team.

In the end, a plan was made to make me an honorary Chief of the Kamloops nation in an elaborate ceremony.

The first part of the event was just theatre. Chief Gottfriedson and about a dozen other Shuswap men rode up Mount Paul, on the Kamloops reserve, on horseback in the mid-afternoon. When they got to the top, they lit a big fire. One of them began to fan it with a blanket, making puffs of smoke that drifted down from the mountain. This wasn't their idea. Smoke signals had never been one of their traditional practices, and the Chief didn't appreciate the gimmick. But he'd been convinced by someone in the team organization that this would make a splash in the papers—the local Chief using smoke signals to call his band members, as well as local Okanagan and Chilcotin, to the arena where a Cree hockey player would be honoured.

Muriel, Peter, Loretta, and I stood outside on the reserve and watched the procession of horses and then the smoke signals forming in the distance. Gus might have thought the whole thing was a bit silly, but I didn't. I thought it was beautiful—grey clouds of smoke drifting off the mountaintop, slowly dissolving in the blue sky.

That evening, after the hockey game, a ceremony like the one they'd had in Edmonton took place. This time, about 200 boys from the band school stood as an honour guard and the girls performed traditional dances to begin the proceedings.

While Kenny MacKenzie, dressed in a kilt in his clan tartan, looked on, Chief Gottfriedson put a beautiful feathered bonnet on my head and pronounced me an honorary Chief of the Kamloops band—Skenknēp-sxts'ēy, Chief Thunderstick. Gus had come up with that name himself.

In Edmonton, I'd felt great pride in being recognized by the Hobbema nation. That ceremony reminded me of what it meant to be Indian. And I loved being honoured with the name Chief Running Deer. But the Kamloops ceremony was something else. Chief Gottfriedson and the band council weren't just bestowing a new name on me in a sacred naming ceremony. They were officially making me part of the Kamloops nation. I had become an "honorary" Chief, but I wasn't just an honorary band member. I was a member like all of the other residents on the reserve. They had made me part of their family. They were giving me a new home.

Reporters had been told about the hilltop spectacle and the arena ceremony, of course, and in the stories they ran before and after the game, they encouraged the Indigenous community to come to the games to see and support "Chief Thunderstick" and his teammates. And, boy, did they come.

The night of the ceremony, the game was completely sold out. And the next game over 3,300 people crowded the Kamloops arena. The local Shuswap people bought hundreds of season's tickets and filled the south end of the stands. Many of these folks hadn't been to a Chiefs game before. Very few would've been season ticket holders previously. The Chiefs management was thrilled. And the presence of so many of my people made the games special for me. The Shuswap fans brought drums, and they beat them at the beginning of each game and every time I scored.

I appreciated all of the enthusiasm in the arena, but I appreciated being part of the community even more. A number of the men took me trapping and hunting for pheasant whenever I was in town and had time to join them. Gus took me out on horseback and showed me how to spot and pick the wild asparagus that grew in the floodlands around Kamloops Lake. Loretta too grew even closer to the Gottfriedsons.

Other neighbours were always there as well, to keep her company or help out when the Chiefs were on the road.

The Chiefs did well that year, narrowly losing the league championship to the Kelowna Packers at the end of March.

That summer, I got a job working on a crew that was building the Yellowhead Highway, which now runs from the BC coast to Winnipeg. I operated one of the powerful diamond-studded drills that cored out holes in the rock for the dynamite sticks. One day, when I was on site, a big fancy car drove up and a well-dressed man got out. He walked over to where we were working. It turned out it was the BC minister of highways himself, Reverend Phil Gaglardi. He was a colourful, well-known figure in the province—a Pentecostal minister who also had a popular radio show. He earned the nickname "Flyin' Phil" for his frequent plane travel all through the province to inspect the massive road building project he was in charge of.

He was also a hockey fan—one of his sons would go on to own the Dallas Stars—and he seemed to know who I was.

He singled me out from the crew.

"Fred, what are you doing operating that drill? That's dangerous work. You could get hurt before next hockey season."

I told him I didn't mind the heavy physical labour. I was grateful for the job.

"No, no, no," he replied. "We'll get you something else."

And sure enough, a few days later I found myself a flagman on a surveying crew. It was certainly safer work, if pretty boring. And, strangely, it paid more money than I'd made as a diamond driller.

Our third year in Kamloops was a good one for our family, but it was a troubled one for the Chiefs. Game attendance for all the teams had dropped so low there was talk that the whole league might fold. And the bump that the Kamloops team had got from the Indigenous fans didn't seem to last. Revenue was so bad that Kenny MacKenzie decided to bail, turning the club over to the community and the players. All the players agreed to take a 25 percent salary cut. Even then, the cheques did not always come through. Some players quit in response. And to top it off, we were knocked out of the semifinals at the end of February. Luckily, I still had my work on the survey crew, so we were okay financially.

Loretta was pregnant again, and in early April 1959, our second son, Garth, was born. Garth struggled right from the beginning. He had terrible asthma. We made many trips to the doctor, and poor Loretta had a lot of sleepless night with him. When I was invited to a late spring tournament in North Battleford, Saskatchewan, Loretta said she wanted to come with me and spend the summer in Sandy Lake with the kids. I thought a summer in Sandy Lake was a good idea for the whole family, so I gave my notice at the contracting company.

We were back in the log cabin, and I decided now was the time to start farming all the land I had cleared over the years. I would plant barley and oats, corn and wheat. But of course, I needed some farm equipment to do that. For most people on the reserve, making big purchases like that was a huge challenge. The banks wouldn't loan us money, because the land we lived and worked on was protected by treaty rights. It wasn't private property that the bank could repossess if loan payments weren't being made. So financial institutions had no interest in lending to us the way they did to other farmers. And there was no guarantee that Indian Affairs would provide that kind of financial service either. But I was lucky—I had a little money from my time with the Kamloops Chiefs. I was able to buy some farm machinery and get started.

I worked hard that summer, but it felt good to be in the fields, to be working so close to home. And in what little spare time I had, I volunteered as the recreation coordinator for the reserve and coached the kids' sports teams.

When the crops were high and harvest was on us, Loretta and I talked about the coming year in Kamloops. Loretta was afraid that the damp West Coast air would make Garth's asthma worse. And Chucky was now three and a half—in a year, he would be going to kindergarten. Loretta felt it was time for her and the kids to put down roots in Sandy Lake.

I understood that.

And besides, I had my doubts about my future with the Kamloops Chiefs. It was hard to imagine that the league would turn around and be profitable again. But we agreed that I should go back and see. I now had three children to support, and even a reduced paycheque from the Chiefs would help.

When I got back to Kamloops, I could sense the desperation of the club's management. They were trying to bring fans back by offering a free Hawaiian vacation for the 30,000th spectator to attend a game. But I don't think they ever made it. Once again, the paycheques often didn't arrive. I figured that the club wouldn't be able to last much longer. (The 1959–60 season would be the Kamloops Chiefs' last in the league.) And living in Kamloops without Loretta and the kids was tough. I always felt secure that the kids were getting everything they needed—Loretta was about the best mother I could imagine. But still. On the phone, Chucky and little Phyllis, just beginning to talk, would ask where I was, when I was coming home. That made me feel rotten. I was willing to spend this time away from Loretta and the kids if I was putting food on the table. I sure couldn't see the point of being a long-distance father if I never knew if there was going to be money to send home.

In January, I told the team management I was done. I said goodbye to Muriel and Peter, to Chief Gottfriedson, to the entire Gottfriedson family. And then I boarded a train heading east.

I wasn't unhappy to be returning to Sandy Lake—it was home. But as the mountains disappeared behind me, I felt a twinge of sadness. I'd thought I would have a few more seasons out west. I had, from time to time, even imagined making it my new home. The Gottfriedsons were there. Our other new friends too.

And I had a good job in BC. I knew I could go back to the highway crews, which would've brought in more money than I could ever earn logging or farming. Leaving behind all of that was bittersweet, sure, but there was something else as well. Kamloops had seemed like a place where I could live in both the môniyâw world and the Indian world at the same time. A place that might hold the kind of future my mother and George Vogan imagined for me—and might also hold my heart. But now my heart was in Saskatchewan.

And I was following it.

12

nikotwāsomitanaw cipahikanis napew

THE SIXTY-MINUTE MAN

When Loretta had stayed back with the three children, she moved in with her father. I joined her in Eldred, but I hadn't been there long when a couple of men from a little town called Glaslyn showed up at our door. They wanted me to play for their Glaslyn Eskimos, in the Big Four league, against teams from Meadow Lake, North Battleford, and Turtleford. The Glaslyn organization would pay me per game, give me a job at the local gas station, and also loan us a house to live in. When I left Kamloops, I thought it was probably the end of hockey for me as a career. I had the beginnings of my small farm started. I could always pick up logging work. A new sort of life was waiting for me. But if Glaslyn was going to provide a steady salary, hockey could still provide more financial security for my family than a winter spent trapping or ice fishing. We set off again for Glaslyn, eighty miles from Eldred, fifty-five miles from Sandy Lake.

It was a bit of shock to find myself in this little town—back in northern Saskatchewan, but not on the reserve. Peter moved back to

Saskatchewan with Muriel for a time, and he played on the Glaslyn team with me for a season. But still, I wasn't in Sandy Lake, and sometimes I found myself thinking, Oh, man, what am I doing here? The money was good, however, so we stayed in Glaslyn for a couple of years. But managers and owners from other teams kept dropping by. The Saskatoon Quakers, of the Saskatchewan Senior League, were interested in me. The Meadow Lake Stampeders. The Kinistino Tigers, of the Carrot River Valley league. The Prince Albert Anavets Intermediate A hockey franchise. Teams in the Big V league, where I had played when I first left Calgary. The most interesting offer I ever received, however, had been when I was in Kamloops. A British couple came to see me and asked me to join a team in England. I was curious about it, but I wasn't going to move my family across the ocean.

I talked with my parents about the offers that came my way. My father never bragged about his NHL-playing son to anyone. He never talked with me about my former pro career. But I could tell he was proud of me—that he wanted me to appreciate my own value.

"poko kotinaman mewasik kīkway ka-meskihk." You have to take the best offers, Toosaw, he said. "e-kīspinatamāsowin oma, mina oma ka-naheyin emistakihtek." You deserve that. Your talent is worth good money.

We did need the income. Our family was continuing to grow. Beverley was born in February 1961. But I couldn't ask Loretta and the four kids to bounce from town to town. Chucky had started school—soon Phyllis and Garth would too. They needed to stay in one spot.

Besides, as much as I had been tempted by a life in Kamloops, I had really always thought my children's home would be Sandy Lake. I knew I wanted to give them the childhood on the reserve that was taken from me. In the sixties, parents were still being pressured to send their children to St. Michael's. But it seemed that the school no longer had the authority to take kids by force, and many parents refused to send them. Frank had not let any of his kids go. I wouldn't let any of mine spend time at that damn place either. Instead, they'd stay at home and go to school in one of the little towns nearby. They'd have as much time as they liked with their kokum and moosum, their aunts, uncles, cousins. They'd learn our Cree traditions and our old ways from the Elders in the community. Loretta and I decided to get funding from Indian Affairs to have a house built for our family down the road from my parents' place.

So Loretta, Chucky, Phyllis, Garth, Beverley, and I moved into our new house in Sandy Lake. It was not much bigger than my parents' old log cabin and had only two rooms—a bedroom and a living room/kitchen. Power had not yet come to the reserve, so the little house had no electricity. And no indoor toilet. Water had to be hauled from the slough for drinking, bathing, cleaning. Loretta had a wringer washer on the porch, powered by a foot pedal. She hung the laundry outside in the summer heat and winter deep freeze. There was a wood stove inside for heat and cooking. It was a simple place, like the houses where Loretta had grown up, or the homes that the rest of my family had on the reserve.

For the next ten years, I followed the money, jumping from team to team, from league to league. I kept playing even when my club was finished for the season. Other teams in other leagues often tapped me to help them out in the playoffs. Sometimes I would be asked to join a team to give them an edge in a tournament. (Once, in my younger days, a junior team even asked me to impersonate an Indian player who was sick and couldn't play. They snuck me in the back door and had me dress in the player's sweater before I went anywhere near the ice. My dad was in the stands that night. One of the fans sitting beside him nodded in my direction. "Boy, that kid can play. He should be in the NHL.")

I was on the move a lot. In some towns, I boarded with families. In others, I lived in hotels and rooming houses. Sometimes I was close enough I could come home every two weeks during hockey season. But sometimes I was living hundreds of miles away from Sandy Lake and hardly saw Loretta and the kids at all during the winter. And as time went on, there were more kids: Derrick, Kevin, Karen. In 1967, Neil was born. Loretta spent about five months of every year raising these eight single-handedly. She was, as I've said, a fantastic mother— loving yet firm, energetic yet patient. But my absences meant I wasn't much of a father. And family life wasn't always smooth when I showed up and tried to step into the role. The kids deserved better.

I used to think of Chucky as my little cowboy. He just loved his horses. He'd spend hours and hours with my father, in his barn and out in the fields. Even as a small boy, Chucky would walk between two huge workhorses without an ounce of fear. He was the same with dogs. He loved all animals, and his gentle nature made him great with them.

Phyllis was good at so many things, but the one I noticed right away was sports. She was a talented athlete—and she loved baseball. She could run, hit, catch, everything. But she worked hard at whatever she did, becoming a good cook and seamstress too. When she hit her teens, she wanted to be a model. I'm sure she could have been, but she went to college instead.

Because of his asthma, Garth stayed pretty close to home when he was young. The poor little guy couldn't play sports or do a lot of the things his friends and siblings did. Over the years, he ended up in the hospital many times. Loretta was, of course, always worried about him. Garth knew his mother doted on him and he often got away with stuff that his brothers and sisters couldn't. The little rascal and Loretta were very close.

Our second daughter ending up getting renamed, because my mother always had trouble pronouncing "Beverley." Little Debbie, as we called her, spent a lot of time with Loretta, as she had a real passion for cooking. Even when she was tiny, she used to tie on one of Loretta's aprons and spend hours in the kitchen. In fact, she became such a good cook that before she was even a teenager, she would often be taking over the meals, making lunches and dinners for the family.

Derrick was our toughest kid. I don't mean he was difficult. One summer afternoon, I got in my truck to go run some errands. Loretta was in the house, cooking. The kids were all off playing somewhere, the older ones looking after the younger ones. My truck was parked on top of a little rise. It idled a bit fast, so as soon as I put it into gear it bounced forwards, over the crest of the slope. I heard a big *thump, thump, thump.* Oh, no, I thought. I've hit the dog. I threw the truck in park and leapt out. As soon as I did, I realized it wasn't a dog I'd run over. Two-year-old Derrick was lying behind the truck, covered in dirt. I shouted, but before I could get to him, he'd popped up on his feet. I picked him up. He was smiling. By that time, Loretta was out of the house. She scooped Derrick out of my arms and headed to the truck. She said we had to take him to the hospital right away. But there he was on his mother's hip, bright-eyed and grinning.

"Let's just take him in the house for a few minutes first," I said.

When we set him down in the living room, he began to run around, laughing, as if nothing had happened to him. He reminded me of my moosum Alexan. That toughness and strength. It wasn't surprising that he grew up to be a tough hockey player.

Karen, who we ended up calling Kerry, was a great athlete, but I remember her best as a little reader. She wasn't the least bit interested in TV. For her, it was always books, books, books. She just loved to learn. She graduated from Canwood High School with the highest honours, and Loretta and I were so proud of her.

Kevin, well Kevin was a child who seemed to have a special connection with our traditional life and practices, even when he was really young. He loved to hunt and trap. When I was home, he would work the traplines with me. And by the time he was in high school, he would go out into the bush by himself with his gun for days. He had one of the best moose calls I have ever heard.

Neil was always my biggest fan in the family. He used to talk about my NHL career all the time. It wasn't just me that Neil looked up to. He was always interested in what the Elders in our community had to say. You could see how well he listened, how he wanted to learn from them, how much respect he had for our history and traditions. And it seemed he was always thinking about the future, and his role in it. Like he knew he wanted to be a leader for his people. Neil was a really smart little boy—I always felt he was one step ahead of me.

And there was also a little guy named Lester. When Christina Ledoux and I dated in the summer of 1954, she got pregnant. I didn't know it at the time. Once she had the baby, there were a few rumours around that I was the father. But I was dating Loretta and caught up in my exciting life. I ignored them. I believe it was around the time we got back from Kamloops that I met Christina again, and little Lester. I knew he was my son. I told Loretta about him then. She was generous, accepting. She said that Lester was one of the family—just the way my mother had accepted my father's first child, Sophia.

Sophia had grown up in Sandy Lake, raised by her maternal grandfather, Baptiste Starblanket, and his wife. Frank and I had known her for most of our lives. It wasn't until I was seventeen or eighteen, however, that my mother told us she was actually our half-sister. After that, Frank and I made an effort to get to know our big sister better, and Sophia and her children eventually became an important part of our family. (Sophia and my mother grew very close as the years went by, and Sophia would nurse Mom during her final days.) But Christina never lived in any of the places I stayed, and Loretta and I wouldn't get to know Lester until he was in his teens. By that time, he had become a terrific hockey player and was well known in northern Saskatchewan for his skill on the ice. Even though he didn't share my last name, people called him "Sackie."

My kids were all so different and so talented. But if I'm being honest, I have to say I didn't always appreciate that or honour it. When I was home in the off-season, there wasn't a lot of time to spend with them. I was away from the house for most of each day, busy clearing land, planting fields, harvesting crops. Fishing in the spring and summer. Hunting in the fall. And in the spring and summer, I still ran the rec programs on the reserve, spending hours with all the local kids, not just my own. And then there were all my evenings out with my friends. But worse, when I did spend some time at home, I could be really hard on my kids, especially the older ones. Used to living like a bachelor so much of the time, I had little patience for their energy, their noise, their small misbehaviours. It didn't take much for me to fly off the handle, to tear a strip off them. And, oh, boy, if they started asking me for things, things that cost money, that would really get me steamed up. I was earning just enough to put food on the table. I didn't have money for the extras. That made me feel bad. And when I felt bad, I lost my temper.

Perhaps if I had spent the winters at home I might have improved my parenting skills a bit, but it wasn't an option. Farming didn't pay enough. Hockey was my bread and butter—it was still what I did best. And besides, it was what everyone wanted me to do.

I think it's sometimes hard for people who have always had televisions and computers and local movie theatres to understand how important live hockey games once were in small-town Canada. In the winter, it was often the only entertainment. And in northern Saskatchewan in the sixties, it could be really good hockey. The amateur leagues were filled with ex-NHLers or other semi-pros who had almost made the big leagues. Like I had done after Calgary, at least one other Saskatchewan man, Gerry Ehman, rode out his NHL suspension playing for the Big V league. He returned to Toronto in time to play for the Leafs when they won the Stanley Cup in 1964. That was the level of play in our little northern towns.

In tiny communities of three or four or five hundred people, 2,000 might show up at the local arena if it was a big game, or if one of the players was someone—like a full-treaty ex-NHLer—who people really wanted to see. With the teams I was playing for in the sixties—just like when I was first playing in Debden—chartered buses full of fans from Saskatoon, North Battleford, and Prince Albert would drive huge distances over the gravel roads to watch our games.

Of course, on these smaller rinks, I could really deliver. But they weren't built for crowds like that. Some of them, like the Debden arena, began to add little balconies inside to make room for the fans. Sometimes more than half the fans would stand for the whole game. This is why the team owners were willing to pay me. Even if admission was only twenty-five cents, they were making money every time I appeared on the ice. After the games, there were often people waiting outside the dressing room to get my autograph.

But, oh, man, the pressure. It didn't matter what team I was on, the message was the same. "Don't get off the ice, Freddy. There are a lot of people who have come here just to see you."

Even the managers of the opposing teams would sometimes come into the dressing room to tell me they expected to see me in play for every minute of the game.

"I got a whole busload of people just pulled up outside," one manager said, pointing his finger at me. "They come to see you, so you'd better give them a damn good show."

Years earlier, when I was playing in Debden, I learned what would happen if I didn't show at all. I was driving from Debden to Blaine Lake, where we were going to be playing. I stopped for a quick drink in Leask. I never made it out of the bar. When I got back to Debden, the team manager lit into me. I could handle his anger, but I felt really bad when he told me about how disappointed the crowd had been. I made sure to show up after that. But just showing up was not enough anymore. People expected a sixty-minute performance.

I tried to play smart so I didn't have to come off. I shifted between forward and defence, trying to control my pace and speed. I told my teammates to go into the corners after the puck, and I would put myself in front of the net for their passes. I had discovered years ago that if I pulled my stick back as if I was going to take a slapshot, players would move out of my way, fearing they were going to get hit by the speeding puck. Then I could put my blade down and skate closer to the net without getting checked. But now I also relied on my slapshot to conserve energy—powering a drive from the blue line to save my legs from long forward dashes. Yet the coaches and team owners never let me forget what they were paying me for.

"Okay, take a breather, Freddy," they'd say, "but just a short one. Then get back on the ice."

Many of the team owners went to crazy lengths to make sure I was there for the paying fans. One March, a huge storm kicked up when I was home at Sandy Lake for a visit with my family. I was supposed to be driving to North Battleford for a Big Four league playoff game. But once I started out, it was clear that the roads weren't in good enough shape for me to make the ninety-mile drive. I stopped in a little town to phone my team manager.

"I'm not going to make it," I said.

"Where are you?"

When I told him, he insisted I stay put.

"I'm sending a plane for you."

Sure enough, a short time later, a small prop plane landed in the field outside of town. I climbed in, and off we flew. The arena was packed when we got there. We won the game and had a party after. Someone flew me back home the following day.

But being the sixty-minute man got tougher and tougher as the years passed. For one thing, being a star also meant being a target. In my early days in the northern Saskatchewan leagues, the opposing teams seldom picked fights with me. That may have been out of respect, but it may also have been because they were a little afraid of how any fight might turn out for them. I had never forgotten my St. Michael's boxing lessons. Now that I was getting older, however, sometimes players from the opposing teams would try to take me out of the game any way they could. Occasionally, it took more than a couple of stitches to fix me up. In one game, I was hit from behind so hard my mind was foggy for days. When I got home to Loretta, I kept trying to piece together what had happened after I was hit.

"What was the score? What was the score?" I asked her.

Of course, she wasn't there, she didn't know. But I was upset, because I could not remember anything of the game or evening that followed.

Another time, the tactics of the opposing team almost did stop me playing for a while. We were facing a juvenile team in an inter-league game, and I got into a scuffle with someone. Before we could skate apart, I looked up and saw a couple of his teammates jumping off the bench and charging towards me. I wasn't going to wait to be knocked down by these big, strong kids. I threw a punch. Just then, the referee skated between us. I heard a crack and the ref crashed to the ground, blood pouring out of his nose. He had to crawl to the boards to get off the ice. I was ejected from the game, and about a month later, at the end of January, the Saskatchewan Amateur Hockey Association announced that I was barred from playing organized hockey in Canada for one year.

Frankly, I don't remember missing any games that year. And I do know that the following fall I was back, playing on another team. Perhaps the team owners decided to look the other way so that the arenas would continue to be full. I have no idea.

As the years went on, so did my accumulated injuries—gashes, twisted muscles, separated shoulders. But it wasn't just hockey that was hard on my body.

One day in early spring, I heard that a big herd of elk had been spotted not far from Sandy Lake. I asked my father to drive me out to the area so I could hunt. The snow was still deep, but I managed to locate the herd and bring down several elk. Before I'd had a chance to get them back to the truck, I spotted a huge bull moose. This was a big bonus— the meat would last my family and friends for months and months. I took a shot. I wounded the beast in the chest, but he didn't go down. He was moving away from me. I thought that if I could get him to walk in the direction of my father's truck, I could finish him off there instead of trying to carry over a thousand pounds of moose meat to the vehicle.

I got close to the moose and began kicking snow to move him along in the right direction. But when we got to a small slough, he refused to cross the water. I was prodding him forwards with a branch when two other hunters approached. They asked what I was doing, and I told them.

When I turned back to the moose, I noticed he had lowered his head and his ears were flattened back. He was mad. But I wasn't going to back down either. And then, before I knew it, he was up, charging towards me. I tried to raise my gun, but his antlers caught me under my left arm, raising me high in the air and sending me soaring about twenty feet backwards. I landed in a small stand of willows and deep snow. The moose was advancing towards me again. He was snorting, his nostrils puffing as he got closer and closer.

I had dropped my gun when I was hit. I could see the impression in the snow where it had fallen. Too far away to reach.

"Don't move, don't move," the hunters were calling at me. "He'll hit you with his hooves!"

"Shoot him!" I yelled at them.

"No, he's too close to you," one of them said. "It's too dangerous."

But lying there, waiting for the moose, seemed pretty dangerous too. I could feel his breath in the air, close to me. I made a decision.

I jumped up and moved towards the hole in the snow where my gun had landed. I dug it out and raised it, rushed towards the moose. I pushed the muzzle into the moose's forehead.

"Get down," I said.

I could feel blood dripping along the inside of my torn jacket. My finger tightened on the trigger.

The moose must have spent his last bit of energy lunging at me. It sank to the ground and died right there at my feet.

I managed to get back to my dad's vehicle, managed eventually to get the elk and the moose into the bed of the truck, but my shoulder was screaming the whole time.

A day or so later, I went to the doctor. My shoulder was separated. It would take about a month before I could really use that arm again.

My left side had been injured one too many times, though. I would never regain the strength on that side.

Hockey—and life—were hard on my body. But I was hard on it in other ways too.

The team management wherever I played always made sure I was taken care of—and that included plenty of cold beer after the third period. In 1951, revisions to the Indian Act allowed for Indians to be served alcohol in licensed establishments. But the federal government required each province to pass their own rules permitting this change. Saskatchewan finally did that in 1960. Indians were still not allowed to take any spirits out of a bar or a store, but that rule didn't apply to me. Anywhere my teammates drank, I could drink. And I sure did.

When I was in my twenties, I could snap back if I drank a little too much. The season after I returned from Calgary, the Debden team were going to a tournament in Prince Albert. The team owner refused to pay me to play, so I decided to sit the game out. I drove to the little town of Shell Lake and had a few drinks. Then I went to another small town, Mont Nebo, and had a few more. By the time the fellows from the Debden team found me, in Canwood, I was completely drunk. They didn't care. They'd changed their minds and were willing to pay me to play—even if I couldn't stand up. They put me in the car and drove me all the way back to Prince Albert. When we got there, they had to prop me up to get me into the arena. They shoved me in a cold shower just as the first period was finishing up. I skated onto the ice for the second period, but I was still drunk. After the second period, they threw me in the shower again. When I stepped onto the ice for the third period, I was ablaze. My skates were flying, and my stick was driving shots in from the blue line. The goalie was the netminder from my days with the

Moose Jaw Canucks—Ray Ethier. He kept shouting at his players to keep me from shooting, but it almost seemed like they were getting out of the way so they wouldn't get hit by the puck. I think, by the end of the game, even Ray was shuffling aside. I scored seven or eight goals that night, and we won the match.

But by the late sixties, life was catching up to me. I was in my mid-thirties, I was drinking too much, and I wasn't bouncing back like I had all those years ago. More than anything, I was tired. I began to look forward to getting penalties, just so I could have a few minutes to sit down. Those short breaks weren't enough, though. After sixty minutes of play, I'd drag myself off the ice, completely drained.

Eventually, at least one person recognized that I was wearing thin. It was 1968, and I was playing for the Kinistino Tigers in the Carrot River Valley league. The team was owned by the town's doctor, who put me up in the local hotel. Almost as soon as I got there, the man who ran the Chinese restaurant showed up with his small boy. He told me I should come to the café and he would feed me. The meals he prepared for me were beautiful, but when the doctor found out where I had been eating, he wasn't pleased. There wasn't enough energy in that food, as far as he was concerned. I told him he might not like what I was eating, but I wasn't happy about where he had me staying. The hotel was one of those places that was really just rooms above a bar—the whole place reeked of alcohol. The doctor moved me into a house to board with an older woman. She gave me a room with a small bed and a TV. She cooked all my meals for me, and I did chores for her. But her cooking didn't seem to have enough energy in it either.

During one of the first games of the playoffs, the doctor came to see me in the dressing room.

"You're getting tired, Freddy," he said.

"Yes, I am," I shot back.

"I'll fix that," he said. "I need you on the ice if we're going to win the playoffs." He told me to come to his office the next day.

An hour before our next game, I followed the instructions he'd given me at his office. I took half each of the small pink pill and little blue pill he'd handed me, and the whole big white pill. By the time I got onto the ice, I was buzzing. My legs were spinning—I was jumping back and forth across the ice like my eighteen-year-old self. The three periods flew by. When the final buzzer rang, I didn't want to get off the ice. I felt as if I could've played a second game. And maybe a third.

But that amped-up energy didn't fade even once I was home. At about four in the morning, the old lady came into the living room wanting to know why I was still up.

I took the same pills before the next game and the sleeplessness happened again. The sun was coming up by the time I finally shut my eyes.

For every team I played with, in every town, part of my responsibilities was to coach the local children's teams and to teach hockey skills. A couple of days after that second playoff game, a Cree father approached me at the rink to say he'd pay me to give his son some private lessons. I told him I didn't really have the time to give private lessons, but his son could join the hockey programs I was giving.

"I want him to play like you, Freddy," he said. "I watched you the other night—your stickhandling, your skating. They were unreal. I want my son to be as fast as you are."

I admitted I'd had a little help before the game—that the doctor had given me some pills for energy. And that I hadn't been able to sleep after.

"Freddy, I know what those pills are!"

The guy sounded alarmed. He told me he raised thoroughbreds and was a chuck wagon racer. Some racers gave their horses the same stuff before the competitions.

"Freddy, that doctor gave you speed."

He told me it was very dangerous, and I shouldn't take it again.

What he said worried me. I'd been given medication in other towns too. When I was hurt or wasn't feeling well, when my legs were tired. Sometimes I felt strange sensations afterwards. Occasionally I felt pain in my chest. Now I wondered what I'd taken. I wondered if any of those managers had been thinking about me or, like the doctor, just about winning.

I didn't say anything to the doctor the next time I saw him. But I wasn't his racehorse. And I wasn't going to take any more of his damn pills.

I was ready for a change the following year. Around the time I was playing for Kinistino, I was offered a spot on the Eastern Hockey League's Jacksonville Rockets, in Florida. The beaches and warm weather would've been nice, but it was too big a move for Loretta and the children—and I couldn't be that far away. Instead, I jumped from Kinistino to Prince Albert to play with the Prince Albert Barons. It wasn't as far away from home as Florida, or even some of the places I already played, but it was far enough. When the season wrapped up, in March 1969, I was done. I packed up my gear and headed for Sandy Lake. I knew I wouldn't be back. I was going home for good.

On the long drive back, I thought of everything I'd done. Everything I'd been through. I was about to turn thirty-six. It had been twenty years since George Vogan had arrived in Blue Heron to tell me he thought I had a shot at the big time. Fifteen long years since I had played my last NHL game. I thought about Bill Mosienko's farewell celebration in Chicago. The look on his face as he stood at centre ice, waving goodbye to the fans. That must have been hard. But was it harder than this? I felt like I had been standing on that ice, saying goodbye, for years.

13

yēkawiskāwikamāhk

SANDY LAKE

The reserve I returned to that spring was very different from the place I had left as a child. For one thing, so many more of our people called it home. At the end of the sixties or beginning of the seventies, electricity had finally come to Sandy Lake (although we wouldn't have water lines or natural gas until the mid-eighties). That encouraged more people to move to the reserve. By the early seventies, the population was probably more than a thousand people. New houses were being built all through the place. Wagon trails had been replaced by graded gravel roads. And a few of the houses had phone lines.

The Indian agent was gone and our band council, under the leadership of our Chief, Paul Ahenakew, was running the reserve. After the 1951 changes to the Indian Act that reversed many restrictions on us, powwows, round dances, Sweat Lodges, and other traditional practices had returned to Sandy Lake, although many of our people still believed these were dangerous pagan customs. The influence of Reverend Hines and residential schools would be lasting. (And sadly, our children were speaking English and being taught French in school. Most of our young people would not be taught Cree by their parents or the schools for decades yet.)

When I came home that spring, I got to work on my farm and jumped back into volunteering as the rec program coordinator. I also joined the band council. But the loss of my hockey income was going to hit us hard. I knew that. I began to look for other earning opportunities.

The little day school on the reserve had closed in the early sixties, as Indian Affairs seemed more interested in funding facilities off the reserve. People were sending their children to school in Canwood, Shell Lake, Debden. Clara, my sister, actually taught in Canwood. St. Michael's was still in operation too. While they no longer had the authority to take Catholic Indigenous children by force, Children's Aid required some families in trouble to send their kids to the facility. Some Indigenous people even sent their kids there willingly. It had a good hockey program, and I guess it may have improved the education it offered.

A white fellow from Prince Albert had a contract with Indian Affairs to run the school buses from Sandy Lake and a lot of other reserves in northern Saskatchewan. The drivers were all from the reserves, but I figured that the busing money might as well stay in our community as well.

With the backing of Indian Affairs, my friend Clifford Ahenakew and I managed to get financing from the local bank to buy our own school buses. I bought three. I drove one, Loretta drove the other, and we hired a local fellow to drive the third. In 1977, Sandy Lake opened its own elementary school, but we would continue to operate our buses until 1995, when the reserve added a high school as well.

Now that I was home in the winter, I could run the skating and hockey programs for the reserve kids. It was something I'd been wanting to do for years. Hockey had been so important to me as I was growing up. It gave me a way to escape grim reality when I needed it. It gave me confidence, self-esteem. It gave me hope. And once I began to play pro, it made me realize that we nēhiyawak could compete in the white society. We could be as good or better than môniyâwak. I wanted more of my people to feel the way I did. To understand what I had learned through hockey.

In fact, the entire time I was playing for all of those northern Saskatchewan towns, I had also been working to help reserves run their own hockey programs. Without those, our kids had a tough time learning to play. Sure, the little towns all over the province had teams for various ages. But those teams also had residency clauses. If you didn't live in the town itself, you couldn't be on the team. So kids and adults from the reserves were kept out of organized hockey. And even if a team or a league didn't have a residency clause, a lot of our families didn't have vehicles, so we couldn't get our kids to games and practices any distance from home. In the early sixties, while playing for the Meadow Lake Stampeders, I had been hired as the sports and recreational director for the Meadow Lake Tribal Council. During that time, and after, I worked with others from reserves across northern Saskatchewan, helping start teams both for kids and adults. We found funding to hire coaches from Saskatoon to come to our communities to teach us how to coach and develop our players. And we created the Northern Indian Hockey League, a senior men's league.

Boy, what a difference that made. The teams created excitement in the communities and drew us together. They provided a great outlet for our young ones. And tournaments for all ages brought people from different reserves together for some healthy rivalry. Our very own NHL (Native Hockey League) championship was an incredibly popular event.

Eventually, the government came to understand the value of supporting recreation for our people. Indian Affairs began to provide funds to build sports facilities on the reserves. In the early seventies, Sandy Lake received such a grant and used the money to build a heated indoor arena near the old community hall. (Three decades later, the band council would decide to name it after me. The Fred Sasakamoose Arena.)

Now that we had a rink, many Sandy Lake kids wanted to play hockey, but it's an expensive sport. Families often couldn't afford proper equipment. For every division, I had to create two little groups—one with kids who had equipment, one for kids who didn't. It was too dangerous to let the children who didn't have proper helmets and pads play against the kids who did. With so many players, divided into so many groups, I spent long, long hours at the rink. Many days, I'd be skating three or four hours myself as I ran the drills.

In 1974, after playing in international competitions in western Canada for a few years, our Indigenous bantam all-star team was invited to a tournament in the Netherlands and Finland over the Christmas break. (Two boys from the Sandy Lake reserve were on that team.) It was the first time any Canadian Indigenous hockey team of any age had made an international trip. As well as our twenty players, we decided to bring along about thirty young Cree drummers, dancers, and singers so we could showcase our culture to the Europeans as well as our hockey skills.

Before we left, I got a message from Howie Meeker, the former Leafs right winger, who was now a *Hockey Night in Canada* commentator and the operator of a hugely successful youth hockey camp business. A year or so before, he'd come to northern Saskatchewan for some reason, and he wanted to go fishing. I guess he remembered me from all those years ago when we had played against each other, Leafs versus Hawks. He got in touch, asking if I could arrange a fishing trip.

So I got a float plane to take me, Howie, and my friends Ray Ahenakew and Cliff Morin north of La Ronge to fish for two or three days. Howie hadn't forgotten that time we spent together. Now he was using his connections in the Hockey Canada organization to invite me and the bantam all-star team to join him in Edmonton to watch a Team Canada practice.

Once we got to Edmonton, I found out Bobby Hull was there too. I introduced myself. He said he had remembered hearing of me. He said he had heard of my slapshot.

Shortly after that, the team was on a flight to Amsterdam. Man, to board a plane with fifty excited young people. None of them had been on a plane before. The kids were buzzing as the aircraft lifted off.

I was about as excited as they were. I'd been in small prop planes before. But nothing like this. To see the white prairie fields disappearing beneath us, to lift up above the clouds. Wow, I kept thinking, as the plane soared higher and higher.

And then landing in Amsterdam and taking the train east through the low water-filled countryside to Nijmegen, on the German border. Another world.

We weren't the only ones at the tournament amazed at all the new things we were seeing. When the team walked into the arena for the first time—the faces of the little Dutch kids! One of our boys said later, "They looked at us like we were from outer space."

But it wasn't like when my St. Michael's Ducks teammates and I had skated onto the môniyâw rinks. These Dutch folks were happy to see us. In the Netherlands, everyone remembered Canada's role in World War II. When the coaches walked into a bar one evening after a game, no one would let us pay for our drinks.

We were in the Netherlands for about a week, and then we flew to Finland. In Finland, the hockey was higher calibre, and the people were just as welcoming as the Dutch. In fact, in Finland, there were more local families who wanted to billet our children than we had children. In the end, we had to move the poor kids from home to home every night so we wouldn't disappoint any of the host families.

It was great to see hockey give the kids an introduction to the wider world, just as it had done for me.

Hockey wasn't a paying gig for me anymore, but I still played in my late thirties and forties. I was the player-coach on the reserve team, the Sandy Lake Chiefs. And often I'd be asked to help out one of the other men's teams in various tournaments.

And, of course, I followed the pro game.

One of the first things I did when electricity came to the reserve was get a TV so I could finally watch *Hockey Night in Canada* at home instead of at friends' houses outside the reserve—or in the bars. It was fascinating to follow the changes in the game, the expansion of the league. And other Indian players who began to appear: Jim Neilson, Reggie Leach, Bryan Trottier, Stan Jonathan, Ron Delorme, Ted Nolan, and others. I loved the game, and on my good days, it was the best entertainment I could imagine. On my bad days, sitting in front of my TV, watching great players test their skills against each other, I sometimes found myself thinking about what might have been.

Because life wasn't easy in the years after I quit hockey. Our youngest child, Ryan, had been born in 1973, making eleven of us. It was tough to provide for a family of eleven, even with my expanding farm and the new, better location of our home.

After a few years in our little house near my parents, I'd realized that the spot wasn't good if I wanted to raise animals as well as crops. The water from the slough needed to be boiled before we could drink it. Cattle and horses wouldn't touch it—they had to be brought several miles to the river or to a little spring to drink. So, in the mid-sixties, I had my house moved south, to an open area nearer to the river, where I could graze and water the cows and horses I eventually acquired. And where I could put in a hand-dug, open-air well. Over the years, I'd increased the fields I worked as well, until I had about 1,100 acres planted. Loretta kept a big vegetable garden. And we had a cow for milk and chickens for eggs. But I didn't have the resources to buy enough equipment to make my farm profitable.

I also hunted, fished, and trapped. It provided food for the table, of course, but I couldn't really make cash that way. Years earlier, I'd tried to earn some big dollars by trapping. There was a high demand for beaver pelts at the time—and they were bringing a good price. I wanted to take advantage of that, but there weren't a lot of the animals around Sandy Lake. I needed to find a place with a lot of beavers so I could make a good haul in a single trip. One of those places was the Prince Albert National Park.

Now, I knew it was against the law to trap in a national park. But I also knew that Lieutenant-Governor Alexander Morris had promised Ahtahkakoop and the other Chiefs at the Treaty 6 negotiations he would never take away my people's right to support themselves by hunting and fishing. When Ahtahkakoop had raised concerns about possible hunting restrictions, Morris had said, "I told you we did not want to take that means of living from you, you have it the same as before, only this, if a man, whether Indian or Half-breed, had a good field of grain, you would not destroy it with your hunt."

The national park did not have fields of grain. I figured it was my right to hunt there, no matter what the authorities said. And I needed the money.

My father dropped me off one morning at the end of the park. I hiked about nine miles into the bush and started to set my traps. Other than that equipment, all I had with me was a gun, some bannock, and my backpack. I spent two or three days by myself in the woods, sleeping in the open air, emptying the traps, and skinning my catch. I didn't light a fire, because I didn't want a park ranger to notice my presence. On the third day, I was ready to hike out of the park with my bounty and went to gather my pelts from the various spots where I'd left them. I reached a little rise in the forest when I saw what I thought was a timber wolf approaching me from below. I raised my rifle in case he decided to come after me. That's when I heard a voice.

"Don't shoot!"

I turned around. Behind me was an RCMP officer and a park ranger. The "wolf" was actually a police dog.

The two men asked where my beaver pelts were. I denied having any. They weren't convinced. I was marched out of the bush and into a police cruiser.

They drove me to the RCMP office in the little village of Waskesiu Lake, in the park. They were going to hold me overnight there, but the office had no cells. Instead, they took me to a large iron cage—a bear cage—outside the building and locked me in. The next morning, they took me out of the cage and brought me to a justice of the peace. I told the JP that I was simply exercising my treaty rights to hunt. He issued me a fine of $104.

I'd gotten off very easy. I knew that. But it wasn't an experience I wanted to repeat. Clearly, trapping and fishing were never going to earn me good money.

So even with the livestock, the crops, and the income from the buses, it was hard to make ends meet. Life became even harder after a fire destroyed our family home on Christmas Eve, 1972.

Loretta and I were in Prince Albert. We'd left sixteen-year-old

Chucky to babysit and were at the mall buying presents for the kids. The Christmas music had me feeling cheerful and silly. I saw a shiny Christmas brooch on a display table.

"I'm going to buy this for you," I said to Loretta.

She shook her head. "Don't do it!"

Loretta never liked fancy clothes or flashy accessories.

But I went to the checkout counter with the brooch anyhow.

"I'm going to decorate my wife for Christmas!" I said.

We were both still feeling merry about our day of shopping together when we turned down the road to our house and saw a billow of smoke. Loretta started to cry right away.

My cousin Jeffrey was standing in front of the smouldering ruins of our home. Loretta was calling out for the kids before her feet even hit the ground. Jeffrey told us they were all safe. They were all at his house.

But we'd lost all of our belongings, including most of my mementos from my junior and NHL days. (I probably had a hundred trophies stored in that basement.) We had to move in with my mom and dad.

Two days after Christmas, Chief Ahenakew called a big meeting. The entire reserve pitched in to provide clothing and other necessities. And then, with funding help of Indian Affairs, they started to build a new house for us, right next to the old one. In some ways, that was a real blessing. Our tiny one-bedroom house was replaced with a bigger three-bedroom one. We loved the new place, but it had been an awful way to get more space.

The strain during those years wasn't just financial. The truth was, I'd been away so long that I really struggled with family life. By the time I'd come home for the winters, Chucky was about thirteen, heading into his teen years. Phyllis was eleven or twelve. I'd missed so much time with them—and the younger ones too.

In all those small towns I'd lived in, I had taught other people's kids how to skate, how to play hockey. But I hadn't been home to teach my own. The older boys joined local teams, learned to skate, but I'd never really guided them the way Father Roussel or George Vogan did with me.

Now that I was back, coaching the Sandy Lake teams, instead of making up for lost time, I was more concerned that people didn't think I was playing favourites with my own kids. When I had to make cuts to the teams or decide which players got to go on trips, my children were always first off the list. The older boys were often really angry about this, but I thought it would teach them to think of others before themselves. I also figured I'd spare them unwanted attention. I knew people expected them to be not just *good* hockey players but *great* ones. Because of me. When they showed up on the ice in other towns, people pointed to them.

"That's Freddy Sasakamoose's boy," they'd say.

But I didn't take into account that those expectations met them on the reserve as well. As time went on, the boys didn't even want to play games in Sandy Lake. By the time they were teens, the older boys had all quit.

It makes me sad to say my failings as a father went further than that. I'd developed bad habits during my years living as a bachelor during hockey season. I would bring those habits home when I came back in the spring—and I didn't abandon them now I was in Sandy Lake year-round. Sometimes I'd go into one of the little towns and buy beer or a bottle and bring it back to Sandy Lake to share with Frank or my friends on the reserve. (I never brought it into my own home. Loretta would only allow alcohol in the house on Christmas Day.) Other times I might drive into Debden or Canwood and pull a stool up to the bar with my white friends. Either way, by the time evening rolled around,

I'd often be drunk. I'd get home after Loretta had put the kids to bed. Poor Loretta had her husband now, but he still wasn't much help to her. More than once, I woke up in the morning to discover that Loretta had spent the night sleeping in a chair in the living room, a sick child in her lap. She'd stayed out there, dozing upright, to let me sleep off all the booze in peace.

Of course, it wasn't just that the drinking kept me away from my family. It also led to blow-ups.

One night, when I was in my mid-twenties, I walked into a bar to see a face from the past. It was one of the fellows who'd dragged me into the bush that terrible afternoon at residential school. I felt flames leap up behind my eyes. My heart was pounding. My fists were clenched. I wanted to walk over to him and beat the living daylights out of him. I knew I could. He was just a tired-looking, out-of-shape guy slouched on a bar stool. I was strong, an athlete. I could finally make him feel a bit of the pain I felt all those years ago.

I stood there, staring at his back, for what seemed like an hour. Then I turned on my heel and walked out of the bar.

As Ray and George told me all those years ago, there was no point in retaliating. It wouldn't make me feel better—it would only hurt my future.

I know I did the right thing that night, but if I'd managed to have a drink before I saw the fellow, I don't know that I would've walked away.

Because the hurt and anger hadn't disappeared. Residential school. And then all those taunts and slurs when I was on the ice in the years that followed. (They continued, off and on, all through my playing days.) I hadn't forgotten. In fact, one evening, when I was out in a bar in one of the small towns near the reserve, a fellow had come up to me, laughing, and said, "Hey, Freddy, remember all those names I used to call you when you played hockey?"

Of course I did. *Squaw humper. F-ing Indian.* I guess that was his clumsy way of apologizing, but he didn't ask for forgiveness. And I didn't give it.

The pain was still there. And now I was also dogged by the feeling I was a failure to my people. No longer playing hockey, I didn't know what to do with those emotions. Because hockey had been my outlet.

Lots of people today complain about the fighting in hockey. I never do. I've always felt it was part of the game. Besides, it worked for me. One of the things I missed when I stopped playing was the way the aggression in the games let me release a bit of my anger, even if I didn't realize that's what I was doing. I often felt a little calmer after a good scrap on the ice. And now that I didn't have hockey, when pain and anger and guilt flared up, there seemed to be no good way to deal with them.

And Frank, my brother Frank, was exactly like me. All through the sixties and seventies, when the two of us would drink, we would get angry about the smallest things and often take it out on each other. My kind, gentle brother, who had protected me during our school days together, the fellow I'd missed so much when he left and all the years I'd been away, he'd find something to argue about, or I'd find some damn thing to be upset about, and then we'd ruin our evening, we'd ruin everyone's evening, by having a raging fight. The next day, we'd always apologize.

"Sorry, I was drunk."

It was such bullshit. Such a waste.

While I spent more time drinking during those years than I care to admit, I tried to avoid being around my kids when I was drunk. As the kids got older and stayed up later, I got an old school bus and parked it on my property. When I came home from a night out, I would sleep there so they didn't have to see me.

But that didn't mean my kids didn't know what was going on, or avoided all the anger I was carrying around with me, now that I wasn't venting it on the rink. Chucky, Phyllis, Garth, and Derrick were well into their teens by the mid-seventies. They were beginning to party themselves, staying out late, pushing back. They weren't going to listen to me lecture them about not drinking after watching me head off to the bars, evening after evening. So we argued. And even a small confrontation with one of them could send me into a rage. I had never believed in punishing kids physically. All my years at St. Michael's had shown me the cruelty of that. Yet more than once, arguing with my older sons, I would find my hands landing on them. Afterwards, I would feel sick with regret. But I could never find the words to admit this to the boys. To apologize and tell them that I *knew* my behaviour was not right. Looking back now, I see so clearly that I failed them. Heck, I abused them. Though we were treated badly at St. Michael's, I had many loving and supportive adults in my life—my moosum, my mom and dad, George Vogan. People who believed in me and showed me how to be in the world. I never did that for my kids.

Loretta shielded the children from my anger as best she could. And while she never voiced her disappointment or disapproval with me, I knew it was there. But one person always let me know exactly what she thought.

"toosaw, ka-pāstāhon." Toosaw, you are going to be punished for your sins, my mother used to say. "nikosis ka-pasastehkosin." God's whip hurts, my son.

When I asked her what she meant, she would usually say, "misawac kika-kiskeyihtān." You'll find out. You'll find out. But once, she was more direct.

"kicawasimsak kawanihawak." Your kids will disappear, Toosaw.

I didn't believe her. But I shouldn't have been so foolish. I should never have doubted her.

———

By the late seventies, the older kids had begun to leave home. Chucky and Phyllis even had children of their own by the time the eighties began. But they lived on the reserve, and I saw them regularly. Everyone was still in my life.

In 1980, however, I would lose one old friend, a man we always called "the Old Chief." Allan Ahenakew had been our band leader for forty-four years before he retired in 1958. He was in his late eighties and had recently been diagnosed with cancer. One afternoon in early October, my father came by our house to say that Allan wanted to talk with me. When I arrived at Allan's house, he was lying in bed, too sick to get up.

"Fred," he said, "I want you to put your name forward to be the new Chief. I want you to lead our people."

Oh, boy, that is going to be tough, I thought.

Allan had been a great Chief. A wise man. He had been only the third Chief of the Sandy Lake band, after Ahtahkakoop and Ahtahkakoop's son, Basil Starblanket. It seemed to me that all of Ahtahkakoop's wisdom had passed to him. Had allowed him to guide our people in good times and bad, even after he retired. And for many in our community, there had been plenty of bad times.

I'd been a councillor for close to ten years by that point. I knew the challenges our community faced. Many of our people were residential school Survivors and carried those deep scars. And childhoods spent away from parents had robbed many of the understanding of how to be parents themselves. So the trauma continued through the generations and sometimes led to child neglect or abuse. But even many who had avoided residential school struggled. Our people had never escaped the yoke of poverty. Unemployment, despair, intergenerational trauma, and PTSD—so many were using alcohol to cope. And then in the seventies, people began sniffing solvent and experimenting with other substances.

By the eighties, that had led to widespread intravenous drug use on the reserve. Of course, all of this had devastating effects on family life. Over the years, I'd often been called to break up family fights, to check in on kids when there was some kind of crisis in the home, or when they had been left alone. And like in so many Indigenous communities across the country, Children's Aid had swooped in and taken kids off, placing many up for adoption.

Being Chief would mean trying to lead the community towards healing. But our growing community also presented plenty of organizational, administrative demands for its leader. Dealing with Indian Affairs. Financial management. Construction projects. Getting services in that we needed.

"There are a few things I have to tell you, Fred," Allan said, after a moment of silence. "To serve your people, you have to avoid drink. You have to go to church. You have to be a role model. Show them a brighter life. We are poor, but poor is nothing. It's what you give that counts."

I knew he was right. I needed to change the direction I was going. I'd been worrying for years that I'd failed my people. I needed to stop thinking the only way I could be a role model was as a hockey player. I could be a different kind of role model. I needed to be a better man to be a good leader. A better husband, a better father, a better grandfather. I vowed not just to quit drinking but to put aside the partying and late nights. And I needed to embrace my heritage more strongly. I'd been quietly going to Sweat Lodges with my friends for years. But now I'd also work on my Cree language so I could once again speak as fluently as Allan did, as so many of the other Elders did.

On October 17, 1980, I ran in the election. I won. A month after that, on November 17, Allan passed away.

Being elected Chief was one of the proudest moments in my life. Yet I knew some people questioned if I deserved the position. I was known for hockey, but also for partying, for things I wasn't proud of. Over the next few years, I worked hard to prove those people wrong. When I faced difficult decisions, I sought out the wisdom of Elders, both in my community and in other bands. I learned a lot from them.

During my time as Chief, we started to construct a log building on the shores of Sandy Lake that we hoped would house a small factory to make traditional Cree buckskin jackets, moccasins, boots, that we could sell to stores throughout the province. The construction created employment for many on the reserve—we logged and prepped all the lumber right in Sandy Lake. Unfortunately, we could never get the funding we needed to get the business off the ground.

While I was Chief, the council took over the welfare office on the reserve, hiring administrative staff to help our families fill out paperwork for social assistance and other government services they needed. I also began the process of taking some of the responsibility for education over from Indian Affairs. And we worked on plans to get addiction treatment services for Sandy Lake.

During those years, the council also moved forward with the arrangements to get water and gas lines into the reserve. It would take many years for all of the houses to get gas furnaces and indoor plumbing, to no longer rely entirely on wood stoves, diesel furnaces, or water drawn from wells and cisterns. By the mid-eighties, however, the reserve began to install the water and gas lines and get those services to many of our community.

Some of the decisions I had to make while Chief were really tough. With the council's agreement, I made the call to have the reserve continue to receive yearly funding from Indian Affairs instead of taking a one-time settlement that was offered. I'd gotten advice from other Chiefs in the area who suggested that while the lump payment was attractive, if it wasn't managed expertly the reserve could face financial disaster. They told me of some reserves where investments had been poorly chosen and where cost overruns for programs and capital projects had quickly eaten through the funds. Those reserve councils, having taken the lump payments, could not apply for financial help or additional aid programs run by Indian Affairs. They were essentially left broke, with no way to generate the needed income for their communities.

One decision, however, required no debate. While I was Chief, our council brought the buffalo back to Ahtahkakoop's land.

The council had been notified about a program that would deliver buffalo from Alberta to reserves interested in reintroducing them to their lands. Buffalo had always been our medicine, the sacred animals that sustained us, whose spirits filled our lives and our land. We knew immediately this was something we wanted. In the early eighties, our application was approved, and about fifty head of buffalo were introduced to Sandy Lake. Boy, what a feeling to see those amazing beasts graze our open fields.

Of course, even as Chief, promoting youth and senior Indigenous hockey continued to be one of my priorities. In the seventies, I had helped to establish the Saskatchewan Summer and Winter Games. In 1980, we had our inaugural First Nation Winter Games in Cote First Nation.

I also decided to try to give some of the folks on the reserve the same kind of opportunities I'd had to see a bit of the world. I found some funding to enter our reserve men's hockey team in a few tournaments in other provinces and even south of the border. Our most memorable trip was to a tournament in Anaheim, California. Many players brought their wives. For most everyone, it was the first air travel they'd ever done. Just like with the bantam team, there were whoops and cheers when the plane took off.

Once in California, we played hockey and were tourists. We visited Knott's Berry Farm theme park and drove past Disneyland, which had just been orange groves and fields when I was there last. Then someone suggested that we take a short detour to Mexico. We wanted to see if we might be able to connect with some Indigenous communities down there.

That detour was an unhappy reminder that racism sure was alive and well. The US border guards refused to let us pass out of the States. They thought we were undocumented Mexican migrants. They kept us sitting on the bus for ten hours before we were allowed to turn around and drive back to LA.

But despite that, it was a good trip, in a year of exciting work as Chief.

And then, on a warm summer morning, everything changed.

It was August 7, 1983. I was on the golf course. My brother Leo had become an excellent golfer, playing in many high-level tournaments, including against Lee Trevino in Hawaii. He'd encouraged me to take up the sport. About five or six years earlier, some of us on the council had organized an annual golf tournament with the local RCMP detachment. We nicknamed it "Cowboys and Indians." I was playing in the tournament and was on the fifth or sixth hole when an RCMP officer drove up in a golf cart.

He wasn't wearing golf clothes. He was wearing his uniform.

"Fred, I need to talk with you."

I walked over to the cart.

"There's been a car accident," he said. "Your daughter Phyllis was killed."

Everything went black.

When I came to, someone was splashing water on my face. I sat up. I couldn't hear a thing. I couldn't say a thing. I couldn't cry.

yēkawiskāwikamāhk

The officer helped me up and told me to leave everything. Someone would bring my clubs and car home.

When we pulled up in front of our house in the police cruiser, I could see a group of friends and relatives clustered on the front porch. I didn't want to get out of the car.

"People are waiting for you, Fred," the officer said gently.

That's when Loretta walked out the door. She came over to the car. Helped me out. Guided me into the house.

If I hadn't appreciated it before, I did then—Loretta, with her small stature and quiet demeanour, has always been stronger than I've ever been.

I didn't want to ask any questions about what had happened to Phyllis. I didn't want her death to become real.

Eventually, however, I'd learn she had been behind the wheel of her car in the early hours of the morning when she lost control. There was alcohol in her system. Her passenger survived.

My girl. My beautiful, talented girl. Gone.

I didn't understand any of it.

I could sit here for days, weeks, months, and I'd never be able to find the right words to describe how that felt. The most I can say is it changed me. Knocked me down and hollowed me out. Left me weak.

Especially in the early weeks after her death, I was adrift. One day, my mother took me aside.

"matotisān itohte, nikosis. asām kitānis, macosteha mīciwin tahkohc asinīyak." Go to the Sweat Lodge, my son. Burn food for your daughter on the rocks. To feed her in the afterlife, she said.

I nodded.

"ekwa itohte o-kihkwahaskān. ekwa wīhkask kastan." And go to her grave. Put sweetgrass there.

I did as my mother suggested. At Phyllis's grave, I left two cigarettes on the stone. A tobacco offering is, of course, a traditional act of respect.

225

But Phyllis loved to smoke, and that's what I was thinking about too. Then I lit some sweetgrass. I waved the smoke over my head and then across the plot where Phyllis lay. I prayed that it would guide her to a better place. I prayed it would help take her soul to God.

14

miywanohk-pimātisiwin

A NEW WAY OF LIFE

Phyllis's three young children moved in with Loretta and me. Our family tried to go on with our lives. But I was finding the demands of being Chief difficult to bear. The practical decisions needed to manage our growing community felt overwhelming. The personal interactions were even tougher.

There were still very few phones on the reserve. A lot of my time involved visiting people in their homes, especially those people who were having trouble. I'd always felt a real connection with people in pain. I understood their struggle. I wanted to listen to them, to try to help them. I wanted to find ways for us to help each other.

But now all that responsibility bore down on me. When I'd started as Chief, I felt I had the focus to make good decisions. The strength to take care of my community. I wasn't so sure about that anymore. It worried me. And I was also facing pressure to step down because of an incident a year or two earlier.

One afternoon, I was out on the tractor in my fields when a car pulled up on the road. A man got out and walked over to me. It was a fellow who sold diesel fuel in one of the little towns outside the reserve. He began to talk about some money I owed him.

Non-band members are not allowed onto reservations unless invited. This man was trespassing.

I told him I would come into town and settle up with him later. I needed to finish seeding my field first.

That answer clearly annoyed him. He kept after me to pay him right then and there. I told him I couldn't do anything until I'd finished seeding.

At that, he came right up to the tractor, pulled himself onto the step, and attempted to get in the cab. I wasn't sure what his intentions were, and my heart started to pump. I reached out and gave him a big shove. That sent him clear off the tractor, onto the ground below.

He picked himself up, got in his car, and drove away.

Unfortunately, he headed straight for the RCMP office and filed a complaint against me. He claimed I had punched him. Around the time Phyllis died, the charges against me were being brought to court.

The judge would eventually dismiss them. There wasn't any evidence to support the man's claims, and he had been trespassing. But the council couldn't have a Chief known to have charges pending against him. I had to step down. Barry Ahenakew came in as Chief, and I wasn't reinstated once the charges were dropped.

I felt that yet again I had let my people down.

The following July 4, my father passed away. Dad and I had never been ones to talk a lot. Our relationship was quiet but steady. Reassuring. His loss was hard for me. Harder was watching how it affected my mother. In her darkest moments, she would go to the graveyard and lie between Phyllis's headstone and my father's. But even on her better days, she would sit alone in their house, quietly suffering.

With the arrival of fall came the time of the next council elections. While some in the community had pushed for my removal from office because of the tractor incident, others were encouraging me to run again. The last couple of years had been difficult, but I did want another chance to serve my people as Chief. I ran against Barry. I lost.

When I heard the election results, I was surprised to realize I wasn't really disappointed. My doctor had told me I shouldn't be Chief. He was concerned about my blood pressure and my heart. I knew he was right. Being Chief again would have been hard on my health. And I was exhausted.

Now that I was no longer Chief, however, I wasn't going back to how I had lived before. When I had started out as Chief, I'd reined in my drinking but didn't stop completely. After Phyllis's death, I vowed never to touch the stuff again. And I didn't. Instead, I found other ways cope.

In the years that followed, the pain of my childhood folded into the pain of my greatest loss. I needed ways to prevent that pain from bursting into anger. I sought strength in my Catholic beliefs. For so many years, I had not wanted to go to church—I'd had enough Sundays at St. Michael's. Yet I'd carried the faith with me. Now I picked up my bible and found comfort there. Eventually, I would even start attending the Anglican church on the reserve.

Like my moosum and my mother, I never thought that a belief in Christ and Reverend Hines's God meant I could not embrace nēhiyaw spirituality. I now tried harder to live in wâhkôhtowin, or kinship, with the land and the living. Attending Sweat Lodges continued to be a way to heal. So was daily smudging. I also went to the spot at the bottom of Lonesome Pine Hill where I understood my moosum had buried his medicine bundle. There I would lie down and drift to sleep, hoping to connect in my dreams with Alexan and his wisdom. And I spent more and more time talking in the tongue I had learned at my mother's knee. Cree was once again my first language.

And I focused on my family.

For years, my mother had warned me about taking my children for granted. I was heartsick that I had shrugged off her wisdom. That it had taken such a loss to make me understand. But now I was reminded of her words again and again—sometimes in the most unexpected ways.

A few years after my daughter passed away, the new buffalo herd on the reserve was established enough that the residents were allowed to hunt them. I decided to go out with my gun and see if I could bring home some buffalo meat. The herd had grown—it wasn't hard to track them down. In no time, I came across a young bull. He was probably about two years old. I took aim and shot him in the neck. He moved a few paces and went down. To my surprise, the gun blast did not scatter the other beasts in the area. Instead, a huge bull came towards the young one. He put his head to the ground and seemed to be trying to get the animal to its feet. The bull snorted and pushed with his nose. When the fallen buffalo didn't move, the big bull lifted his head and stared in my direction. His gaze cut right through me. I knew then that the buffalo was the father, and I had shot his son.

Later, Loretta told me she'd read that the buffalo were easily slaughtered by the white trophy hunters because they wouldn't leave their dying brothers and sisters when one was shot. I could believe that. Because, oh, man, looking at that great bull, I swear I could see tears in those giant eyes. It just broke my heart.

I knew exactly how he felt.

When the bull eventually moved off, I took my kill. It would be a great sin to waste the life of the sacred animal I'd brought down. But I swore I would never hunt buffalo again.

I had always loved all of my children. I sure had. But it wasn't until I lost one that I truly appreciated how God had blessed me with them. Ryan, who was only eleven when I quit as Chief, was still at home. I spent more time with him than I had with the older kids. He was a great hockey player. When I coached him, I tried to make sure I wasn't being harder on him than on any of the other players.

With the arrival of Phyllis's three children and the visits from grandchildren, our house was never empty. That made Loretta very glad—and I recognized it for the gift it was. I was being given another opportunity to be a good parent.

I taught my grandchildren how to skate and play hockey, but like with Ryan, I tried to be more supportive than I had been with my older boys. I also tried to share other things I knew with them. I took many of them out in the bush and taught them to hunt. I took them fishing and trapping as well.

Most importantly, I didn't allow myself to lose my temper—although time and grief had softened me and I didn't need to work so hard to do this.

As my children earned college and university degrees, took up jobs, found partners, built homes, had children of their own, I tried to celebrate their achievements, even though I still had trouble sharing my feelings with them in words. When they struggled, and some of them did, I didn't judge. Instead, I tried to be kind and supportive. I made sure our door was always open.

Yes, some of my older children were having a tough time in those days. And they weren't the only ones.

While the reserve had been dealing with alcohol for years, drugs were flooding into northern Saskatchewan. Many reserves found members of all ages becoming hooked on opioids and intravenous drugs. Sandy Lake was no different.

Drug use was so widespread that, decades later, the reserve would be home to many people with drug-related illnesses. A 2013 Health Canada study told us that sixty people on our reserve were HIV positive. That meant 3.5 percent of residents had contracted the virus—most likely from intravenous drug use. That number was seventeen times the national average, and higher than the HIV rate in some of the hardest hit African countries. (Nigeria's HIV rate for the same period was 3.17 percent.)

Those numbers were sad, even shocking, but anyone living in Sandy Lake in the eighties and nineties saw plenty of things that might have prepared them for the statistics. Alcohol abuse had gotten so bad in the eighties, the council cancelled the public dances. They were just getting too out of control. The damage being done by opioid drugs was public too—but in a different way. Even if you didn't have someone close to you who was using, it was easy to see that something troublesome was going on in the community.

We all noticed that there was a rise in theft. But more upsetting was what we were spotting day in and day out: lost souls wandering the reserve or showing up on our doorsteps. You'd be driving in the middle of the day, and there would be a young man or woman, skinny, ill-looking, stumbling along the gravel road or sitting on the shoulder. Or you'd see a thin figure walking aimlessly around the shores of the lake. Sometimes there'd be a knock on your door and some sad soul would be asking if you could spare a bit of food or a little water. I came to understand that some of these folks had been asked to leave their homes. Many were sleeping out of doors, in tents or with no shelter at all. I couldn't imagine what would happen to them in the winter.

In the mid-eighties, I had constructed a new two-bedroom log-frame house at the north end of Sandy Lake, overlooking the water. It was a beautiful spot, surrounded by plenty of property. I decided to build a little cabin a short distance from the house. I outfitted it with a simple bed. When the next young man knocked at my door, looking for food, I told him he could spend the night in the cabin if he needed shelter. Word got around the reserve.

For the next dozen years or so, men and women moved in and out of the place. Sometimes I was shocked to realize I recognized one of them from my coaching days. Their once young, energetic faces now grey and drawn. Their hope spent. Some stayed a night or two—some stayed longer. Those who rested at the cabin for a few days tended to go away looking much healthier and brighter. That gave me comfort.

I was happy to be able to help this way, but I couldn't afford to feed everyone who stayed at the cabin. (I was working my fields, running the buses, and later running the water delivery service for the reserve. But I was far from well-to-do.) Besides, I knew that these men and women needed something more than a free dinner. Instead, I tried to help them help themselves. If the people were at the cabin more than a night, I showed them where I left my boat and my fishing equipment. I encouraged them to get out onto the lake and fish for their own supper. I also pointed out where they could build a fire outside at night and cook their catch. My chainsaw was always left where they could find it, so they could go into the wood and cut firewood. Many brought back enough logs to keep my wood stove burning as well as make their own fires. And I always insisted that they clean up the cabin each day—that they leave it as they found it so others could move in after they were gone.

For many years, dozens of people moved in and out. I hope they found a little peace there, and that the shelter kept them alive long enough to get real help.

The cabin was one small thing I could do, but of course, it was just a drop in the bucket. What we needed was some way to stop the kids from abusing alcohol and drugs in the first place.

I had been promoting sports for children and adults in my community my whole adult life. As Chief, I'd been able to step that up so we had hockey teams for just about every age group. I knew sports was a self-esteem booster. Physical activity could be a good outlet for anyone struggling with troubling emotions. Team sports provided great opportunities to travel a bit, see a little more of the world. And for kids heading into their teens, being involved in sports might keep them away from more dangerous activities.

But even I could see that hockey and baseball teams weren't going to be enough to protect our kids. I decided to give those young people the only other thing I had—my story.

I went into the Sandy Lake school to talk to the kids. I travelled to schools on other reserves, all through northern Saskatchewan. And every time I went to a tournament or ran a hockey clinic, I spoke to the young people there. I shared my story to let them know that they too could achieve, that there was a good life out there for them, if they worked for it. But I also told them that part of that work involved living a healthy life. Staying away from alcohol and drugs. Taking care of their bodies and their spirits. I told them that I regretted the hours, days, and years I'd wasted drinking, and that I now knew that booze and drugs did nothing to help with difficult times and with pain. I told them I believed in them, but in order to have a bright future, they had to find ways to stop hurting themselves.

Sometimes these talks were done on hunting and fishing trips with the kids. Some of the kids weren't learning about our traditional ways. I began to take small groups out in the woods and teach them how to track and shoot, or out onto the lake with nets to show them how to fish.

Eugene Arcand heard about what I was doing and reached out to me. Eugene is from Muskeg Lake Cree Nation, in Saskatchewan. Like me, he attended St. Michael's Residential School, although I was long gone by the time he arrived at the school. Also like me, he found comfort, strength, and hope through hockey, which he played at St. Michael's and, after, in the Saskatchewan junior and intermediate leagues. He had gone on to work in a variety of roles in Indigenous organizations. His focus was on promoting our culture and encouraging our youth to choose sports over alcohol and drugs.

Sometime around 1990, Eugene invited me to speak at a college in Saskatoon. I shared my story and my advice with about 200 of the students there. Afterwards, someone from a local newspaper interviewed me.

After that, Eugene continued to invite me to work with him to promote sports, recreation, and culture for Indigenous kids across the province. The more appearances I made, the more invitations I seemed to get. I spoke to hockey teams and youth organizations, at conferences and meetings, to Indigenous groups and government officials. Like I had done with the kids in Sandy Lake and on the other reserves, I told my story and talked about the damage of drug addiction and substance abuse, about the importance of a healthy active lifestyle, hard work, and pursuing your dreams. I drove all over the province to speak and made several longer trips as well.

In later years, I even got other NHL players, including Reggie Leach and Theo Fleury, to come to the local schools and hockey clubs and talk to the kids about reaching their goals and living their best lives.

Other members of my extended family have also worked in this area. In 2014, my daughter-in-law JoLee Sasakamoose (Derrick's wife), a professor at the University of Regina, started the Fred Sasakamoose Indigenous Youth Leadership and Wellness Program. The three-day camp, for youth aged fourteen to seventeen, provides guidance about healthy living and community involvement. I tell my story and share my point of view in an opening speech every year.

Oh, man, I'm sure I've talked to thousands and thousands of kids over the years about clean living. But I also had the privilege of working again with the band council as they tried to tackle the drug problem. I returned to the position of councillor a few years after I stepped down as Chief. In 1987, the Cree Treatment Centre was opened on the Ahtahkakoop Cree Nation reserve (the name was changed from Sandy Lake in 1986). The centre would serve the Ahtahkakoop residents and Indigenous people from the surrounding area. And it was housed in the log-frame building that was supposed to have been the arts and crafts centre. Located right on the wooded shores of Sandy Lake, it was the perfect place to heal.

By the time the new century was underway, the Ahtahkakoop health centre had also started an intensive education program, providing information to everyone on the reserve, including school kids, about harm reduction when it comes to drug use and disease. The health service also began to offer a needle distribution program and HIV and hepatitis C tests, which they encouraged residents to take. People who had positive results could then start treatment.

In 2017, we also got a brand new health clinic. And around the same time, a methadone clinic was introduced. The first such clinic on a reserve in Canada. No longer would people from Ahtahkakoop have to walk or hitchhike the eighty kilometres to Prince Albert for treatment. (Methadone makes you drowsy, so you can't drive after you've taken it. It was a terrible thing to see people try to walk back down the highway to Ahtahkakoop, tired and cold, in the middle of winter.)

As a result of all these efforts, new cases of HIV and hep C have dropped dramatically in recent years, and antiviral medications have helped 90 percent of those with HIV manage the illness.

My community is still struggling with drugs. In recent years, members of gangs from the bigger cities have been coming onto the reserve to sell opioids, crystal meth, and other narcotics. We have an RCMP office on the reserve, but it seems as soon as one group is arrested, other gang members take their place.

We are making progress, though. Indeed, by the early 2000s, my little cabin sat empty most of the time. I decided it had served its purpose and could use another. So I gave it to my son Derrick and his wife, JoLee. They lived in Regina, and I knew they would like a little spot on the lake where they could spend their summers.

Drug use might be the most alarming challenge our people have faced in the last several decades, but there have been lots of other issues too. In June of 2009, I was asked to serve as a senator for the Federation of Saskatchewan Indian Nations (FSIN). The federation is an advisory board that represents the seventy-four Indigenous bands of Saskatchewan. We work on many things on behalf of our people. I chose, however, to sit on a committee that administers our Treaty Protection Fund. I had never forgotten the stories my Elders told me when I was just a boy, the stories about Ahtahkakoop putting his hand to the treaty paper with the Queen. Stories about how his trust had been broken, how the agreement he thought he'd made had been twisted by the môniyâwak, right from the start. And this is still happening.

Despite Lieutenant-Governor Morris's assurances that our nations could continue to hunt and fish through the province, every year our people are charged with hunting and fishing "illegally." I was nabbed, of course, trapping in a national park. And in the mid-nineties, I faced a charge of fishing illegally, after I attempted to sell fish I'd caught on my own reserve. Again I argued that the charges violated the treaty that Ahtahkakoop made with Alexander Morris. The judge dismissed the case against me.

Our committee looks at cases like mine and will often fund their defence. It's an important process, but one I feel shouldn't be necessary. Our treaties shouldn't be negotiated in the courts. The original terms should simply be honoured. *As long as the sun shines, the grass grows, and the rivers flow.*

Through the FSIN, I also served as an advisor with the Aboriginal Healing Foundation. For the sixteen years of its operation, the organization worked to address the damage done to the health and well-being of generations of our people. Funding for the healing programs it developed came at first entirely from the Canadian government, but in 2007 the Catholic Church was also required to contribute. I told my story during the gathering of testimonies about residential schools. And I attended the meetings of the foundation held all over Canada. But it was tough work, spending so much time listening to the terrible things my people had gone through, and I only lasted a few years before I had to give it up.

I've had my hand in a lot of things in the last three decades. But always there was hockey. Hockey was the thread that seemed to hold my life, my story, together. What started on that frozen slough with my moosum Alexan has always been part of who I am. Even though I gave up playing when I closed in on my fifties, I never forgot hockey. And as I entered my sixth decade, I would discover it had never forgotten me.

15

okimāw kā-pitihkwēk mistik

CHIEF THUNDERSTICK

In 1998, the NHL organization invited me to join the diversity task force that was being led by Willie O'Ree. Willie O'Ree was the first Black NHL player when he became a rookie for the Boston Bruins in 1958. I was to help young people in western Canada get involved in the sport or improve their skills.

For four or five years, I travelled around to reserves all over the north and west, talking with young people there and watching them play. I then identified kids, ten to fourteen years old, who had potential and could benefit from special training. The NHL would send these kids to hockey camps run by the NHL teams themselves. I often accompanied the parents and kids to the camps, which meant trips to Los Angeles, Denver, Minnesota, even Florida. (Strangely, no Canadian teams seemed to run these camps for the kids.) About three times a year, I also attended meetings with Willie and other NHL officials at these camps and in cities in Canada.

Two young boys I selected from Meadow Lake for this training ended up making the NHL in the 2000s—D.J. King played for the St. Louis Blues and the Washington Capitals, and his brother Dwight played for the Los Angeles Kings and earned two Stanley Cup rings.

My renewed relationship with the NHL provided a nice benefit—I got to reconnect with a number of players I had crossed paths with during my Hawks days, including Gordie Howe, Bobby Hull, and Murray Costello. It also allowed me to build relationships with league organizers and club managers. And those connections made it possible for me to provide a great opportunity for our young Indigenous players. In 2002, I started a practice I would continue for many years: I brought a children's team to Edmonton to watch an NHL game. The first time I did this, I took the Beardy's Blackhawks midget team to see Edmonton play Chicago. Before the game, the team got to skate around the ice with the pros and were taken for a tour of the dressing rooms. They were so excited to see the stalls with the names of the players over each one. It all reminded me of the first time I stepped into the Hawks' dressing room in Chicago that November afternoon so many years ago. The kids also got to have their pictures taken with Chris Simon, who was playing for the Hawks that season.

Around this time, I also became involved with Saskatoon's All Nations Hockey School, and started the Fred Sasakamoose All Star Hockey Week. It was a camp for young Indigenous hopefuls to polish their skills, but I kept it open for non-Native kids as well. It seemed important not to create barriers between the young players. We ran the school for about eight years, even adding a girls-only school for one year, but we fell victim to our own success. We had too many kids wanting to join us and couldn't find enough affordable ice time.

But I continued to be involved in various efforts to promote and support Indigenous hockey, including the Saskatchewan Indian Winter

Games—where, in 1998, I had the joy of watching one of my grandsons compete in hockey—and the Aboriginal Hockey Showcase in the lead-up to the 2010 World Junior Championship in Regina and Saskatoon (they even featured my photo on the game tickets). Most recently, my son Neil and I helped organize the first Indigenous Hockey Summit, which was to be held in April 2020 to promote hockey in our communities and encourage community reconciliation through sport. Along with NHL officials, like Commissioner Gary Bettman, ten Indigenous players were going to speak, including the King brothers, Ron Delorme, Stan Jonathan, and me. But unfortunately, the COVID-19 outbreak forced us to cancel the event. And in recent years I've worked with the non-profit organization KidSport and the Canadian Tire charitable organization Jumpstart to help our Indigenous kids get the financial assistance and equipment they need to play hockey.

The NHL Diversity Task Force appointment, some of the other honours that would come my way during the next few years—I would never have expected any of that if you'd asked me what life had in store for me when I stepped down as Chief. My life back then was full. But quiet too. Sure, every hockey fan in the towns, villages, and reserves around my home knew my name, knew my hockey history. But the rest of the world? Well, if they had ever heard about an Indian NHL player named Sasakamoose, they seemed to have forgotten about him. And then, one day in the late eighties, someone changed that just a bit.

I was in the band office at an all-day council meeting when one of the office staff came into the council room.

"Freddy, there's someone out here who wants to talk to you."

What could be so urgent that I'd have to leave the meeting?

When I came out, I saw a middle-aged white woman—waiting for me, it seemed.

She told me her name was Brenda Zeman, and she was a writer. Working on a book about Indigenous athletes. She wanted to include my story.

"You think I have a story?" I said.

"I sure do," she replied.

I was amazed she had heard of me. And I was impressed that she had managed to track me down. I still didn't have a phone at home, and she had travelled all the way to the reserve without knowing where she might find me. I decided to sit down and tell my story to this stranger. I was talking to young kids about my past at this point, but when I did, I didn't really get into details. Brenda asked a lot of questions about my Moose Jaw and NHL days. I was a bit surprised at how much joy and excitement I got from remembering everything I had done back then. How talking to her reminded me of things I had almost forgotten.

I didn't tell Brenda everything I remembered, however. Not a word about my abuse or suffering at St. Michael's. I just wasn't ready for that.

Brenda's book, *To Run with Longboat*, was published in 1988. It seemed to be the beginning of public interest in my story, in me.

Over the next few decades, many people outside of my northern Saskatchewan community began to seek me out. Doug Cuthand featured me in his 2005 documentary series *Chiefs and Champions*, narrated by Tom Jackson. I also appeared in Don Marks's film *They Call Me Chief*, and in an episode of the TSN documentary series *For the Love of the Game*. The books *Life after Hockey* and *They Call Me Chief* also tell some of my story.

And there was another book. But I didn't find out about it until it was turned into a movie.

In 2017, the film *Indian Horse* came out, and the following year I was invited to a screening in Gatineau, Quebec, at the Canadian Museum of History. I understood that the movie was about an Indigenous boy who plays hockey. What I didn't know was that it was based on a novel written by the Ojibway writer Richard Wagamese. When I got to the screening, a reporter asked to take my photo in front of one of the movie posters. Then one of the organizers asked me to come up on stage. He introduced me as "the real Indian Horse." I was confused. When the movie started to play, I could see that it was not really my life. But then the scenes in the residential school started— and they seemed very familiar. My memories became too painful. I told the fellow sitting next to me to come and get me when the school stuff was over. I headed to the lobby.

I went back into the theatre when the school scenes were done. I enjoyed the movie. But I wasn't sure what to make of the suggestion that the film was connected to my story.

I found out later from my brother Peter and his wife, Muriel, that Wagamese was a neighbour of theirs for years in Kamloops. He used to come over to their place, ask them questions about me. Listen to their stories. But Muriel and Peter didn't know he was writing a novel about a hockey player, and he never talked to me. After the book came out, he told them that my story had inspired *Indian Horse*, although the main character is Ojibway and the details of our lives are quite different.

One of the movie's producers was Clint Eastwood. So the film was a big deal, released in theatres across Canada and the US. It was good to think that many people might become aware of Canada's residential school history through the book and film. Good to think I had a tiny part in making that happen. But I worried that people would really believe I was Indian Horse. That it was *my* story. It wasn't. And I wanted to tell *my* story myself.

———

Over the last three decades, I've had many opportunities to do that. There have been a lot of profiles written about me, often written when one honour or another has come my way. In January 2007, I was inducted into the Saskatchewan Sports Hall of Fame, in the Builder category. In 2012, I was inducted into the new Saskatchewan Hockey Hall of Fame, in the Player category (I'm glad at least some people seem to remember my slapshot). I've also made it into a number of local halls of fame, and into the Canadian Native Hockey Hall of Fame. In 2011, I received a National Aboriginal Achievement Award (now called the Indspire Awards). I also received a Federation of Saskatchewan Indian Nations Circle of Honour Award. The Queen Elizabeth II Diamond Jubilee Medal was awarded to me in 2012. In 2017, Saskatchewan Polytechnic bestowed on me an honorary diploma, and in 2020 the University of Saskatchewan gave me an honorary doctorate of laws.

Probably my greatest honour came in 2018. In May, I travelled to Ottawa to receive the Order of Canada. None of my family members could go with me, so I asked my friends Chief Larry Ahenakew, FSIN Vice-Chief Dutch Lerat, and Delores Greyeyes to join me on the trip. Man, that was something.

The ceremony was held in Rideau Hall, the governor general's residence. The whole place spoke of a rich and powerful past. The marble floors. The pink-and-white striped wallpaper. The chandeliers. And everyone who moved through the hall was dressed to the nines— many of the men in tuxedoes, the women in gowns.

It felt unreal to be sitting there, surrounded by so many accomplished people—including hockey great Mark Messier. More strange and thrilling still to walk up to the dais, to have the medal put around my deck. I was glad to have friends there to watch it all happening.

After the ceremony, there was a formal lunch. While Governor General Julie Payette travelled around the room, talking to the recipients, uniformed servers waited on us—two a table.

Of course, the ceremony, the medal and pin, the fancy lunch, it's all meant to make you feel honoured and appreciated. And it sure made me feel that way. But I also couldn't help thinking how strange it was for me and the other Indigenous people in that room. The residential schools and the rules and governance of Indian Affairs (now called Indigenous and Northern Affairs) have always made it clear that we are second-class citizens. And while recognition of Indigenous individuals is a good thing, a thing that does make me feel hopeful, it's not really enough. Chatting with Julie Payette, I thanked her for the honour. But what I really wanted to say was that she and the rest of the government should go beyond honouring a few people. They should honour all of us. They should honour us as the nations we are. That's what I would really like to see. That is what I hope for. I have spent so much of my life promoting Indigenous sport, and one of my aims has always been to have more of our athletes competing at the highest levels—like at the Olympics. But I'd like to see us competing as representatives of our own proud, independent nations. I think we deserve that.

I am always a little stunned when I think of that list of awards, awards that have come after so many years of living quietly and largely unknown in Sandy Lake. And there continue to be many less formal honours. Since the nineties, I've done televised shootouts for charity, been honoured at several Edmonton Oilers games, and participated in many celebrity charity hockey and golf tournaments. I can't tell you how many times I've had the fun of dropping the puck at a tournament or even an NHL game.

But there's one puck drop I've come to look forward to every year. And that's the one at the Fred Sasakamoose "Chief Thunderstick" National Hockey Championship.

In 2016, Chief Larry Ahenakew and the Ahtahkakoop band council organized a hockey tournament for local Indigenous teams, and they named it after me. It was a great event—one that my son Neil thought should become an annual thing. So he and other family members got involved with Larry and the council, and for the last several years we've held a tournament in Saskatoon for Indigenous teams, men's and women's, from across Canada.

Boy, how it's grown. The first tournament had a dozen teams playing. In 2020, forty men's teams and eight women's teams were signed up to participate. They would have come from as far away as Rankin Inlet, northern Quebec, and New Brunswick. One hundred and ten games on six sheets of ice were planned for the two and a half days of the tournament. We used to have a banquet as part of the event, but we didn't plan for one in 2020—with so many games to be played, we couldn't fit an evening dinner into the schedule. Unfortunately, the COVID-19 pandemic meant we had to cancel the 2020 tournament. But I hope it will continue in the future. It's been such a great event for our First Nations players—and for me.

In the past, at the tournament, one of the things I've enjoyed most is the time I have to visit with the fans and players—Neil always sets up a booth for me in one of the arenas, and people can come up to chat or sit and have a cup of coffee with me. Old friends and family join me there. My brothers Leo and Peter have attended many of the tournaments. But I meet plenty of new folks too. People like to introduce themselves to me and talk about what I've done or what the tournament means to them. A lot of older folks like to reminisce about their own residential school teams or the Indian hockey heroes in their own communities. About the great Indian leagues and tournaments of decades past. Stories like these are shared with young fans and players. Pride, connection, community— the days of the tournament are really a big celebration of our past, present, and future. A coming together over a shared history and a passion for the game. And I'm there for all of it, talking to the fans, watching the players, who love the sport every bit as much as I do, getting excited about the future of all of these people. It's been the highlight of my year.

Perhaps the biggest thrill I've had since putting on that Black Hawks sweater all those years ago came on April 25, 2019. That night, my son Neil made it possible for me to turn over the hourglass.

A number of years before, Neil had heard that there might be a videotape of some of those early games I played in the NHL. When he investigated, he found that there was one—of my debut game in Toronto, February 27, 1954. After some negotiating with the NHL, he managed to get a copy—and the permission to screen it once, and only once, for the public.

Neil booked the Roxy Theatre in Saskatoon. He advertised the showing in the local papers. And then he took the soundless tape to Clarence "Tsi-Boy" Iron. Clarence has been calling local Indigenous hockey games in Cree for decades for Saskatchewan radio stations. In March 2019, he joined Rogers Hometown Hockey to call games in Cree for APTN, the Aboriginal Peoples Television Network. Clarence recorded a play-by-play for my game in our native tongue.

When I got to the theatre that night, it was packed—over 300 people filled every seat in the place. My cousin Herb Seeseequasis, who, of course, played with me on the St. Michael's Ducks, was there.

Loretta and I were taken to seats in the front of the theatre. Before the movie was about to start, Neil announced that there was a surprise presentation. Members of Father Roussel's extended family had heard about the screening. And they had brought with them the 1949 Saskatchewan midget championship trophy, which they had found amongst the old priest's things after he passed away. Two of them went to the stage with the cup. Herb and I were called to join them and receive the trophy and a photo of our championship team. What a moment. There were tears in my eyes as I thanked them. But it was nothing compared to what would come next.

Once I sat back down, the screen lit up with a picture of my mom and dad—the Cree-dubbed film had been dedicated to them. And then the image transformed into a grainy shot of the ice in Maple Leaf Gardens—and the starting faceoff.

My eyes were glued to the screen as the first period unfolded. Shift after shift went on the ice (the game reminded me that lines stayed out for a lot longer in those days). I could feel the whole audience in that theatre, waiting, waiting to catch a glimpse of Freddy Sasakamoose.

And then I saw it. Wavy black hair, rising in the front like a sharply peaked cap, the number—21—across the back of a dark sweater. *Me.*

It was like being hit by a bright bolt of energy. I was twenty-one years old again. Young, strong. Full of blazing hope and crazy joy.

I didn't even realize I had jumped to my feet in the theatre. Because I wasn't really there anymore. I was on the ice.

I could feel myself dashing forwards, twisting away from a defence-man, snapping a pass to a teammate.

And then I was back in the theatre. Number 21 had spun around on the ice, towards the camera, and for a split second I felt my young self looking straight at the old me. It sent shivers down my spine.

The tape ran for over an hour. But it felt as if just five minutes had passed when Hawks goalie Al Rollins plucked a high shot out of the air and Clarence Iron announced the game was over. On the screen, the camera focused on the Leafs players heading off the ice, and then on the old analog clock hanging from the Gardens rafters, with the score 4–2 for the Leafs.

Watching that game was probably the most extraordinary moment of my life. I had gone back in time. I was young again for over sixty minutes. Young and old at the same moment. Full of ambition and energy, yet with the wisdom to know what a rare and wonderful experience it was to have played at all. Watching myself on the ice had also finally given me peace about something.

For years and years, I had been wondering how I actually did with the Hawks. Was I really good enough to be on that ice? To play with those players?

And now, six decades later, I could finally answer that question.

Yes. I was good enough.

That evening at the Roxy was an extraordinary high. In the last few years, there have been so *many* highs. But there have also continued to be moments of great sadness. And worse, devastating lows.

In January 1993, my dear brother Frank passed away. He was only sixty-two years old. Oh, boy, do I miss him. What I wouldn't give to go back and reclaim all that time we squandered venting our anger at each other. Next, in 1996, my beautiful, strong, outspoken mother left this world. That punched a hole in my heart. And it loosened the ties of my family. My mother had been the magnet that drew my brothers and sisters, my nieces and nephews together. Without her, our large family get-togethers happened less and less often. That made me miss her all the more.

And then I lost another old friend.

In 2005, our family held a fiftieth wedding anniversary party for Loretta and me. Phyllis Vogan travelled from Moose Jaw for the event.

I hadn't seen her since I'd left that city in 1954. When I asked about George, she told me that he'd passed some years earlier.

I was crushed.

I'd talked to George on and off over the years, but once I was back on the reserve, once my responsibilities had begun to fill my life, I hadn't been very good about staying in touch. I'd never even managed to make it back to Moose Jaw. It made me sad that I hadn't said good-bye, that the moment in his driveway so many years ago—the moment George said, "Anytime you want, you come home"—was the last time we would see each other.

So many losses, but none was as shocking as my daughter Phyllis's death. Not until March 29, 2016.

I was three hours away at a conference, in Lloydminster, Alberta. Loretta had joined me, but I was surprised when she appeared beside me during one of the presentations.

She put her hand on my back.

"We have to go home," she said.

I could barely understand what she told me. Our gentle, loving eldest son, Chucky, was being accused of shooting and killing a man. And now he was missing.

We raced back to our hotel room, threw our clothes in suitcases, and got on the highway.

Police officers met us at our house. They wanted to know if we had any idea where Chucky might be.

I knew exactly where he was. I wanted to take them there. The officers said they couldn't allow that. I told them about Chucky's teepee down by the lake. It was where he went to pray and to smudge. Where he found peace when he needed it.

"Please don't shoot him," I begged. "He's not a violent man."

Loretta and I were forced to sit in our house, staring out across the lake, hoping and praying, while police helicopters beat the air above us.

Hours later, the police returned. Chucky had taken my hunting rifle down to the teepee. He had, they said, taken his own life.

Eventually, we found out who Chucky was accused of killing. He was a white newcomer to the reserve. A man who had served many years in prison for violent crimes. We don't know what passed between him and Chucky, but we do know Chucky had talked to others about his fear of the man. He was terrified about the safety of his wife and kids.

The murder and suicide shocked everyone who knew my son. No one could believe he could ever be involved in something like that. Loretta was hurt beyond anything I can describe. So were the rest of us. And the whole reserve too.

My heart aches for Chucky and his family. And I worry for him. "God's whip hurts, my son," my mother told me. Chucky broke God's most important law. *Thou shalt not kill.* I wonder where he is now. I pray every day that God has taken him in his arms, has forgiven him.

There have been other terrible losses in the last few years. My lovely sister Clara passed away in May 2017. And in February 2019, my tough little guy, Derrick, left this world. He had been suffering from a long-undiagnosed illness, and his death was shattering, an enormous shock to all of us. He was only fifty-six.

It seems strange to end a book with such tragedies, or to write about all the good times I've had during these last few years, with the deaths of Phyllis, Chucky, and Derrick hovering in the background. But I think it's important to share all of my story. So many profiles have been written about me in the last thirty years. Some mention my residential school pain, although I carried that silently for decades and decades. But most only skate over the difficult parts of my later life. I don't want to be silent about that anymore. It's a great privilege to be asked to share your story with the world. And when you have that opportunity, it's important to convey the heartache, the mistakes, the darkness. Perhaps it may help others to see that they are not alone. If nothing else, it's honest. My mother always insisted on that. She told us not to worry about people judging us or looking down on us. It was more important to be honest and ask the forgiveness of God.

These tragedies. Well, one thing they've taught me is I need to appreciate my many blessings. To enjoy the wonderful people I have in my life. I am now eighty-six. I have been married for sixty-six years to a wonderful woman. And I have fifty-one grandchildren, eighty-eight great-grandchildren, and two great-great-grandchildren. Added to my ten kids, that makes 151 riches in my life. Not many people can say that.

My children have stayed close. Neil lives in Saskatoon. Kerry divides her time between North Battleford and Sandy Lake. But the rest of my kids are on the reserve. Great-grandchildren drop by almost every day after school for snacks and conversation. And Loretta and I also visit them and attend their sporting events. Some of my grandchildren and great-grandchildren have become terrific hockey players. Nothing makes me more aware of my good fortune than Christmas. This past year, Loretta and I went shopping for gifts for the youngest family members. We bought seventy or eighty presents. That's a lot of shopping, but, boy, it's sure fun to hand the parcels out and watch our little ones' excitement.

Loretta and I have our health setbacks these days, but we are nearing the end of our eighties living in our own home and pretty much as active as ever. I can still walk miles. My phone rings steadily with exciting invitations. I accept almost every one. My calendar is full, but my gas tank empties quickly.

The reserve, now called Ahtahkakoop Cree Nation, is a wonderful home, a vibrant community. It's one of the very few rural Saskatchewan towns whose population is actually growing. At the time I am writing this, over 2,000 band members live here. And I know everyone. The kids at the school and the rink, they all greet me with smiles and questions. These days, they often ask me about my book.

We have wonderful people in our community committed to making this reserve a good place to live. The most recent Chiefs—Barry, Clifford, and Larry Ahenakew—have done a great job of making the reserve more and more self-sufficient.

A cultural studies program operates out of the school, teaching our children about our heritage and history, working hard to reverse those warped lessons their parents and grandparents were taught about who we are. As well as the school, we have a family centre, a health centre, a community hall, and a radio station. And, of course, there's the Fred Sasakamoose Recreation Centre, where I often go to watch the kids play or have lunch at Kookum's Kitchen—a little café staffed by young people interested in learning traditional cooking from their Elders.

Many, many mornings, I get into my truck and drive up to the top of Lonesome Pine Hill. There is a tiny chapel up there now and a monument to all the children of the reserve who were sent to residential schools. My name is on it.

On cold days, I park my truck so I can see out across the wooded valley and the little slough on the west side of the hill. On warm days, I get out and walk around and feel the breezes that brush the top of the hill. I never tire of looking out at the land Ahtahkakoop chose for us. I think he would be pleased with how his people have taken care of it. And how it has taken care of them.

———

I do a lot of my thinking up on Lonesome Pine Hill. I spent some time there in the fall of 2002. Before I flew to Chicago. My first trip back since 1954.

The Chicago management had invited me, as a representative of the NHL Diversity Task Force, to present a cheque to a local midget hockey team and perform the opening puck drop. Eugene Arcand went down with me. When I got to the new arena—the United Center—the team management made quite a fuss over me. Owner Bill Wirtz invited me to his office and presented me with a bottle of Scotch that had been bottled in 1954. Eugene Arcand and I were taken outside to see the new sculpture outside the arena. On one side are six hockey players from different eras of the club. Engraved in stone on the other sides are the names of every player who ever played for the team. My name is on it.

Then I was presented with a brand new Hawks sweater with my name and number across the back. These days, the team name is the Blackhawks, not the Black Hawks, but the logo and the colours are just like I remembered them.

The sweater was a beautiful thing. I accepted it with gratitude.

I know they were thinking I would put on the new sweater right away. Get dressed for the opening ceremony at centre ice. But I didn't.

"I'm going to wear what I have on," I said. "But thanks anyway."

I'd come down to Chicago wearing a fringed buckskin jacket. It was decorated on the shoulders, pockets, and sleeves with blue and yellow beadwork. It reminded me of the ones nēhiyawak used to wear when I was a boy. Like the one my mother made for me and brought to Saskatoon when she watched me play hockey for the very first time. It was a jacket that meant a lot to me.

I was going to wear it out on centre ice. I wanted everyone watching from the stands and on television to see it.

I had always wanted to come back to Chicago. But I now knew what was really important. It wasn't coming back as a Black Hawk.

It was coming back as mamihcihiwêw. A proud Cree man.

EPILOGUE

A few years ago, a US sports network wanted to do a segment on me. When the interviewer showed up at my place, he said, "We want a happy story, Fred."

"Well, you've come to the wrong place, then," I said.

His request made me think he didn't know much about what it's been like to be Indian on this continent for the last couple of centuries. Or maybe he did, and he was telling me he and his viewers didn't care, didn't want to hear about it. But it is part of my story, and I want people to understand that. I am a lucky man. One of those rare people who had a dream come true. Who did something that so many people would like to do but can't. But I am also an Indian trying to survive in a world that has not always recognized our rights or given us the freedom and honour we are owed.

I will never forget how difficult it has been for my people. Our freedom was stolen. Whole generations were crippled by the restrictions of the Indian Act and by childhoods destroyed in residential schools. Even since those institutions disappeared, anti-Indigenous racism remains strong. I know why people drink to bury their past or numb themselves to the present. I spent a lot of my own days that way, but I came out of that dark time. For the unlucky, however, alcohol and drugs destroyed any chance they had to live a good life after their traumatic youth.

A number of years ago, I passed a man sitting on the sidewalk in Saskatoon. He was selling twists of sweetgrass. When I looked down at him, I was shocked to realize he had no legs—and that I knew him. It was Albert Seenookeesick. My teammate on the St. Michael's hockey team. The fellow who had hitchhiked all the way to Detroit to see me.

The man who liked to imagine himself trying out for the Detroit Red Wings. When I asked what happened, how he had lost his legs, he said he'd been drunk and fallen asleep on the railroad tracks. My old friend, who'd once been so swift and skilled on his skates, could now get around only by crawling.

I don't know what happened to Albert at St. Michael's. We never talked about what was being done to us when we were at that school. And no one talked about it after. I don't even know what happened to Clara, to Leo, to Peter.

In 2008, the Canadian government launched the Truth and Reconciliation Commission of Canada, inviting residential school Survivors from across the country to tell their stories. When they held their hearings in Saskatoon, in June 2012, I decided I needed to attend. That I needed to testify. I heard that a group of about twenty or thirty people from Ahtahkakoop and the surrounding area were going to walk from Duck Lake all the way to Saskatoon. We'd camp overnight in Duck Lake before starting out. On the journey, we'd sleep where we could, eat when possible.

On that first night, we set up our tents at the site of St. Michael's school. The school had closed in 1996, then caught fire and been demolished. Spending the night near the ruins of a place that had ruined our childhoods seemed like an appropriate way to bear witness. But as I lay in my sleeping bag that night, I couldn't drift off. Every time I closed my eyes, I'd see my classmates' faces. And a terrible sound would thread its way through the tent. The sound of crying children. I heard it all night long.

The eighty-five-kilometre walk to Saskatoon took us four days. As each day passed, more and more walkers joined us. Farmers and residents from the little towns and villages along the highway fed us and brought us water. When the days grew late, people invited us to pitch our tents in their baseball fields and town parks. When we got close to Saskatoon, the police arrived to escort the walkers, who now numbered in the hundreds, into the city. We were greeted in the town centre by a huge crowd of Indigenous and non-Indigenous supporters. It was extraordinary to see that so many people wanted to honour us and our experiences. I was moved beyond words.

At the hearings themselves, I joined a sharing circle. I wasn't sure I'd be able to speak of my experiences, but the bravery of the other Survivors uplifted me, inspired me. On the second day, my old St. Michael's Ducks teammate Azarie Bird spoke. Memories of him, our small but poisonous goalie, made me smile. Then the story he told at the hearing made me cry. I knew I had to share what happened to me. I could no longer pretend I had left it behind.

Clara, my sister, also spoke. She chose to testify in a private hearing. Several family members offered to sit with her during the process, but she refused. She wanted *someone* to know what horror she had lived through, but she didn't want to burden any of the family with it. She did not want to cause us any more pain.

When I talked at the hearings, I described my hockey experiences as well as my sexual assault. It seemed important to speak about the sport that helped me cope with the awfulness of those years, and the sport that helped me build a life after I left the school. It felt important to talk about both pain and success. The dreadful lows, the bittersweet highs. About the many blessings I've been given, including the men and women who helped me achieve what I did. And my most important gifts—my many children, grandchildren, and great-grandchildren. I told the panel and the other listeners that it was time for all of us to enjoy our blessings. We deserve that. We may not have "happy stories," but we need to celebrate all the good things in them.

———

I am an old man now, with time to wonder about the past and the future. Sometimes I ask myself, if I had done things a bit differently, could I have returned to the NHL? Could I have had a long career like so many of the players of my generation?

A number of things probably made that a long shot.

That very first game I played in Toronto should have told me something. At that point in the franchise history, the Chicago Black Hawks wasn't a team where it was easy, or maybe even possible, to develop as a player. As fellow Hawks rookie Murray Costello said to me recently, "It's hard to play well on a bad team. It's much easier on a good team."

With so little passing and playmaking, it was almost impossible to really improve. And with the urgent need to bring in new blood, the Hawks probably didn't nurture new players the way they should have.

I'm not the only one who has felt this way. Just recently, someone showed me an article from December 18, 1953, by the sports columnist Tom Melville for the *Edmonton Journal*. Melville quotes Sid Abel saying, "There isn't a potential NHL player in the Chicago farm system who is less than two years away from the big time." Then he writes, "Fred Sasakamoose and Wally Blaisdell of the Moose Jaw Canucks appear to be the best prospects." Melville quotes Sid Abel again: "Maybe they'll have to be turned pro next season and used by the Hawks when they should be in the minors." Wally and I would be better off, Melville writes, if we went from junior hockey to playing for the Moose Jaw Millers, the senior team, before we jumped to even minor professional hockey. Melville believed that we needed time to fully develop as players. We needed additional training and mentoring to be the very best we could be. So that when we did hit the pros, we would have a real chance.

When Metro Prystai was interviewed in 1988 for an article about me, he said pretty much the same thing: "If he'd been with a better organization, maybe like Toronto or Montreal or Detroit, they could have afforded to bring him along more slowly, they could've groomed him better. . . . [Freddy] was most likely with the wrong organization."

Of course, I didn't understand this at the time. In fact, the article reminded me of an exchange I'd had in Chicago when I first went down.

I can't remember what we were talking about, but Jerry Toppazzini shook his head and said, "Freddy, you're too young. At your age, I was playing with the Hershey Bears."

I didn't know why it mattered that I'd made it up before he did. I didn't understand what he was getting at. So I shrugged my shoulders and didn't think about it again. But I realize now that being brought into the pros so early made me impatient. It raised my expectations and then dashed them again. Perhaps this is part of what Sid Abel was worried about. He must have understood how crushing it is to be sent down, once you've played pro. How the experience can ruin your self-confidence and sour you on the system—even if you feel more accepted and at ease than I did. And George—for all his love and support—he had such high hopes for me that we never sat down and discussed how playing in the lower leagues was part of the process of becoming an NHL professional. So, when it happened, being sent down made me feel as if I was failing, falling further and further from my NHL dreams.

But then again, if I had been offered a spot on the Moose Jaw Millers before I'd ever gone to the Hawks training camp or had a game in the pros, would things have turned out so differently? I probably would have accepted it, but I'm really not sure how long I would have lasted. I had already met Loretta, after all. I would have gone home for visits, and I imagine I would have fallen for her exactly the way I did. Now, I'm not trying to say that Loretta held me back. I'm trying to say that I fell in love with someone I understood. Someone who held dear something that was important to me. Loretta never wanted to leave northern Saskatchewan. In fact, she never wanted to leave the Ahtahkakoop reserve once she settled there. When we moved to our new house on the north side of the lake, she was worried she'd be homesick for our house on the south side of the lake. She is a homebody, someone who understands how attached you can be to a place. Like me.

Ever since I was taken away when I was seven, all I wanted to do was go home, to be in the arms of this land. No matter how comfortable I became in Moose Jaw. No matter how much I dreamed of an NHL career. In Toronto, Chicago, New York, with all the lights and excitement. Standing toe to toe, at centre ice, looking my hockey heroes in the eyes. Flying over the big ice while tens of thousands of people watched. All that time, part of me was back here, back in Sandy Lake. Back where my mother and father lived. Back where my moosum held my hand during those long, silent walks. I always felt this place was waiting for me. Always.

In the last few years, I received so many awards and honours. But still, sometimes I wonder if my life will leave a lasting mark behind for future generations.

In several recent newspaper articles, writers have described my hockey career as "trailblazing." They have suggested that I broke some kind of barrier for Indigenous players and players of colour. It pleases me to think that might be true—that I am someone whose experience made things just a little easier for those who followed.

In April 1993, Doug Cuthand, who would go on to make that documentary *Chiefs and Champions*, authored a column in the *Lethbridge Post* talking about the importance of hockey and hockey tournaments to Indigenous communities of Saskatchewan. In it, he said that growing up, he and his buddies worshipped me and then the Indigenous players who followed. When someone showed me that article, I was comforted as much as flattered.

I had the same feeling in February 2003, when I was the guest of honour at a luncheon for Aboriginal youth, along with Jordin Tootoo. There I met a young Saulteaux First Nation hockey player named Adam Houle, who was playing for the Saskatoon Blades. He said that when he was growing up, his mother used to tell him he had a wrist shot like Fred Sasakamoose. That made me so happy. Sure, he was young enough that he would have heard of many other Indian players in the NHL. But I thought maybe his mom followed hockey and encouraged her son just a bit more because she knew that someone just like them had made the big leagues.

There've been many Indigenous players since I started, but it's good to think I inspired Indian kids way back then. Showed them, showed everyone, that we could make it in the white world. That's more important than any award.

And I hope by sharing my story now, non-Indigenous readers might have a better understanding of the hurdles we have to overcome to succeed.

I hope by telling my people about the vision of my grandfather Alexan, they will see how their own belief in the future can strengthen those around them.

I hope by telling them about the friendship of men like Ray, like Dave, like Jerry, about the selflessness and generosity of people like George, they will see that there is goodness in the outside world too.

And finally, I hope my story reminds my people that while it might not be a world made for us, it's a world we can make better by being proud of who we are and where we come from.

ACKNOWLEDGMENTS

I have many people to thank, so I better get started.

My wife, Loretta, and my children—Lester Ledoux, Algin (Chucky), Phyllis, Garth, Beverley (Debbie), Derrick, Kevin, Karen, Neil, and Ryan—and their families. I dearly miss those who have left us, but am grateful to have had you in my life. My children, grandchildren, and great-grandchildren are my riches and my blessings—the best part of my story.

Whatever I accomplished in my life, I did because of the people who loved and raised me: my mom and dad, Sugil and Roderick Sasakamoose; my moosums and kokums, Veronica Bear, Gaspar Morin, Julia and Alexander Sasakamoose. (I never met my mother's father, Joe Morin, yet through my love for kokum Veronica, I felt his influence.)

My siblings and their families are also a huge part of who I am: Sapphire (Sophia) Masuskapoe, Frank, Peter, Leo, and Clara. Even when we didn't all live in the same place, my parents and my brothers and sisters were home to me. (And all the little ones who passed away before I could ever know them—they too were part of that.)

I am a lucky man to have had in my life so many aunts and uncles, cousin, nieces, and nephews—a wide and wonderful kinship. On my mother's side: her sisters and their families, Aunty Veronica and William Duquette, Aunt Beatrice Morin, Aunt Philim Morin, Aunt Virginia Bear, Aunt Tchipuck Bear, Aunt Mariah Lachance, Aunt Louleech; her brothers and their families, Uncle Felix Morin, Uncle Albert Morin, Uncle Philip Morin, Uncle Chief John Keenatch, Uncle Dick Keenatch; as well as Lewis Keenatch, Paul Morin, John and Jimmy Dreaver, William Beads, the Snake family, and all of Whitefish and Green Lake.

And on my dad's side: Uncle Joe Sasakamoose and family, Jeffrey, Daniel, and Steven Sasakamoose and family, Aunt Annie Isbister (Roddie's sister), the Cameron family of Mont Nebo, Senator Hilliard and Myrtle Gardypie, Ralph "Bulldozer" Gamble and family, Kenny Cameron and family, Uncle James Seeseequasis, Uncle Joseph Seesequasis, Herbert Seesequasis, Gilbert Seeseequasis, Albert Seeseequasis, Kenny Seesequasis, Gilbert Favel, Arthur Favel, Richard and Nellie Gamble, Grace Greyeyes, Ron Delorme, and Olive Robinson.

In my people's tradition, I was guided and educated by many Elders in my community. I am profoundly grateful for the wisdom of Chief Allan and Bertha Ahenakew, Myrtle (Meegwais) Duquette, of Mistawasis, Solomon and Maria Masuskapoe, Peter Vandall and family, Jacob Masuskapoe, Peter and Matilda Knife, James Peekeekoot, Samuel Peekeekoot, Norman Benjamin, Angus Knife, James Starblanket, Austin Ahenakew, Thomas and Cecelia Masuskapoe, Simon Williams, Jacob Williams, Edward Little, George Bird, Samuel Joseph, Douglas Joseph, Frank Ahenakew, Henry Bowman, Stewart Bowman, John Nayneecassum (Martin), and Solomon Martin.

Charlie Martin (Nayneecassum), a dear lifelong friend, is very much missed. But I'm lucky to have many others friends who have been by my side over the years: Lawrence and Priscilla Joseph, Chief Eddie Head, Ron Michelle, Chief Larry Ahenakew, Chief Kenny Moccasin, Tammy Cook, Gus and Mildred Gottfriedson, Joe Leonard, George Leonard, Joe Camille, Joseph Jules, Allan Manuel, Billy Eng, Danny Seymour, Joe Lavolette, Father Allan Noonan, Louis Marchand, the Cheecho family, John Tootoosis (founder of FSIN), Chief Bruce Morin, Allan Starblanket, Eugene and Lorna Arcand, Peter Chief, Tony Cote, and all the staff and players of participating teams in the "Chief Thunderstick" National Hockey Championship, particularly the 2019 champions, the Waswanipi Chiefs from Quebec.

My moosum Alexan may have ignited my early love of hockey, but a number of people kept that flame rising. I will be forever grateful to Father Roussel, George Vogan and the entire Vogan family, and all of the staff, trainers, and coaches who accompanied me on my journey in sports. A special note of thanks to those who have kept my hockey story alive through the Fred Sasakamoose "Chief Thunderstick" National Hockey Championship: committee members Neil Sasakamoose, Kim Michael, Kerry Sasakamoose, Mel Paranteau, Curtis Standing, Alexis Christensen, Vince Sauvie, Clarence Iron, and many more.

One of the joys of writing this book was remembering the time I spent with teammates on and off the ice. I can't thank these men enough for their friendship and companionship: Dave Rusnell, Ray Leacock, Jimmy Chow, Ray Ahenakew, Philip Morin, Jerry Toppazzini, Bill Mosienko, Bill Gadsby, Ray Frederick, Pete Conacher, Kenny Wharram, Herb Greyeyes, Alex Greyeyes, Harris Wichihin, Robert Mike, Azarie Bird, Narcisse Daniels, Ivan Daniels, George Daniels, Noel Daniels, Gus Kyle, and Jim Shirley.

Thank you also to all of the hockey organizations that became a home away from home over the years: the St. Michael's Ducks (the Mighty Ducks), the Moose Jaw Canucks, the Chicago Blackhawks, the Debden Rockets, the Kamloops Chiefs, the Sandy Lake Chiefs, the New Westminster Royals, the Meadow Lake Stampeders, the Glaslyn Eskimos, the Kinistino Tigers, and the Saskatoon Quakers.

In the many years since I left the Chicago Blackhawks, a number of NHL players have reached out to me. I am so appreciative of the friendships of Theo Fleury, Jim Neilson, Gordie Howe, Ted Nolan, Reggie Leach, Jordin Tootoo, George Armstrong, and Scott Daniels, from the neighbouring reserve of Mistawasis.

I also have to say a word about those who helped get this book into your hands.

Call Me Indian was the idea of Alanna McMullen at Penguin Canada. I will always be grateful that Alanna gave me the opportunity to tell my own story and then encouraged me to dig deep to express everything that needed to be said.

Meg Masters listened to me carefully and helped me put my story on paper. Whenever she said, "Just a few more questions, Fred," I knew she was lying. There were always *many* more questions. But I'm glad she asked them.

Thanks also go to Darwin "Pete" Chief for his confirmation of Cree spellings, copyeditor Alex Schultz for his careful eye, Paul Patskou for fact-checking, Matthew Flute for his beautiful cover design, managing editor David Ross for keeping everything on track, and marketing manager Beth Cockeram and publicist Steve Myers for getting the word out.

My son Neil deserves a special mention. The time and energy he has spent celebrating my life and accomplishments has kept my story alive. Without his help, this book wouldn't have happened.

Neil's son Zaine Michael also deserves a huge thank you. Zaine is the family historian, and his dogged research into the Sasakamoose clan reminded me of so many of the stories my Elders shared and gave me details that I never knew. Zaine loves a good story, and prompted by his questions, I retrieved a good number of my own that were about to slip into the mist.

And finally, to the Ahtahkakoop Cree Nation: I am so happy to call this place home.

© Battlefords Agency Tribal Chiefs Inc.

AYAHKOKOPAWIWIYIN or FRED SASAKAMOOSE was born in 1933 on what is now called Ahtahkakoop Cree Nation in Saskatchewan. A residential school Survivor, Fred is known as the first Indigenous player with Treaty status to play in the NHL. After retiring from hockey, Fred dedicated his time to activism in order to improve the lives of Indigenous peoples through the power of sport. Sasakamoose is recognized for his achievements by the Assembly of First Nations and the Federation of Saskatchewan Indian Nations. He has been inducted into four different sports Halls of Fame, served on the NHL Diversity Task Force, and was a board member for the Aboriginal Healing Foundvation. Sasakamoose became a member of the Order of Canada in 2017. He passed away in 2020.

MEG MASTERS, a Toronto-based writer and editor, worked with Fred Sasakamoose to put his story on paper. She is also the co-author of the bestselling *A Good Wife: Escaping the Life I Never Chose* by Samra Zafar and Andrea Constand's *The Moment: Standing Up to Bill Cosby; Speaking Up for Women*, as well as nine other books. Her best-selling children's book *Five Minute Hockey Stories* was published under the pen-name Meg Braithwaite. As an editor, she has worked with many of Canada's bestselling authors, and for twenty-five years, was the story editor for both Stuart McLean's award-winning books and his enormously popular "The Vinyl Cafe" show on CBC radio.